PENTAGON PRESS

COMMITTED TO SERVE THE ARMED FORCES

SOUTH CHINA SEA

Emerging Scenario

SOUTH CHINA SEA

Emerging Scenario

Editor

G. Jayachandra Reddy

PENTAGON PRESS

SOUTH CHINA SEA: **Emerging Scenario**

Editor: G. Jayachandra Reddy

First Published in 2018

ISBN 978-93-86618-57-3

Disclaimer: The views expressed in this book are those of the authors and do not necessarily reflect those of the editor.

Published by
PENTAGON PRESS
206, Peacock Lane, Shahpur Jat
New Delhi-110049
Phones: 011-64706243, 26491568
Telefax: 011-26490600
email: rajan@pentagonpress.in
website: www.pentagonpress.in

Printed at Avantika Printers Private Limited.

Contents

Preface

The twenty-first century Asia has begun to be considered an 'Economic Pivot' of the globe on account of its huge size and resource base manifesting in commendable economic growth. At the same time, Asia carries the distinction of being a centre for many conflicts and flashpoints like the Korean Peninsula, the India-Pakistan rivalry and the South China Sea (SCS) imbroglio with well-discernible geopolitical nuances. Certainly there is a lot of difference between the issues of the SCS and other conflicts in Asia, majority of which are in the form of international border disputes between two or three countries. The SCS roughly with 250 small islands is bound by several littoral states, viz., China and Taiwan (to the north of SCS), the Philippines (east), Sabah/Sarawak of Malaysia, Brunei and Indonesia (south), Malay Peninsula and Singapore (southwest) and Vietnam (west). The overlapping claims of the littoral states on the jurisdiction of territorial waters and sovereignty of smaller islands have made the SCS a geopolitical lake.

The SCS assumes international strategic significance not merely because of its geographical location but also on account of it being the major sea lanes of communication endowed with rich oil and natural gas reserves. The SCS, however, has been transformed into a geopolitical and strategic mess due to its huge number of rival claimants. Scholars across the world have considered four major factors for the escalating tensions in SCS: one, the nationalistic sentiment among rival claimants; two, the lack of ability in orchestrating the challenges with a positive diplomatic approach; three, the desire to control offshore resources; and four, the ongoing unhealthy military competition.

The SCS security dilemma is not only complex but challenging. Given their role and policy-perceptions, the US and China have begun to emerge as the major powers capable of deciding the destiny of SCS. However, the constructive role of other littoral states cannot be reduced to lesser significance, in view of their increased sense of faith in multilateral dialogue option. Economic inter-dependability is emerging as a vital ground to shun war.

This volume, *South China Sea: Emerging Scenario*, is a compendium of papers presented by eminent scholars at the international conference organized by the UGC Centre for Southeast Asian and Pacific Studies, Sri Venkateswara University, Tirupati, in July 2017. The facts and figures presented in different articles of this book serve a valuable source of information for the scholars concerned with multilateral engagements across the world.

The responsibility for facts and opinions presented in the articles rests exclusively with the individual authors. Their interpretations do not necessarily reflect the view or the policy of the UGC Centre for Southeast Asian and Pacific Studies or the Editor of this work.

In the capacity of the Director of the Centre for Southeast Asian and Pacific Studies, I had the opportunity of organising the International Conference on "South China Sea: Emerging Scenario" on 22–24 July 2017. Consequently, as the editor of this book, I am deeply indebted, among others, to Prof. A. Damodaram, Vice-Chancellor, Sri Venkateswara University; Amb. Nelakantan Ravi, Former Secretary (East), Ministry of External Affairs, New Delhi; Shri Piyush Srivastava, IFS, Joint Secretary, ICWA, New Delhi and Dr. Upendra Choudhry, Director, ICSSR, New Delhi, for guiding and extending their scholarly support in organising the conference. I owe a debt of gratitude to the former directors of our Centre—Prof. A. Lakshmana Chetty, Prof. Y. Yagama Reddy, Prof. K. Raja Reddy, Prof. C. Ravindrantha Reddy and Prof. P. Munirathnam Reddy—for their expert guidance. I sincerely thank my colleagues in the Centre—Dr. M. Prayaga, Dr. G. Vijay Kumar Reddy, Dr. V. Ramesh Babu and Dr. M. Padmaja—for extending their unstinted support to bring together a wide range of view points on the South China Sea at this moment of changing global order. I thank all the scholars, both from India and abroad who participated and presented papers in the conference. My appreciation is due in large part to the UGC, New Delhi; ICWA, New Delhi; ICSSR, New Delhi; and Sri Venkateswara University, Tirupati, for their financial support to organize the conference. Pentagon Press, New Delhi, deserves a special mention for working hard in printing this book elegantly. Finally, I wish to thank my office staff for their assistance at ground level for making the conference a success.

G. Jayachandra Reddy

1

South China Sea: Historical Background and International Order

Jayachandra Reddy G

Since the end of the Cold War, disputes in the South China Sea (SCS) have dominated the headlines, and they seem to continue to generate fresh national security issues among its littoral states. Of course, scholars and legal experts across the world have raised a variety of legal and geopolitical equations which may impact the future course and the nature of conflicts in the region. The SCS has emerged as one of the serious flash points of the world. It is not only due to conflicts but it has huge resource potentialities under the blue waters. In fact, the conflict of the SCS has many dimensions, primarily international trade route and its oil reserves in addition to its huge fishing stocks. National interests are another sentiment as each claimant attaches symbolic value to the SCS islands that far exceeds their objective material wealth. Of course, it has become a pivot of international power politics as China and the US began to jostle each other for their control over the international order.[1]

The geography of the SCS may play a direct or indirect role for such conflicts. The entire SCS may be divided into two archipelagos—Paracel Islands and Spratly Islands located in northwest and southeast of the sea respectively. Irrespective of geographical proximity, there are bitter arguments or claims based on the history of these islands. All the littoral states of the sea argue that these islands are being a source for regular fishing apart from shelter for their fishermen. But, China whose, argument has been totally different, tries to find evidence of its exclusive usage of the Sea's many features since time immemorial. Undoubtedly, the interests and the claims of each country are geographically overlapping in terms of Exclusive Economic Zones (EEZ) and China's U-shaped line. Moreover, the entire scenario of conflict did not happen overnight but it has the history of more than six decades. Seans Mirski stated that:

> In fact, at the end of World War II, no claimant occupied a single island in the entire SCS. Then, in 1946, China established itself on a few features in the Spratlys, and in early 1947, it also snapped up Woody Island, part of the Paracel Islands chain, only two weeks before the French and Vietnamese intended to make landfall. Denied their first pick, the French and Vietnamese settled for the nearby Pattle Island.[2]

This phase of occupying or claiming islands was a period of inertia for many reasons. It was only in early 1970s many countries initiated the process of claims and made an issue of national interest. The first maritime claims became vaguer in January 1974, just before the Battle of the Paracels in which Chinese forces evicted Vietnam from the western half of those islands.[3] This time, though, the scramble was spurred by indications that oil lurked beneath the waters of the SCS. The Philippines was the first to move. China followed shortly thereafter with a carefully coordinated seaborne invasion of several islands. In the Battle of the Paracel Islands, it wrested several features out from under South Vietnam's control, killing several dozens of Vietnamese and sinking a corvette in the process. In response, both South and North Vietnam reinforced their remaining garrisons and seized several other unoccupied features. Another decade of relative inaction was punctuated once again with violence in 1988, when Beijing moved into the Spratlys and set off another round of occupations by the claimants. Tensions crested when Beijing forcibly occupied Johnson Reef, killing Vietnamese sailors in the process. Once again, tensions deescalated for a few years, only to rise again in 1995, when Beijing built bunkers above Mischief Reef in the wake of the Philippine oil concession.[4]

Surprisingly, China didn't claim "historic rights" in the SCS in 1946-48 and either in its 1958 decree or in its 1974 statement, at the UNCLOS negotiations, or subsequently in its 1992 Law concerning Territorial Waters and Adjacent Regions. Something changed in the 1990s, however. By the time the PRC passed its Law on the Exclusive Economic Zone and the Continental Shelf in June 1998, officials felt it necessary to include the wording that, "the provisions of this Law shall not affect the historic rights enjoyed by the People's Republic of China."[5] But, Malaysia, the Philippines, Vietnam, and now China have correctly understood that the key to sovereignty is not legal arguments but physical possession and control—a continuous human presence. Whether an island generates an EEZ or simply a twelve-mile territorial sea is determined by whether or not it is able naturally to support human life. Hence, the rush to seize and settle any and all land features in the SCS and to demonstrate that people can live on them.[6]

This entire history has been overshadowed by China's claims in the form of U-shaped line or nine-line. It has asserted claims to the reefs and islands and to "surrounding" or "relevant" waters—but never spelled out their exact extent. In May 2009, Chinese diplomats attached a map of the U-shaped line to an official submission to the United Nations Commission on the Limits of the Continental Shelf but didn't explain its significance.[7] The most coherent formulation of what it might mean comes from Wu Shicun, President, National Institute for South China Sea Studies (an organization jointly sponsored by China's Ministry of Foreign Affairs and Hainan Province). For Wu, the U-shaped line claim contains three elements:

- sovereignty over the features within the line;
- sovereign rights and jurisdiction over water as defined by the Law of the Sea (UNCLOS);
- "historic rights" over fishing, navigation, and resource development.[8]

U-shaped Line

The U-shaped line in the SCS is the line with nine segments displayed on Chinese maps. Its official Chinese name is "traditional maritime boundary line" (*chuantong haijiang xian*) though it was referred in different ways, such as the 'U-shaped line',[9] 'nine interrupted-lines',[10] the 'nine-dashed intermittent line',[11] the 'line of national boundary',[12] the 'dotted-line',[13] the 'dashed lines',[14] the 'tongue-shaped line',[15] as well as 'the Chinese border'.[16] The so-called line (cartographically drawn) of claim of China, is surrounded by six countries—China, Vietnam, the Philippines, Brunei, Malaysia, and Taiwan—with a geographical area of 648,000 square nautical miles, twice the area of the Sea of Japan. There are numerous insular features like reefs, islands, islets, banks, etc. All such features are considered into four groups like Pratas Islands (*Dongsha Qundao*), the Paracel Islands (*Xisha Qundao*), the Macclesfield Bank (*Zhongsha

Qundao), and the Spratly Islands (*Nansha Qundao*). The Pratas Islands are under the firm control of Taiwan and for the Macclesfield Bank, the only claimant is China (mainland China and Taiwan).[17] Whereas the Paracel Islands are under the control of the People's Republic of China, and contested by the Vietnamese. The dispute over the Spratly Islands is the most complicated since it involves as many as six parties (mainland China, Taiwan, Malaysia, Vietnam, the Philippines, and Brunei).

The U-shaped line first appeared on the map in December 1914, which was compiled by Hu Jinjie, a Chinese cartographer, but only included the Pratas and the Paracels.[18] On 1 December 1947, the Chinese Ministry of Interior renamed the islands in the SCS and incorporated them into the administration of the Chinese Hainan Special Region.[19]

Christopher Chung, a PhD student, University of Toronto, who examined the archives of the ROC (U-shape line) with the help of forensic technology, has stated: "On September 25, 1946, representatives of the Ministry of Foreign Affairs, Ministry of the Interior, Ministry of National Defense, and ROC Navy General Headquarters (NHQ) convened in the Ministry of the Interior to resolve several issues pertaining to the SCS islands."[20] In February 1948, the ROC formally concluded four decades of internal Chinese arguments about where its borders lay with the publication of the Atlas of Administrative Areas of the Republic of China. The Atlas included the new official map of the SCS—the first public document produced by any Chinese government to include the line. Again, it was only about islands; there were no references to "historic rights."[21]

There is no official evidence or substantial argument from China regarding the U-shaped line, yet China has been reinforcing its claims within the line, consistently. In addition to fisheries operations carried out by the Chinese fishermen in the SCS, China has made numerous moves in support of the line. One of the major moves of China is Maritime Surveillance which was established in 1998. Its prime objectives are: to cruise and safeguard the national maritime interest; protect the maritime environment; and to monitor the laying of submarine cables and pipelines.[22] In this regard, *China Haijian 83* and *China Haijan 84*, vessels joined the SCS Bridge of the China Maritime Surveillance in May 2011. According to the *Law Enforcement Bulletin 2008*, China Maritime Surveillance sent 113 vessels and 242 aircraft, monitoring 285 foreign vessels and 43 foreign aircraft, including stopping illegal foreign activities in outer continental shelf investigations in 2008.[23] Curiously in 2010, the numbers increased to 188 vessels, 523 aircraft, monitoring 1303 foreign vessels, and 214 foreign aircraft.[24] In addition, two China Maritime Surveillance branches were created in 2010 for the SCS—the 10th Branch stationed in Haikou and the Law Enforcement Branch for the Paracel, Spratly, and Macclesfield Islands.[25]

Despite its existence on the Chinese maps for more than six decades, the U-shaped line, as a traditional maritime boundary line of China in the SCS, has never received a wide recognition in the world community, much less by the other claimant states in the SCS. The U-shaped line is a legal conundrum not only for China but also for the world community. But, China has not given up maritime claims based on the U-shaped line and recent practice has demonstrated that China is attempting to further consolidate the claim based on the line; in particular by undertaking regular and intensified law enforcement patrols in the SCS within the line. There is no doubt that the U-shaped line carries some legal implications for the settlement of territorial and maritime disputes in the SCS and may extend to the other regions of the world.

International Order

The end of World War II marked the advent of the construction of contemporary international order. The core reason was that World War II was triggered by the contradictions among imperialists left by World War I and later turned into the global war against Fascism. After World War II, the United Nations was founded primarily to address common security issues. Therefore, the end of World War II means the end of the age where imperialists could partition the territories of other countries by means of war.[26]

Today military and economic strength persists as the conventional source of power, although demography and globalisation have driven significant reformulation of that power for our modern age. It is true that China's military modernisation programme, pursued now for many decades with considerable resources and speed, has improved its ability to leverage force as a source of influence. More importantly, however, China has marshalled a source of power arguably more potent to our contemporary world: its economic demography. It is true that China is still a developing country, with economic challenges and many millions of the world's poor. In fact, it is not relevant for discussion about the present context, but it is indirectly responsible for escalating tensions/

conflicts through the bulldozing attitude of China's maritime policy in the SCS.

Such attitude has taken many forms, such as Chinese island building and maritime confrontations. Citing historic rights to vast swathes of the SCS within its so-called Nine-Dash Line. Prior to an UNCLOS-chartered Permanent Court of Arbitration decision clarifying the definition of legal islands, China has engaged in extraordinary dredging operations to build islands in strategic locations throughout the SCS, especially inside the Paracel and Spratley islands. This may be for two purposes: i) they could reinforce Chinese claims inside the Nine-Dash Line by way of the maritime entitlements; ii) the various reef-made islands could serve as strategic staging grounds, serving as host to weapons and sensors that would enhance conventional force projection in the region.[27]

The appearance of the SCS issue shows that the emerging oil crisis in the 1970s prodded the surrounding countries to pay attention to the oil reserves beneath the SCS. Interests alone cannot lead to conflict, though. The evolution of the maritime system is a vital factor complicating the SCS issue. The United Nations Convention on the Law of the Sea (UNCLOS) was launched in 1982. The regulation of UNCLOS on the 200 nautical mile exclusive economic zone of the coastal countries brings two problems to "the big lake" of the SCS, which has very complicated geomorphology and maritime conditions and is surrounded by many countries. The first problem is the overlapping of the exclusive economic zones and their conflicts with traditional rights and interests. The second problem is that the status of islands in maritime rights is an uncertain factor. On the one hand, islands can possibly bring tremendous maritime rights and interests. On the other hand, the claim of maritime rights of 200 nautical miles can possibly cover some islands which don't belong to the countries.[28] This entire argument seems to be misinterpretation of the UNCLOS and in favour of China's claims in the SCS.

There are arguments from some of the Chinese scholars that the US is taking advantage of the SCS issue to reshape East Asia, primarily by hijacking international law to justify its military deployment. Against this backdrop, Chinese perception is that the award by the Permanent Court of Arbitration in the Philippines' arbitration case is astonishing, and shows obvious signs of political influence. They believed the unfair arbitration award has increased the possibility of conflict in the SCS. They also held that the so-called process of establishing rule of law in the SCS has reached a dead end since the US and the Philippines have abused international law.[29]

It is true that international arbitration rulings prohibit unilateral actions in disputed areas that "change the nature of the area"—such as drilling. However, in both these cases, the only rationale that China might have for claiming the areas in question has already been rejected by an arbitration panel. Nevertheless, it would appear that despite the arbitration panel's ruling, China's nine-dash line historical claim to sovereignty over the resources and features encompassed by it—or alternatively, a potential claim to 200 nautical mile exclusive economic zones (EEZs) around some of these features, which was also rejected—is still very much alive. If this is truly the position China is taking—that it still claims the nine-dash line or EEZs and will use force to enforce its claim—it will have serious implications for China-ASEAN and China-U.S. relations. Indeed, the United States argued that this is a violation of the existing international order, which it helped build and still leads. Moreover, the United States, Japan, and Vietnam are likely to use these aggressive moves of China to unite ASEAN against China, at least on this set of issues. Contributing to the increased tension, the United States has resumed its Freedom of Navigation Operations (FONOPs) against China's claims in the SCS and U.S. FONOPs are now likely to become more frequent and provocative under the Trump administration—much to China's chagrin.[30]

At the 31st ASEAN Summit Meetings in Manila, the leaders of ASEAN and China formally announced the start of negotiations on the fine print of the Code of Conduct (COC) in the SCS. The agreement comes just three months after the foreign ministers from both sides endorsed the framework on the COC earlier in August 2017. Recent progress made on the COC is seen by many as a milestone development, in light of the brinkmanship in the lead-up to the arbitral tribunal ruling in July 2016. Tension certainly appears to have calmed down significantly since, and discussions on the COC have been actively going on since the meeting of the 19th ASEAN-China Joint Working Group on Implementation of the Declaration of Conduct in the SCS. Compared with the history of strenuous negotiations, the relatively fast pace of recent developments does appear encouraging.[31]

However, the 2002 ASEAN-China Declaration on the Conduct of Parties in the South China Sea (DOC) made explicit that: "the Parties (nations) reaffirm their commitment to the purposes and principles of the Charter of the United Nations". Further the statement read: "the 1982 UN Convention on the Law of the Sea, the Treaty of Amity and Cooperation in Southeast Asia, the Five Principles of Peaceful Coexistence, and other universally recognized principles of international law shall also serve as the basic norms governing state-to-state relations",[32] yet to be fully implemented more than a decade after its adoption. How different would the COC be from the DOC? Is this another tactic by China to buy time? How united would ASEAN be in negotiating with China?

NOTES AND REFERENCES

1. Sean Mirski (2015), "The South China Sea Dispute: A Brief History", *Lawfare*, https://www.lawfareblog.com/south-china-sea-dispute-brief-history (accessed on 31 December 2017)
2. Ibid
3. Chris P.C. Chung (2015), "Drawing the U-Shaped Line: China's Claim in the South China Sea, 1946–1974", *Modern China*, vol. 2(1), pp.1–35
4. Sean Mirski (2015), no.1
5. Zou Keyuan (2001), "Historic Rights in International Law and in China's Practice", *Ocean Development and International Law*, vol. 32, pp.149–68
6. Shannon Tiezzi (2015), "The Real History of the South China Sea Disputes", *The Diplomat*, https://thediplomat.com/2015/04/the-real-history-of-the-south-china-sea-disputes/, (accessed on 31 December 2017)
7. Bill Hayton, "China's 'Historic Rights' in the South China Sea: Made in America?", *The Diplomat*, https://thediplomat.com/2016/06/chinas-historic-rights-in-the-south-china-sea-made-in-america/, (accessed on 31 December 2017)
8. Shicun Wu, Keyuan Zou (2016), *Arbitration Concerning the South China Sea: Philippines Versus China*, Routledge, 2 March 2016, p.132.
9. See Steven Kuan-Tsyh Yu (1995), "Legal Nature and Status of the U-Shaped Line and the Inside Waters in Our South China Sea" (in Chinese), paper presented at the Conference on the South China Sea, Taipei, 16–18 October 1995, pp.1–13.
10. M.J. Valencia, J.M. van Dyke, and N.A. Ludwig (1997), *Sharing the Resources of the South China Sea,* Martinus Nijhoff, Dordrecht, p. 24.
11. Ji Guoxing (1998), "China Versus South China Sea Security," *Security Dialogue*, Vol.291, p.103.
12. Chi-kin Lo (1989), *China's Policy Towards Territorial Disputes: The Case of the South China Sea Islands,* Routledge, London, p.45.
13. Ian Townsend-Gault (1996), "China Ratifies UNCLOS," available at www.ibru.dur.ac.uk/cgi-bin/data.
14. Robert W. Smith (2010), "Maritime Delimitation in the South China Sea: Potentiality and Challenges," *Ocean Development and International,* Vol.41, p.224.
15. Daniel J. Dzurek (1996), "The Spratly Islands Dispute: Who's on First?", *IBRU Maritime Briefing,* Vol.2, p.11.
16. Hanns J. Buchholz (1987), *Law of the Sea Zones in the Pacific Ocean,* Institute of Southeast Asian Studies, Singapore, p. 43.
17. A reason that there is no other claimant for the Macclesfield Bank is that it is permanently

submerged. Otherwise, Vietnam or the Philippines might also have claimed the feature.

18. The map was named "the Chinese territorial map before the Qianglong-Jiaqing period" (AD 1736–1820) of the Qing Dynasty in Hu Jinjie's compilation, *New Geographical Atlas of the Republic of China*. See Han Zhenhua, ed., *A Compilation of Historical Materials on China's South China Sea Islands* (Beijing: Oriental Press, 1988) (in Chinese), 355.
19. See Ministry of Interior, *An Outline of the Geography of the South China Sea Islands*, National Territory Series, 1947, Fig. 11, 861, as cited in J.K.T. Chao, "South China Sea: Boundary Problems Relating to the Nansha and Hsisha Islands," in *Fishing in Troubled Waters*, eds. R.D. Hill, N.G. Owen, and E.V. Roberts (Hong Kong: Centre for Asian Studies, University of Hong Kong, 1991), 88.
20. Bill Hayton (2016), no. 7.
21. Ibid
22. See Lu Shouben, ed., *The Marine Legal System* (Beijing: Guangming Daily, 1992) (in Chinese), 231–232.
23. *China Maritime Law Enforcement Bulletin 2008*, supra note 28.
24. *China Maritime Law Enforcement Bulletin 2010*, supra note 32.
25. *Ibid.*
26. Shi Yongming (2017), "South China Sea Issue: A Dispute over the Order in East Asia, 20, May 2017",*China International Studies*, https://www.pressreader.com/china/china-international-studies-english/20170520/2824885 93740668 (accessed on 24 January 2018)
27. Harry Krejsa (2016), "The South China Sea: A Challenging Test of the International Order", *Maritime Issues*, 27 December 2016, http://www.maritimeissues.com/politics/the-south-china-sea-a-challenging-test-of-the-international-order.html (accessed on 24 Jan 2018)
28. Shi Yongming, 2017, no.26
29. Ibid
30. Mark J. Valencia (2017), "The ASEAN Summits and the South China Sea", *The Diplomat*, July 31, 2017, https://thediplomat.com/2017/07/the-asean-summits-and-the-south-china-sea/ (accessed on 23 January 2018)
31. Lee Ying Hui (2017), "A South China Sea Code of Conduct: Is Real Progress Possible?", *The Diplomat*, November 18, 2017, https://thediplomat.com/2017/11/a-south-china-sea-code-of-conduct-is-real-progress-possible/ (accessed on 20 December 2017)
32. Declaration on the Conduct of Parties in the South China Sea, ASEAN Official Website, http://asean.org/?static_post=declaration-on-the-conduct-of-parties-in-the-south-china-sea-2 (accessed on 4 November 2002)

2

The Troubled Waters of the South China Sea

Fabian KP

The first question to ask is etymological: Who called the expanse of water in question the South China Sea (SCS)? That name was given by the Portuguese sailors who went to China from India in the 16th century. They first called it *Mara da China* (Sea of China), and later, as they wanted to distinguish it from the other seas, called it the *South China Sea.* China calls it *Nanhai* (the South Sea); Vietnam calls it *The East Sea* and the Philippines calls it *The West Philippine Sea*. Before the 16th century, it was known as the *Champa Sea* after the kingdom of the same name in Vietnam.[1]

It is important to bear in mind that the term SCS does not bestow any title of possession or ownership on China. We may note that India has made no claims based on etymology or nomenclature on *The Indian Ocean*, called the *Hindmahasagar* in Hindi. In the 1970s, Indonesia under Soekarno tried to change the name to *Indonesian Ocean* but in vain.

What is at Stake?

The SCS is important for world trade as sea-borne trade worth $5 trillion (about 1/3rd of the global trade) passes through it. The SCS is rich in marine life, accounting for 12 per cent of the global catch. It has enormous hydrocarbon resources, probably 11 billion barrels of crude oil and 190 trillion cubic feet of natural gas.[2] National security considerations, exaggerated or not, and considerations of 'prestige', play an important role in the unfolding contestation. Finally, for China with its ambition to emerge first as a superpower co-equal to US, and later as *the superpower*, SCS is of crucial significance. China wants to know to what extent it can successfully intimidate, cajole, seduce, outwit, and cheat other powers for securing its interests in SCS. If China gets away with flouting international law in SCS, the rule-based world order will be damaged. Other big powers too will be tempted to disregard international law and generally accepted norms of behaviour.

China's Claim

A look at the map below shows the extent of China's claim obviously in violation of UNCLOS (United Nations Convention on the Law of the Seas) as China ignores the existence of other states and their claims under UNCLOS in the area in question.

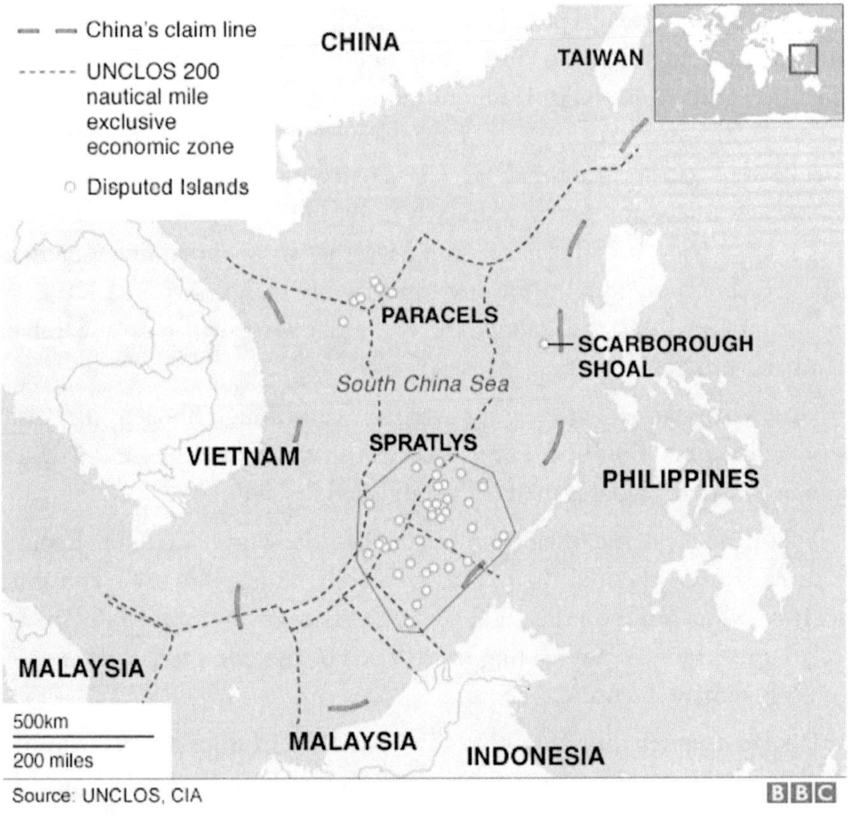

To take one example, China has disputed the claim of the Philippines over the *Scarborough Shoal.* It is 230 km from the Philippines and 650 km from the nearest major Chinese land mass, the southern island province of Hainan. The name *Scarborough Shoal* comes from an East India Company ship *Scarborough* that grounded on one of the rocks on 12 September 1748.[3]

Since the exclusive economic zone (EEZ) under UNCLOS is 200 nautical miles, equal to 370.4 km, it follows that the Scarborough Shoal falls within the EEZ of the Philippines and therefore cannot be under the sovereignty of China. As a matter of fact, The Philippines has exercised sovereignty over the Scarborough Shoal since its independence under the 1946 Treaty of Manila.

The Philippines has solid cartographic evidence to support its claim of sovereignty. Several official maps of The Philippine published by Spain and United States in 18th, 19th and 20th centuries show Scarborough Shoal as Philippine territory. The 18th-century map "*Carta hydrographica y chorographica de las Islas Filipinas*" (1734) shows the Scarborough Shoal then named as Panacot Shoal. The map also shows the shape of the shoal as consistent with the current maps. In 1792, another map drawn by the Malaspina expedition and published in 1808 in Madrid also showed Bajo de Masinloc as part of Philippine territory. The map showed the route of the Malaspina expedition to and around the shoal. It was reproduced in the *Atlas of the 1939 Philippine Census*, published in Manila in 1940, and it predates the controversial 1947 Chinese South China Sea Claim Map that shows no Chinese name on it (the Scarborough Shoal). Another topographic map drawn in 1820 shows the shoal, named there as "*Bajo Scarburo*," as a constituent part of Sambalez (Zambales province).[4]

China has claimed sovereignty over the Scarborough Shoal as it is inside the so-called nine-dash line. Let us look at the validity of the nine-dash-line claim, a line that predates the PRC established in 1949.

Following the defeat of Japan in August 1945 in World War 2, the Republic of China (ROC) claimed the islands—Paracels, Pratas, Spratly—and much else. It based its claim on the 1943 Cairo Declaration and the 1945 Potsdam Declaration.[5] However, a reading of the texts of the two Declarations shows that such a claim is invalid.[6]

Japan surrendered in August 1945 and ROC sent ships to take control of the islands. In December 1947, ROC came out with an eleven-dash-line that was later amended by removing two dashes to exclude the Gulf of Tonkin. The change was carried out by Zhou En Lai in 1953 in favour of North Vietnam.

In short, China's nine-dash-line claim is arbitrary and without any sound legal or historical reasoning behind it as the international tribunal pointed out in its verdict in 2016 which we shall examine soon.

Essentially, the Chinese claim is based on a play with words. It calls the Scarborough Shoal as *Zhongsha Islands* as in a declaration it made in 1985:

> "The breadth of the Territorial Sea of the People's Republic of China shall be twelve nautical miles. This applies to all territories of the People's Republic of China, including the Chinese mainland and its coastal islands, as well as Taiwan and its surrounding islands, the Penghu Islands, the Dongsha Islands, the Xisha Islands, *the Zhongsha Islands*, the Nansha Islands and all other islands belonging to China which are separated from the mainland and its coastal islands by the high seas."[7]

We shall come back to this question of calling reefs and shoals as islands shortly. Meanwhile, we should note that there are areas claimed by two countries and also areas claimed by more than two countries as can be seen in the map that follows.[8]

Let us look at another map[9]:

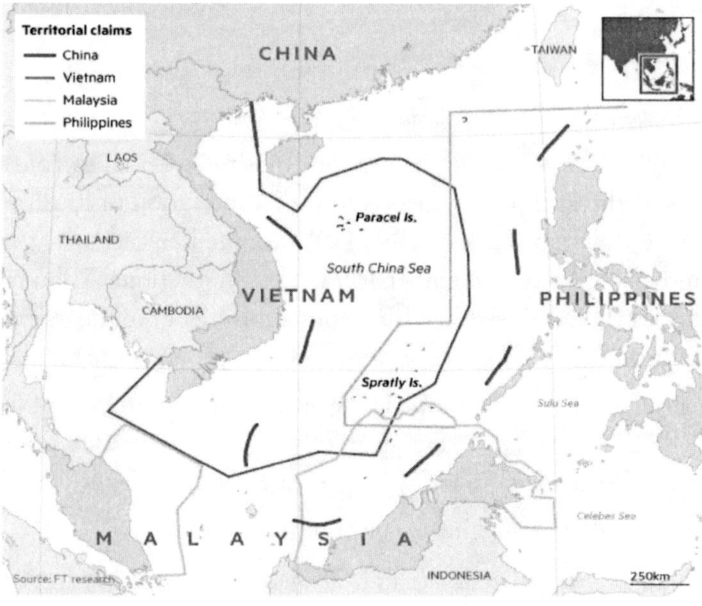

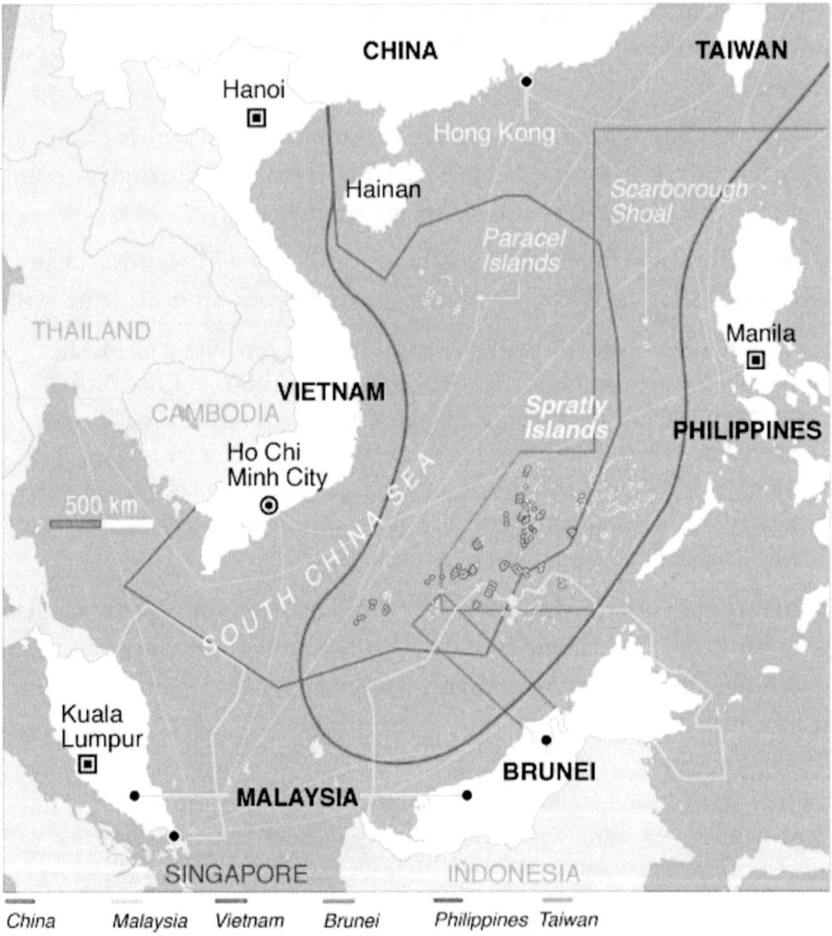

The Philippines is the only contestant that took China to court. Let us briefly look at the Philippines' efforts to seek a resolution of its dispute with China within the framework of UNCLOS, adopted on 30 April 1982 , and coming into force on 16 November 1994. The International Tribunal for the Law of the Sea (ITLOS) to deal with disputes arising out of the interpretation and application of UNCLOS also came into existence on the same date.

For a brief history of the complaint against China lodged by the Philippines before the ITLOS and the verdict given it is necessary to read in full the press release by the Permanent Court of Justice based at The Hague since 1898.[10]

We may note the following salient points:

- China contested that the ITLOS had no jurisdiction in the matter.

But, China did send documents elucidating its position on the complaint.

- The ITLOS did not accept China's plea about jurisdiction.
- The ITLOS did not accept China's argument about its 'historical claims' and ruled that such claims ceased to be valid in case of contradiction with UNCLOS as will be clear from the excerpt below:

Historic Rights and the 'Nine-Dash Line': The Tribunal found that it has jurisdiction to consider

> *Parties' dispute concerning historic rights and the source of maritime entitlements in the South China Sea. On the merits, the Tribunal concluded that the Convention comprehensively allocates rights to maritime areas and that protections for pre-existing rights to resources were considered, but not adopted in the Convention. Accordingly, the Tribunal concluded that, to the extent China had historic rights to resources in the waters of the South China Sea, such rights were extinguished to the extent they were incompatible with the exclusive economic zones provided for in the Convention. The Tribunal also noted that, although Chinese navigators and fishermen, as well as those of other States, had historically made use of the islands in South China Sea, there was no evidence that China had historically exercised exclusive control over the waters or their resources. The Tribunal concluded that there was no legal basis for China to claim historic rights to resources within the sea areas falling within the 'nine-dash line'.*

We give another excerpt from the ITLOS press note on the status of features:

> *"Status of Features: The Tribunal next considered entitlements to maritime areas and the status of features. The Tribunal first undertook an evaluation of whether certain reefs claimed by China are above water at high tide. Features that are above water at high tide generate an entitlement to at least a 12-nautical mile territorial sea, whereas features that are submerged at high tide do not. The Tribunal noted that the reefs have been heavily modified by land reclamation and construction, recalled that the Convention classifies features on their natural condition, and relied on historical materials in evaluating the features. The Tribunal then considered whether any of the features claimed by China could generate maritime zones beyond 12 nautical miles. Under the Convention, islands generate an exclusive economic zone of 200 nautical miles and a continental shelf, but "[r]ocks which cannot sustain human habitation or economic life of their own shall have no exclusive economic zone or continental shelf." The Tribunal concluded that this provision depends upon*

the objective capacity of a feature, in its natural condition, to sustain either a stable community of people or economic activity that is not dependent on outside resources or purely extractive in nature.

The tribunal noted that the current presence of official personnel on many of the features is dependent on outside support and not reflective of the capacity of the features. The Tribunal found historical evidence to be more relevant and noted that the Spratly Islands were historically used by small groups of fishermen and that several Japanese fishing and guano mining enterprises were attempted. The Tribunal concluded that such transient use does not constitute inhabitation by a stable community and that all the historical economic activity had been extractive. Accordingly, the Tribunal concluded that none of the Spratly Islands is capable of generating extended maritime zones. The Tribunal also held that the Spratly Islands cannot generate maritime zones collectively as a unit. Having found that none of the features claimed by China was capable of generating an exclusive economic zone, the Tribunal found that it could—without delimiting a boundary—declare that certain sea areas are within the exclusive economic zone of the Philippines, because those areas are not overlapped by any possible entitlement of China."

The Tribunal's verdict on structures built by China is categorical.

"Lawfulness of Chinese Actions: The Tribunal next considered the lawfulness of Chinese actions in the South China Sea. Having found that certain areas are within the exclusive economic zone of the Philippines, the Tribunal found that China had violated the Philippines' sovereign rights in its exclusive economic zone by (a) interfering with Philippine fishing and petroleum exploration, (b) constructing artificial islands and (c) failing to prevent Chinese fishermen from fishing in the zone. The Tribunal also held that fishermen from Philippines (like those from China) had traditional fishing rights at Scarborough Shoal and that China had interfered with these rights in restricting access. The Tribunal further held that Chinese law enforcement had interfered with these rights in restricting access."

We conclude that the Philippines got the relief it asked for from ITLOS. However, let us look at what followed the verdict given in July 2016.

China rejected the ITLOS verdict with its Foreign Ministry saying that it was "null and void" with "no binding force".[11]

China had good reason to reject the verdict. The new Philippine President Duterte elected in May 2016 had told China months before the verdict that he was not going to make use of the verdict to confront China diplomatically.

In a TV interview to a Chinese reporter in February/March 2016, Duterte said that if he had been in office he would have withdrawn the case from the ITLOS.[12]

Duterte who assumed office on 30th June 2016, chose to make his first official visit to China in a departure from an established custom of making the first visit to Washington. It is believed that China had funded Duterte's election. While in China, Duterte said that he was taking his country away from the seven decades old alliance with US. In April 2017, Duterte announced that he was going to the island Thitu and raise his country's flag there. Later, he changed his plans and said that he might send his son there.

Many senior officials in Manila and a good part of the Manila elite are not in agreement with President Duterte on his approach to China regarding SCS. We do not know whether there will be any change in Manila's approach towards the SCS issue when Duterte ceases to be in office or even before that.

China, ASEAN, and SCS

Obviously, no ASEAN member state can afford to confront China single-handedly. Even as a group ASEAN gets intimidated by China.

Is there any scope for resolving the SCS disputes through negotiations between China and ASEAN? Not really, unless the four member states of ASEAN (Brunei, Malaysia, Philippines, and Vietnam) agree to sign on the dotted line of a text dictated by China. Indonesia has stated that it is not a claimant and hence it has no dispute with any one. This is a diplomatic fiction which might or might not serve Indonesia's interests in the area surrounding the Natuna Islands though as a matter of fact its claims fall within the nine-dash line.

Obviously, those who have no disputes with China on SCS do not want to spoil their relations with the regional hegemon on its way to be a global hegemon by supporting the four. Nor are the four, for that matter, seriously coordinating among themselves in the matter. The Philippines approached the ITLOS without any consultations with others. Even those who have the disputes do not want to confront China beyond a point.

Since China is in a better position to pursue a well-crafted policy over a period as compared to ASEAN, a partially integrated group, with issues among themselves, and understandably fearful of China, it makes sense to recall the words of Sun Tzu, China's equivalent of Chanakya and Machiavelli:

> *If your enemy is secure at all points, be prepared for him. If he is in superior strength, evade him. If your opponent is temperamental, seek to irritate him. Pretend to be weak, that he may grow arrogant. If he is taking his ease, give him no rest. If his forces are united, separate them. If sovereign and subject are in accord, put division between them. Attack him where he is unprepared, appear where you are not expected.*[13]

We should bear in mind that Taiwan is also a claimant. Thus, in all there are 7 claimants (Brunei, China, Indonesia, Malaysia, the Philippines, and Vietnam). Let us look at a timeline of claims followed by physical occupation or other actions from 1956 to 2014.[14]

1956: Taiwan sets up a garrison on Itu Aba, a part of the Spratly group of Islands.

1970: The Philippines occupied five features in the Spratly group.

1974: Vietnam occupied seven features in the Spratly group and claimed it as a province of Vietnam.
China took back the Crescent group (a part of the Spratly) from the Philippines by force.

1983: Malaysia occupied three features of the Spratly Group.

1986: Malaysia claimed two more features.

1988: China attacked Vietnamese forces on the Johnson South Reef.

1994: China evicted the Philippines from the Mischief Reef.

1997: China and the Philippines put flags and markers on the Scarborough Shoal.

2012: China virtually annexed the Scarborough Shoal.

2014: China put an oil rig (Haiyang Shiyou 981) in the EEZ of Vietnam.

The above timeline shows that China is not the only claimant that has resorted to physical occupation. But, China has been the most assertive and aggressive in physical occupation even by evicting other claimants by force.

Let us look at ASEAN's track record in resolving disputes among its own member states.

In 1992, ASEAN came out with a declaration on SCS that had the following operative paragraph:

1. *EMPHASIZE the necessity to resolve all sovereignty and jurisdictional issues pertaining to the South China Sea by peaceful means, without resort to force;*
2. *URGE all parties concerned to exercise restraint with the view to creating a positive climate for the eventual resolution of all disputes;*
3. *RESOLVE, without prejudicing the sovereignty and jurisdiction of countries having direct interests in the area, to explore the possibility of cooperation in the South China Sea relating to the safety of maritime navigation and communication, protection against pollution of the marine environment, coordination of search and rescue operations, efforts towards combatting piracy and armed robbery as well as collaboration in the campaign against illicit trafficking in drugs;*
4. *COMMEND all parties concerned to apply the principles contained in the Treaty of Amity and Cooperation in Southeast Asia as the basis for establishing a code of international conduct over the South China Sea;*
5. *INVITE all parties concerned to subscribe to this Declaration of principles.*[15]

A few intra-ASEAN disputes among ASEAN members were settled in accordance with the 1992 Declaration. For example, in 2002, Indonesia and Malaysia settled their dispute over Sipadan Island and Ligitan Reef. In 2008, Malaysia and Singapore agreed to settle their dispute over Pedra Brance/Pulau Batu Puteh, Middle Rocks and South Ledge through the International Court of Justice.[16]

The appeal for restraint was not heeded by China. In 2002, ASEAN and China signed a Declaration of Conduct that promised to promote favorable conditions for peace and find a durable solution to the differences and disputes among the countries concerned.[17]

The ASEAN–China dialogue has gone on for a long time without any concrete results. ASEAN is far from united and China has been busy manufacturing islands and using force to gain more and more maritime territory.

Recently, when ASEAN met at the summit level in Manila (29th April 2017) President Duterte did not permit any discussion on China's violation of UNCLOS. The summit met against a background of much uncertainty over US policy under Trump towards China's assertiveness and aggressiveness on SCS. ASEAN has always taken care not to criticise China directly. In the past, it has vaguely referred to 'land reclamation and militarisation' as in the 2016 summit. In Manila, the Chinese Embassy worked overtime to eliminate even such oblique references. A draft of Chair's statement leaked to the media did contain the words "land reclamation and militarization". In the end, China prevailed as the Philippines President Duterte, the chairman of the summit, was keen to please China. The section on SCS reads as follows.[18]

Regional and International Issues and Developments

South China Sea

We reaffirmed the importance of maintaining peace, stability, security and freedom of navigation and over-flight in and above the South China Sea. We welcomed the operationalization of the Guidelines for Hotline Communications among Senior Officials of the Ministries of Foreign Affairs of ASEAN Member States and China in Response to Maritime Emergencies in the Implementation of the Declaration on the Conduct of Parties in the South China Sea and look forward to the early operationalization of the other early harvest measure which is the Joint Statement on the Application of the Code for Unplanned Encounters at Sea (CUES) in the South China Sea. We took note of concerns expressed by some Leaders over recent developments in the area. We reaffirmed the importance of the need to enhance mutual trust and confidence, exercising self-restraint in the conduct of activities, and avoiding actions that may further complicate the situation, and pursuing the peaceful resolution of disputes, without resorting to the threat or use of force.

We underscored the importance of the full and effective implementation of the Declaration on the Conduct of Parties in the South China Sea (DOC) in its entirety. We took note of the improving cooperation between ASEAN and China. We welcomed the progress to complete a framework of the Code of Conduct in the South China Sea (COC) by middle of this year, in order to facilitate the early conclusion of an effective COC. We recognized the long-term benefits that would be gained from having the South China Sea as a sea of peace, stability and sustainable development.

By way of comment, the words "We took note of concerns expressed by some Leaders over recent developments in the area" omit any reference to "land reclamation and militarization".

The latest is that ASEAN and China have agreed on a draft of Code of

Conduct at a senior officials' meeting in Guiyang (China). No text has been released and the draft will be put up to another meeting at the level of foreign ministers later in the year. It may be recalled that ASEAN and China had agreed to work on such a Code of Conduct way back in 2002. There is no good reason to believe that China's signing on to such a document will make any difference to its behaviour. We may recall that signing of the 1954 agreement on Tibet that included a pledge to adhere to Panchsheel did not influence China's aggressive intent and behaviour culminating in the 1962 invasion to 'teach India a lesson'.

The Attitude of US

The attitude of US on SCS is of crucial importance. If ASEAN countries that have contested China's claims can be confident of a coherent and lasting US policy of support, including military support if necessary, they might consider standing up to China. If they assess that US cannot be relied upon to lend them such support, they will not be able or willing to stand up to China.

US policy on SCS has been inconsistent to put it mildly. In 2011, President Obama announced a 'rebalancing' in Asia with much fanfare. That policy had the following elements:

1) By 2020, it was planned that 60 per cent of US naval assets will be positioned in the Pacific.
2) TPP (Trans Pacific Partnership) linking 12 countries excluding China (Australia, Brunei, Canada, Chile, Japan, Malaysia, Mexico, New Zealand, Peru, Singapore, United States, and Vietnam).

The transfer of naval assets to the Pacific Ocean did not take place as the Middle East claimed more of resources than anticipated. Obama could not get TPP ratified by the Congress and Trump has walked out of it.

However, Obama as recently as September 2016, said, "I reiterated that the United States will stand with allies and partners in upholding fundamental interests, among them the freedom of navigation and overflight, lawful commerce that is not impeded, and peaceful resolution of disputes."[19] Obama was speaking after the ITLOS order on the complaint of the Philippines. By then the 'rebalancing' had lost its momentum.

Till President Trump, US policy on SCS was to insist on freedom of navigation not only for commerce but also for military ISR (intelligence, surveillance, and reconnaissance). At his Senate confirmation hearings, Secretary of State Tillerson said that US should send a clear signal that island building should stop and that US might not allow access to islands already made. Later, Secretary of Defence Mattis also made similar statements. China signalled its displeasure and Washington started climbing down.

Obviously, US policy on SCS is part of US policy towards China. Trump as candidate and even as President did project the impression of his wanting to be tough with China, "the currency manipulator" who has resorted to unfair trade practices with US. He even threatened to stop adhering to 'One China Policy' after he talked by phone with the President of Taiwan.

China was watching carefully the Trump White House. Beijing cultivated Trump's daughter Ivanka and her husband Kushner who is also senior adviser to the President. China signalled that it would grant trade concessions to Ivanka's business. Trump must have recognized the huge value of the Chinese market not only for his daughter's company but also for his own real estate company.

Fortunately for Xi Jinping, North Korea carried out a missile test days before he came on a state visit to the US on 6th April 2017. Trump, true to his style, had already announced that he would deal sternly with North Korea. His advisers took a while to convince him that there was no military solution as a provoked North Korea can kill thousands in South Korea before US administers a decisive strike that might cause destruction in toto of that country. Trump decided to seek Xi Jinping's help to stop further tests by Pyongyang. Again, true to his style Trump declared that he had sought Xi Jinping. Though he agreed to do his best, Xi Jinping pointed out to Trump the complexities of the situation and the limits to what China can do.

Trump is determined to push China further on the North Korean matter and for that reason, added to the business interests that he has, he decided on a U turn in policy towards China. We are perhaps witnessing the likely emergence of a G2 of US and China working together.

The net result on SCS is that US has stopped FONOPs (Freedom of Navigation Operations) in SCS. At least for now, China can do what it wants in SCS without any opposition from the US provided it does not do anything that will embarrass the US. But, given the volatile nature of Trump it will be hazardous to say that there will not be a second U-turn.

Recent actions by China in SCS

Since 2003 China has been engaged in making artificial islands in SCS reefs. One think tank has found out that so far there are 7 such islands: Subi, Mischief, Ferry Cross, Gaven, Hughes, Johnson, and Curateron. The first three are bigger than others. China has also militarized the islands by placing anti-aircraft missiles, anti-missile systems, concrete hangars for fighter jets, and much more.[20]

In short, China has been changing the facts on the ground without any opposition from any other country.

China's National Off Shore Oil Corporation has put out a tender inviting quotations for exploring and exploiting 22 oil and gas blocks. Sixteen out of the twenty-two are close to China's coastline. Apart from exploration cum exploitation, China is seeking to interest big companies so that its claim on SCS gets additional acceptance. Already a Canadian company by name Husky has signed a contract. The tender will remain open till September 2017.[21]

India's Stakes in South China Sea

First, India has accepted the UNCLOS and believes in a rule based international order. If China violates successfully the UNCLOS, India and other countries that want to uphold a rule-based international order will lose out.

Second, India firmly believes in the freedom of navigation and cannot accept China's claims that do not agree with UNCLOS.

Third, India has entered into contracts with Vietnam for oil exploration/production despite strident protests and rather stiff warnings from China.

Fourth, if China succeeds in getting its nine-dash line accepted, and goes ahead with its militarization and resource exploration/exploitation, the asymmetry between India and China will change to India's disadvantage.

The Prospects

We need to see SCS in perspective considering what might happen in East China Sea, and, more importantly, the changing geopolitical power equations, including China's rise vis-à-vis US and India's rise vis-à-vis the rest of the world.

The think tank Stockholm International Peace Research Institute (SIPRI) has listed the top defence spenders in 2016 as follows:[22]

US	$611 billion
China	$ 215 billion
Russia	$69.2 billion
Saudi Arabia	$63.7 billion
India	$55.9 billion

We may take it that SIPRI might not have considered the purchasing power of the currencies in the respective countries. It is likely that $1 spent in India or China will go a longer way than in the US.

We need to recognize that China's total clout in terms military, economic, diplomatic, and soft-power is growing by leaps and bounds. Recently when the US and South Korea agreed to the deployment of THADD (Terminal High Altitude Area Defence) China hit back by stopping Chinese tourists from going to South Korea. Earlier, China hit at Japan by stopping export of rare earths, an essential component for cell phones and much else.

As we said earlier we need to take into account the policy of US under Trump. The trend towards forming a G2 might or might not continue. That trend might be reversed post-Trump as America always needs an enemy.

The G2 can be of four types: cordial, competitive without hostility, hostile, or a combination of all three in different proportions.

Japan has started improving its military strength. If China turns out to be overbearing Japan might even start making nuclear weapons.

If the regime in North Korea falls and the two Koreas get united the new Korea will have its own geopolitical weight.

India is a growing power. We do not know how Sino-India relations might evolve. We might see increased cooperation between India and Japan. Though there is much historical bad blood between Korea and Japan, under India's leadership the two may come around to working together for agreed common purposes.

We might look at a few possible scenarios:

1) With a cordial G2 between US and China, SCS and East China Sea become Chinese lakes over time. Other countries accept the hegemony willy-nilly.
2) With a hostile G2, US will mobilize others to oppose China's hegemony in SCS.

3) Even with a cordial G2, India, Vietnam, Japan, Australia, Malaysia and others get together and oppose China's hegemony.

We have listed the scenarios in the descending order of probability. As of now, the first scenario looks to be the likely one. But, as Shakespeare put it, who can look into the seeds of time and say which grain will grow and which will not? For all that we know, scenario 1 might hold for a while to be followed by scenario 2.

NOTES AND REFERENCES

1. http://news.nationalgeographic.com/news/2014/06/140616-south-china-sea-vietnam-china-cambodia-champa/
2. https://www.crisisgroup.org/asia/south-east-asia/south-china-sea/south-china-sea-positions-and-facts
3. W. Gilbert (1804), *A New Nautical Directory for the East-India and China Navigation*, pp. 480-482
4. http://globalnation.inquirer.net/34369/scarborough-belongs-to-ph-old-maps-show
5. Florian, Dupuy; Pierre, Marie (January 2013), "A Legal Analysis of China's Historic Rights Claim in the South China Sea": 124.
6. The text of the Cairo Declaration is at http://www.ndl.go.jp/constitution/e/shiryo/01/002_46/002_46tx.html. The text of the Potsdam Declaration is at http://afe.easia.columbia.edu/ps/japan/potsdam.pdf
7. https://www.dur.ac.uk/resources/ibru/publications/full/bsb7-2_keyuan.pdf
8. https://www.ft.com/content/aa32a224-480e-11e6-8d68-72e9211e86ab
9. https://thewire.in/51045/the-hague-verdict-is-a-big-victory-for-the-philippines-but-not-for-the-south-china-sea-dispute/
10. https://pca-cpa.org/wp-content/uploads/sites/175/2016/07/PH-CN-20160712-Press-Release-No-11-English.pdf
11. http://www.japantimes.co.jp/news/2016/07/12/asia-pacific/tribunal-rules-chinese-claims-south-china-sea/
12. https://qz.com/818637/long-before-he-was-elected-president-philippines-president-rodrigo-duterte-let-beijing-know-the-south-china-sea-was-theirs/
13. Sun Tzu, The Art of War , quoted by Commodore Augus Rustandi, Australian Defence College, http://www.defence.gov.au/ADC/Publications/IndoPac/Rustandi_IPSP.pdf
14. Ibid.
15. https://cil.nus.edu.sg/rp/pdf/1992%20ASEAN%20Declaration%20on%20the%20South%20China%20Sea-pdf.pdf
16. Ramses Amer, 'Dispute Management in the South China Sea', National Institute for South China Sea Studies, No. 1, March 2015, pp. 15-20, available at <http://en.nanhai.org.cn/uploads/file/file/20150302_Ramses.pdf
17. ASEAN, 'Declaration on the Conduct of Parties in the South China Sea', *ASEAN* [website], available at <http://www.asean.org/asean/external-relations/china/item/declaration-on-the-conduct-of-parties-in-the-south-china-sea> accessed 12 September 2015. The declaration was signed by ASEAN members and the Government of the People's Republic of China on 4 November 2002 in Phnom Penh, Cambodia.

18. http://www.philstar.com/headlines/2017/04/30/1695400/full-text-chairmans-statement-30th-asean-summit
19. http://www.voanews.com/a/southeast-asia-summit-leaders-express-concern-about-south-china-sea/3498519.html
20. http://www.reuters.com/article/us-southchinasea-china-arms-exclusive-idUSKBN1431OK
21. http://oilprice.com/Energy/Crude-Oil/China-Offers-Contested-South-China-Sea-Oil-And-Gas-Blocks.html
22. https://www.sipri.org/sites/default/files/Trends-world-military-expenditure-2016.pdf

3

Is South China Sea the Potential Flashpoint?

Alok Datta

ABSTRACT

South China Sea is one of the hotspots in the current international scenario. It has been making regular media headlines over the last few years. Many experts on international relations apprehend, the tension in the South China Sea has the potential to flare up into a major conflagration involving, apart from small countries, great powers like the United States and China.

The area is rich in fuels such as oil mineral and gas and is a bone of contention involving seven nations. The United States which is an outside power stresses the importance of freedom of navigation. Many experts fear an outbreak of hostilities among the disputants resulting in the intervention of the USA but against the backdrop of current international situation and USA's military engagements in a number of countries and Sino-American collaboration covering political and economic fields, a military showdown between them does not seem plausible, although occasional skirmishes among parties to the disputes cannot be discounted.

Introduction

The South China Sea disputes involve both island and maritime claims among several sovereign states within the region, namely the Nation of Brunei, the People's Republic of China, Taiwan, Malaysia, Indonesia, the Republic of the Philippines, and the Socialist Republic of Vietnam. As a high proportion of global trade—estimated $5 trillion—passes through the South China Sea, there are many non-claimant nations that want the South China Sea to remain as international waters, with several nations (e.g. the United States of America) conducting "freedom of navigation" operations.[1]

The disputes include the islands, reefs and banks of the South China Sea, including the Spratly and Paracel islands, the various boundaries, including those in the Gulf of Tonkin. There is a further dispute in the waters near the Indonesian Natuna Islands which by most definitions are not part of the South China Sea.[2] The interests of the nations include retaining or acquiring the rights to fishing areas; the exploration and potential exploitation of crude oil and natural gas under the waters of various parts of the South China Sea, and the strategic control of important shipping lanes.

In July 2016, an arbitral tribunal constituted under Annex VII of the United Nations Convention on the Law of the Sea ruled against China's maritime claims in *Philippines v. China*,[3] although it is not enforceable. China does not acknowledge the tribunal nor abide by its ruling, insisting that any resolution should be through bilateral negotiations with other claimants.[4]

The disputes involve both maritime boundaries and islands.[5] There are several disputes, each of which involving a different collection of countries:

1. The nine-dash line area claimed by the Republic of China, later the People's Republic of China which covers most of the South China sea and overlaps the exclusive economic zone claims of Brunei, Indonesia, Malaysia, the Philippines, Taiwan, and Vietnam.
2. Maritime boundary along the Vietnamese coast between the PRC, Taiwan, and Vietnam.
3. Maritime boundary north of Borneo between China, Malaysia, the Philippines, and Taiwan.
4. Islands, reefs, banks and shoals in the South China Sea, including the Paracel Islands, the Pratas Islands, Macclesfield Bank, Scarborough Shoal and the Spratly Islands between China, Taiwan, and Vietnam, and parts of the area also contested by Malaysia and the Philippines.
5. Maritime boundary in the waters north of the Natuna Islands between China, Indonesia and Taiwan.[6]
6. Maritime boundary off the coast of Palawan and Luzon between China, the Philippines, and Taiwan.

7. Maritime boundary, land territory, and the islands of Sabah, including Ambalat, between Indonesia, Malaysia, and the Philippines.
8. Maritime boundary and islands in the Luzon Strait between China, the Philippines, and Taiwan.

Background

The area may be rich in oil and natural gas deposits; however, the estimates are highly varied. The Ministry of Geological Resources and Mining of the People's Republic of China estimated that the South China Sea may contain 17.7 billion tons of crude oil[7] (compared to Kuwait with 13 billion tons). In the years following the announcement by the ministry, the claims regarding the South China Sea islands intensified. However, other sources claim that the proven reserve of oil in the South China Sea may only be 7.5 billion barrels, or about 1.1 billion tons.[8] According to the US Energy Information Administration (EIA)'s profile of the South China Sea region, a US Geological Survey estimate puts the region's discovered and undiscovered oil reserves at 11 billion barrels, as opposed to a Chinese figure of 125 billion barrels. The same EIA report also points to the wide variety of natural gas resource estimations, ranging from 190 trillion cubic feet to 500 trillion cubic feet, likely located in the contested Reed Bank".[9]

The South China Sea is dubbed by China as the "second Persian Sea".[10] The state-owned China Offshore Exploration Corp. planned to spend 200 billion RMB (US$30 billion) in the next 20 years to exploit oil in the region, with the estimated production of 25 million metric tons of crude oil and natural gas per annum, at a depth of 2000 meters within the next five years.[11]

2011 Agreement

On 20 July 2011, the PRC, Brunei, Malaysia, the Philippines and Vietnam agreed to a set of preliminary guidelines which would help resolve the dispute. The agreement was described by the PRC's assistant foreign minister, Liu Zhenmin, as "an important milestone document for cooperation among China and ASEAN countries".[12] Some of the early drafts acknowledged aspects such as "marine environmental protection, scientific research, safety of navigation and communication, search and rescue and combating transnational crime," although the issue of oil and natural gas drilling remains unresolved.

Chinese Objection to Indian Naval Presence and Oil Exploration

On 22 July 2011, the INS Airavat, an Indian amphibious assault vessel on a friendly visit to Vietnam, was reportedly contacted 45 nautical miles from the Vietnamese coast in the disputed South China Sea by a party identifying itself as the Chinese Navy and stating that the ship was entering Chinese waters. A spokesperson for the Indian Navy explained that as no ship or aircraft was visible, the INS Airavat proceeded on her onward journey as scheduled. The Indian Navy further clarified that "there was no confrontation involving the INS Airavat. India supports freedom of navigation in international waters, including in the South China Sea, and the right of passage in accordance with accepted principles of international law. These principles should be respected by all."[13]

Retrenchment

In Spring 2010, Chinese officials reportedly communicated to US officials that the South China Sea is "an area of 'core interest' that is as non-negotiable" and on par with Taiwan and Tibet on the national agenda,[14] but may have backed away from that assertion in 2011.[15]

In October 2011, China's *Global Times* newspaper, published by the Communist Party, *People's Daily*, editorialised on South China Sea territorial disputes under the banner "Don't take peaceful approach for granted". The article referenced recent incidents involving the Philippines and South Korea detaining Chinese fishing boats in the region.[16]

"If these countries don't want to change their ways with China, they will need to prepare for the sounds of cannons. We need to be ready for that, as it may be the only way for the disputes in the sea to be resolved." Warned *Global Times* (China), 25 October 2011. Responding to questions about whether this reflected official policy, a Chinese Foreign Ministry spokeswoman stated the country's commitment "to resolving the maritime dispute through peaceful means."[17]

Alan Dupont of the University of New South Wales has said that the Chinese government appears to be directing its fishing fleet into disputed waters as a matter of policy.[18]

Oil Development

China's first independently designed and constructed oil drilling platform in the South China Sea is the *Ocean Oil 981* (海洋石油 981). The major shareholders are J.P. Morgan Chase & Co. (19%), Commonwealth Bank of Australia (14%), T. Rowe Price Associates, Inc. and affiliates (6%), and Black Rock, Inc. (5%).[19] It began operation on 9 May 2012 in the South China Sea, 320 kilometres (200 mi) southeast of Hong Kong, at a depth of 1,500 m and employing 160 people.[20] On 2 May 2014 the platform was moved near to the Paracel Islands,[21] a move Vietnam stated violated their territorial claims.[22] Chinese officials said it was legal, stating that the area lies in waters surrounding the Paracel Islands which China occupies and militarily controls.[23]

United States

The United States and China are currently in disagreement over the South China Sea.[24] This disagreement is exacerbated by the fact that the US is not a member of the United Nations Convention on the Law of the Sea (UNCLOS).[25] Nevertheless, the US has stood by its manoeuvres, claiming that "peaceful surveillance activities and other military activities without permission in a country's Exclusive Economic Zone (EEZ),"[26] are allowed under the convention. Additionally, a South China Sea free to access is in the US's economic and geopolitical interests.[27] In relation to the dispute, Secretary Clinton voiced her support for fair access by reiterating that freedom of navigation and respect of international law is a matter of national interest to the United States.[28] Her comments were countered by China's Foreign Minister Yang Jiechi as "in effect an attack on China," who warned the United States against making the South China Sea an international issue or multilateral issue.[29]

In July 2012, the United States Senate passed resolution 524, initially sponsored by Senator John Kerry, stating (among other things) the United States' strong support for the 2002 declaration of conduct of parties in the South China Sea, reaffirms the United States' commitment to assist the nations of Southeast Asia to remain strong and independent, and supports enhanced operations by the United States armed forces in the Western Pacific.[30]

In 2014, the United States responded to China's claims over the fishing grounds of other nations by saying that "China has not offered any explanation or basis under international law for these extensive maritime claims."[31] US

Navy Chief of Naval Operations Jonathan Greenert then pledged American support to the Philippines in its territorial conflicts with the PRC.[32] The Chinese Foreign Ministry asked the United States to maintain a neutral position on the issue.[33] In 2014 and 2015, the United States continued freedom of navigation operations, including in the South China Sea.[34] Sources close to the Pentagon have also said that the US administration is planning to deploy some naval assets within 12 nautical miles of the Spratly Islands. In response to this announcement, Beijing issued a strict warning and said that she would not allow any country to violate China's territorial waters in the name of "Freedom of Navigation".[35] On 27 October 2015, the US destroyer USS Lassen navigated within 12 nautical miles of reclaimed land in the Subi Reef as the first in a series of "Freedom of Navigation Operations".[36] This is the first time since 2012 that the US directly challenged China's claims of the island's territorial limit.[37] On 8–9 November 2015, two US B-52 strategic bombers flew near artificial Chinese-built islands in the area of the Spratly Islands and were contacted by Chinese ground controllers but continued their mission undeterred.[38]

The United States itself has not signed UNCLOS, but has accepted all but Part XI as customary international law.[39]

Independent Analysis

The position of China on its maritime claims based on UNCLOS and history has been ambiguous, particularly with the nine dash line map. For example, in its *notes verbales* in 2011, the first phrase stated that China has undisputed sovereignty over the islands and the adjacent waters, suggesting China is claiming sovereignty over its territorial waters, a position consistent with UNCLOS. However, the second phrase in its *notes verbales* stated that China enjoys sovereign rights and jurisdiction over the relevant waters along with the seabed and subsoil contained in this region, suggesting that China is claiming sovereignty over all of the maritime space (includes all the geographic features and the waters within the nine dash line). The third phrase indicates support for basing their claims on historical basis as well.[40] Recently in its *notes verbales* in 2011, China has explicitly stated that it claims the territorial waters and all of the islands in which each island has its own exclusive economic zone and continental shelf. A major problem with this claim is that it fails to distinguish between geographic features considered as "islands" or "rocks" under

UNCLOS. The vast majority of international legal experts have concluded that China's claims based on historical claims are invalid. Many ambiguities arise from the notion of historical claims as a basis for claiming sovereignty and is inherently ambiguous.[41]

Japanese scholar Taoka Shunji criticised Japanese Prime Minister Shinzo Abe for trying to falsely portray China as a threat to Japan and that it was invading its neighbours like the Philippines. He pointed out that the Spratly islands were not part of the Philippines when the US acquired the Philippines from Spain in the Treaty of Paris in 1898, and the Japanese-ruled Taiwan itself had annexed the Spratly islands in 1938, a move that was never challenged by the US-ruled Philippines, which never asserted that it was their territory. He also pointed out that other countries did not need to do full land reclamation since they already controlled islands and that the reason China engaged in extensive land reclamation is because they needed it to build airfields since China only has control over reefs.[42]

- Clashes have occurred between China and Vietnam over South China Sea. Besides, China's stand-offs with Philippines till recently. In 1974, the Chinese seized the Paracels from Vietnam, killing more than 70 Vietnamese troops.
- In 1988, the two sides clashed in the Spratlys, with Vietnam again coming off worse, losing about 60 sailors.
- In early 2012, China and the Philippines engaged in a lengthy maritime stand-off, accusing each other of intrusions in the Scarborough Shoal.
- Unverified claims that the Chinese navy sabotaged two Vietnamese exploration operations in late 2012 led to large anti-China protests on Vietnam's streets.
- In January 2013, Manila said it was taking China to a UN tribunal under the auspices of the UN Convention on the Laws of the Sea, to challenge its claims.
- In May 2014, the introduction by China of a drilling rig into waters near the Paracel Islands led to multiple collisions between Vietnamese and Chinese ships.

In July 2016, the tribunal backed the Philippines' case, saying China had violated the Philippines' sovereign rights. China had boycotted the proceedings, and called the ruling "ill-founded". It says it will not be bound by it.[43]

The Philippines president paid a visit to China in October 2016 the press contextualized the trip as part of his jarring U-turn away from the US alliance and towards China's lucrative embrace. That narrative and Duterte's apparent determination to restructure the regional order, have received no shortage of coverage and analysis.[44]

President Rodrigo Duterte announced his "separation" from the United States on 20 October 2016, declaring he had realigned with China as the two agreed to resolve their South China Sea dispute through talks. Duterte made his comments in Beijing, where he was visiting with at least 200 business people to pave the way for what he called a new commercial alliance as relations with longtime ally Washington deteriorated.[45]

From the US point of view, it has significant political, security, and economic interests at stake if one of the contingencies occur. It holds that the United States has important interests in the peaceful resolution of South China Sea disputes according to international law. With the exception of China, all the claimants of the South China Sea have attempted to justify their claims based on their coastlines and the provisions of UNCLOS. China, however, relies on a mix of historic rights and legal claims, while remaining ambiguous about the meaning of the "nine-dashed line" around the sea that is drawn on Chinese maps. The US believes, failure to uphold international law and norms could harm the US interests elsewhere in the region and beyond. Ensuring freedom of navigation is another critical interest of the United States and other regional states. Although China claims that it supports freedom of navigation, its insistence that foreign militaries seek advance permission to sail in its two-hundred-mile EEZ casts doubt on its stance. China's development of capabilities to deny American naval access to those waters in a conflict provides evidence of possible Chinese intentions to block freedom of navigation in specific contingencies.

From the point of view of trade and commerce, the importance of South China Sea can hardly be exaggerated. Each year, $5.3 trillion of trade passes through the South China Sea; U.S. trade accounts for $1.2 trillion of this total. Should a crisis occur, the diversion of cargo ships to other routes would harm regional economies as a result of an increase in insurance rates and longer transits. Conflict of any scale in the South China Sea would hamper the claimants from benefiting from the South China's Sea's proven and potential riches.[46]

Despite tension over South China Sea between the US and the PRC, the stakes and implications of any U.S.-China incident are far greater than in other scenarios. The United States has an abiding interest in preserving stability in the U.S.-China relationship so that it can continue to secure Beijing's cooperation on an expanding list of regional and global issues and more tightly integrate China into the prevailing international system.

Despite the apprehensions of a Sino-American show down over South China Sea, the realities of the current international situation do not corroborate such a fear. First, the contiguity of the area to mainland China gives it a logistic advantage over the U.S. in the event of major confrontation between the two great powers. Consequently, it is difficult for the U.S. to engage in any military conflict with a major power like China in an area so close to its maritime boundaries. Thus, in spite of saber-rattling and belligerent statements, the two countries will definitely go the whole hog to avoid any military confrontation.

Moreover, the US is currently engaged in military operations in vast swaths of territory particularly in the Middle East which stretch its resources to the limit. The US carries out regular military operations in Syria, Libya, Yemen, Iraq, Afghanistan, Pakistan and Somalia. Furthermore, it has military commitments to many other countries such as South Korea, Israel, Saudi Arabia and so on. Under such circumstances it cannot afford hostilities in the South China Sea. In Afghanistan and Iraq, the US has been fighting protracted battles for over a decade and no end is in sight.

Second, the US needs China to settle scores with North Korea over its Nuclear and Missile Programs. The UN Security Council adopted several resolutions condemning North Korea's nuclear tests and Missile launch program and imposing economic sanctions on DPRK at the initiative of the US which received Chinese support. This is why America and China will not be willing to militarily confront each other leaving the nuclear armed North Korea behind their backs. The U.S often identifies North Korea as a major threat to its security. For this reason, the United States seeks and gets China's support to hold down North Korea.

Third, the role of Russia in any probable confrontation can by no means be downplayed.

Growing Sino-Russian collaboration encompassing political economic and military fields poses a serious challenge to American unilateralism. The latest manifestation of Sino-Russian military cooperation is the joint military exercises conducted by these two countries, according to the following report:

"Chinese and Russian naval forces began joint exercises in the South China Sea on Monday (12 September 2016), adding a new twist to ongoing tensions over Chinese island-building in the region.

The eight-day exercises will highlight marine corps units in "live-fire drills, sea crossing and island landing operations, and island defense and offense exercises," Chinese navy spokesperson Liang Yang said in a report from China's official Xinhua News Agency.[47]

China and Russia are also bound by the "**Treaty of Good-Neighborliness and Friendly Cooperation**". The twenty-year strategic treaty was signed by the leaders of the two international powers, Jiang Zemin and Vladimir Putin, on 16 July 2001.[48]

Both countries are members of BRICS and Shanghai Cooperation Organisation. These two countries have also coordinated their positions on Syria both inside and outside the UNO. Trade between Russia and China has grown rapidly as the leaders of both countries have committed to advancing bilateral economic cooperation. The two countries are reducing the use of US dollar in bilateral trade in favour of their own currencies, calling attention to the importance of their economic relationship.

Bilateral trade volume between the two countries, which amounted to $15.8 billion in 2003, has increased more than 6 times over the last 10 years, reaching $95.3 billion in 2014.

According to forecasts, bilateral commerce could grow up to $100 billion in 2015 and if the two countries continue to nurture the right conditions for trade investment growth, it is likely to reach $200 billion by 2020. The total trading value between China and Russia has grown 17.8 per cent p.a. in the past 11 year.[49]

Russia's growing clout in Europe and the Middle-East—its support to the forces in Eastern Ukraine fighting the Ukrainian government seeking autonomy, the incorporation of Crimea into Russia, military intervention in Syria and victories of government forces backed by Russian airpower, its growing ties with Iran and desertion by Turkey from the Western camp and bonhomie with Russia and latest peace initiative in Syria by Russia along with Iran and Turkey excluding the USA are unmistakable signs of a resurgent Russia which is a matter of concern to the United States. Meanwhile, America launched its first missile attack on Syria after Trump assumed office. 59 Tomahawk missiles were fired on 7 April 2017 in retaliation against alleged chemical attack by Syrian air force on rebel-held areas.[50]

But the charge was vehemently rejected by both Syria and Russia. They argued that there was growing evidence that this was (chemical attack) staged.[51] Russia also warned the US of 'extremely serious' consequences of this for regional and international stability.[52] Meanwhile, in the growing sign of Russia's assertiveness, Russia played host to six party talks involving Afghanistan, Pakistan, India, Iran, China and Russia itself on the future of Afghanistan in Moscow 15 February 2017. Earlier in December 2016, the first meeting on Afghanistan had been hosted by Russia in Moscow in which, apart from Russia, China and Pakistan took part.[53]

China and the United States have political differences particularly over American sale of sophisticated weapons to Taiwan violating the provisions of Sino-American agreement in 1979 which established diplomatic relations between the two countries, Chinese sovereignty over Tibet and frequent references by the US to China's human right records. But in the economic field, the two countries share more or less a cooperative relationship.

Monetary policy has been one of the biggest issues surrounding relations between the United States and China in the past decades. At the heart of the issue is the question of whether or not each country's currency is at the proper value. Each country has pinned the blame on the other. Most monetary and trade experts agree that China's currency has been and is still undervalued,[54] but an article by Business Insider argues that China raising the value of their currency would have a large effect on the trade balance between the two countries.[55]

China is a major creditor and the second largest foreign holder of US public debt[56] and has been critical of US deficits and fiscal policy calling for policies that maintain the purchasing value of the dollar,[57] although it had little few options other than to continue to buy United States Treasury bonds.[58] China condemned the US monetary policy of quantitative easing,[59] responding to S&P's downgrade of the U.S credit rating, and advised the United States not to continue with the accumulation of debt, concluding with the statement that America cannot continue to borrow to solve financial problems.[60]

The US faces other hurdles in going to war with other countries, China included. It is true that armament industry is an important component of the US economy, i.e. the militarization of its economy is a significant factor in keeping it afloat, nevertheless growing anti-war sentiments at home and abroad act as a hindrance to US efforts to commit its troops to other countries for military operations. Since World War II, the US has been involved directly or indirectly in almost all major hostilities causing a drain on its economic resources and taking a heavy toll on human lives including those of the US itself. The people's power asserted itself again when the Obama's administration went all-out to launch military strikes on Syria in September 2013 alleging use of chemical weapons by the Assad regime against its own people on 21 August 2013. It was reported that 71 per cent of Americans opposed US involvement in Syria situation, a poll revealed.[61]

The possibility of the countries locked in disputes with China over South China Sea breaking ranks with the USA cannot be ruled out. As the Philippines case illustrates, these countries, or at least some of them, may not consider it wise to incur the wrath of China and invite troubles for them, given China's economic and military might and their geographical proximity to China and distance from the United States. In fact, China and Vietnam have initiated negotiations to resolve their differences and avert untoward incidents.

On 14 January 2017, China and Vietnam pledged to manage maritime differences over the South China Sea and safeguard peace and stability as Beijing sought to scale up bilateral ties amid Hanoi's push to forge close relations with India.

China and Vietnam had "a candid exchange of views" on maritime issues, a joint communiqué was issued at the end of the General Secretary of the Communist Party of Vietnam (CPV) Central Committee Nguyen Phu Trong's visit to China.

On Friday (13 January 2017), during his meeting with Phu, Chinese President Xi Jingping, who also heads the ruling Communist Party of China, termed China and Vietnam as "comrades and brothers", highlighting fraternal ties between the two countries ruled by the Communist Parties.

With regards to the South China Sea row, Xi said both sides should increase communications and consolidate mutual trust in order to lay solid political foundation for the settlement of disputes and work together on maritime exploration and cooperation.[62]

The above observations of course, do not altogether negate the likelihood of occasional skirmishes between the disputants including the US and China.

On 15 December 2016, China seized a US Navy underwater drone in the South China Sea and the Pentagon demanded it back, raising a new point of tension between the US and Chinese military forces in the disputed waters as relations between the two countries entered uncharted territory.

On 19 December 2016, China returned the US underwater drone taken by Chinese naval vessels in the disputed South China Sea after what China's Defence Ministry said were "friendly" talks between the two countries.[63]

Conclusion

The question of South China Sea cannot be viewed in isolation from the current volatile international relations. Presently, alignment and realignment of forces are taking place in the context of rapidly changing international situation. Newer areas of conflict are arising and the countries, adversaries to each other only the other day, are switching sides and forming new equations. Turkey and Russia backing opposite forces in Syria and engaged in mutual recrimination have now buried their hatchet, even after Turkey had shot down a Russian military plane on 24 November 2015 taking part in the operation in Syria in support of Assad forces and against the rebel groups who received Turkey's help. Likewise, Russia and Pakistan cool to each other are now edging closer forging a new equation in Asia which also includes China. Such fluidity in relations among nations notwithstanding, no great power is willing to militarily take on others, given the devastating consequences that will follow. Important developments in Sino-American ties have been witnessed since Trump's assumption of office. Notwithstanding Trump's high-sounding anti-China rhetoric during his election campaign which cast doubts on continued pursuit of One-China Policy by the US under Trump, he reassured Chinese President Xi Jinping of his adherence to the policy when he called up the Chinese President on 10 February 2017 (*Al Jazeera*, 10 Feb 2017). China strongly opposes any truck between the USA and Taiwan which it considers as its breakaway province, but an integral part.

In a further sign of improving Sino-American ties, the Chinese President paid a two-day official visit to America 6-7 April 2017. "Tremendous progress" has been made in talks with Chinese President Xi Jinping, Donald Trump said on the summit's second and final day (7 April 2017).[64] However, the visit was marred by what is widely regarded as a snub and humiliation to the Chinese President and breach of diplomatic niceties when America carried out its missile attack on Sharyat Air base in Syria alleging the use by Assad forces of chemical weapons against rebels in the Syrian province of Idlib on 4 April 2017.[65] Chinese President was informed of the missile strike by the US president after the dinner at Mar-a-Lago. The US also wants China to help it in its current stand-off with North Korea. The above discussion boils down to the conclusion that as an important sea route South China Sea facilitates a large volume of world trade, the area is also rich in oil and gas resources and a vital strategic point which make the countries adjacent to it and the power like the US covetous of it. All these put the stakeholders at odds over its control. However, given the current global scenario, it is highly unlikely that they will engage in any large-scale military operations. But, this doesn't altogether negate the possibility of small skirmishes between them over this area which is a bone of contention among these countries.

NOTES AND REFERENCES

1. Fensom, Anthony, "$5 Trillion Meltdown: What If China Shuts Down the South China Sea?", *The National Interest*, Retrieved 2017-03-21. "U.S. protests Chinese action in South China Sea" CNN-CNNPolitics.com.
2. Keck, Zachary (20 March 2014), "China's Newest Maritime Dispute", *The Diplomat*, Retrieved 12 February 2015.
   Vaswani, Karishma (19 October 2014), "The sleepy island Indonesia is guarding from China", Retrieved 19 October 2014.
   R.C. Marshall, Andrew (25 August 2014), "Remote, gas-rich islands on Indonesia's South China Sea frontline", *Reuters*, Retrieved 12 February 2015.
3. The South China Sea Arbitration (The Republic of the Philippines v. The People's Republic of China), PCA Press Release, 12 July 2016,
4. David Tweed; Ting Shi (12 July 2016), "China's South China Sea Claims Dashed by Hague Court Ruling", Bloomberg. Retrieved 11 December 2016.
5. "An interactive look at claims on the South China Sea", *The Straits Times*, Retrieved 29 February 2016.
6. John Pike, "Natuna Islands", www.globalsecurity.org, Retrieved 30 July 2015.
7. "China's Multilateralism and the South China Sea Conflict: Quest for Hegemonic Stability?" (PDF), Thesis for M.S.Sc, National University of Singapore, 2006. Retrieved 4 October 2014. quoting Mark. J Valencia, "China and South China Sea Disputes: Claims and Potential Solutions in the South China Sea", Adelphi paper 298 (Oxford University Press, Oxford, 1995).
8. John Pike, "South China Sea Oil and Natural Gas", www.globalsecurity.org. Retrieved 4 October 2014.
9. "South China Sea – Analysis", U.S. Energy Information Administration (EIA), 7 February 2013. Retrieved 11 December 2016.
10. http://news.qq.com/a/20110620/000254.htm

11. http://special.globaltimes.cn/2011-04/645909.html.Missing or empty |title= (help) [dead link]
12. Martina, Michael (20 July 2011), "RPT-China, ASEAN set 'guidelines' on sea row, but no deal expected", *Reuters*, 20 July 2011. Retrieved 20 July 2011.
13. "China face-off in South China Sea", DNA India report, http://www.southasiaanalysis.org/papers47/paper4677.html. Missing or empty |title= (help)[dead link]
14. "U.S., China Relations: Policy Issues Congressional Research Service", 12 January 2011
15. Edward Wong (30 March 2011), "China Hedges Over Whether South China Sea Is a 'Core Interest' Worth War", *New York Times*. Retrieved 1 September 2012.
Bonnie S. Glaser (April 2012), "Armed Clash in the South China Sea", East Asia, Council on Foreign Relations. Retrieved 1 September 2012. For example, China may explicitly refer to the South China Sea as a core interest; in 2010 Beijing hinted this was the case but subsequently backed away from the assertion.
Phil Stewart; John Ruwitch (12 October 2010), "U.S. sees crisis fears easing over South China Sea", *Reuters*, Hanoi. Retrieved 1 September 2012.
16. "Don't take peaceful approach for granted", *Global Times*, China, 25 October 2011. Retrieved 25 October 2011.
17. Wadhams, Nicholas (25 October 2011), "China May Resort to Force in Sea Disputes Global Times Says", *Bloomberg Businessweek*. Retrieved 25 October 2011. Foreign Ministry spokeswoman Jiang Yu told reporters today in Beijing that China "adheres to the strategy of peaceful development. ... Sowing discord and hostility will only complicate" the issue, Jiang said.
18. Pasick, Adam (29 July 2014), "How China's Enormous Fishing Fleet Is Being Used As a Surrogate Navy", www.defenseone.com. Quartz. Retrieved 29 July 2014.
19. "chiefgroup.com.hk 02883 CHINA OILFIELD SERVICES LIMITED Company Profile". Retrieved 4 October 2014.
20. 11 May 2012, 南海钻井平台上工人直升机上下班, NetEase News (Chinese).
21. "Not the usual drill", Singapore: *The Economist*, 10 May 2014. Retrieved 14 May 2014.
22. "Vietnam says China's oil rig movement into South China Sea is "illegal"," *Reuters*.
23. Zhu, Ningzhu (7 May 2014), "China urges against Vietnamese interference in territorial water exploration", *Xinhuanet*. Retrieved 16 May 2014.
24. Diola, Camille (5 November 2014), "US won't 'agree to disagree' with China on sea row", *Philippine Star*. Retrieved 14 March 2015.
25. Etzioni, Amitai (July 2016), "Freedom of Navigation Assertions: The United States as the World's Policeman" (PDF), Armed Forces & Society, 42 (3): 501–517.
26. Lawrence, Susan V.; Thomas Lum (11 March 2011), U.S.-China Relations: Policy Issues, CRS Report for Congress R41108, Washington, DC: Library of Congress, Congressional Research Service, p. 26. Retrieved 25 October 2013.
27. Bouchat, Clarence J. (June 2014), "The Paracel Islands and U.S. Interests and Approaches in the South China Sea" (PDF), Strategic Studies Institute, United States Army. Retrieved 13 March 2015.
Yujuico, Emmanuel, "The real story behind the South China Sea dispute" (PDF), London School of Economics and Political Science, Retrieved 13 March 2015.
28. Landler, Mark (23 July 2010), "Offering to Aid Talks, U.S. Challenges China on Disputed Islands", *New York Times*. Retrieved 15 March 2015.
29. David Martin Jones; Michael Lawrence Rowan Smith; Nicholas Khoo (1 January 2013), Asian Security and the Rise of China: International Relations in an Age of Volatility, Edward Elgar Publishing, p. 57. ISBN 978-1-78100-462-3.
Denny Roy (20 August 2013), Return of the Dragon: Rising China and Regional Security,

Columbia University Press, p. 219. ISBN 978-0-231-52815-3.
30. John Kerry (23 July 2012), "S. Res. 524: A resolution reaffirming the strong support of the United States for the 2002 declaration of conduct of parties...". govtrack.us. Civic Impulse, LLC. Retrieved 3 September 2012.
31. Williams, Carol J. (10 January 2014), "China asserts control over vast sea area, angering neighbors, US", *Los Angeles Times*. Retrieved 12 January 2014.
32. Mogato, Manuel (13 February 2014), "U.S. admiral assures Philippines of help in disputed sea", *Reuters*, Retrieved 13 February 2014.
33. "Beijing slams US Navy official for 'aiding Philippines' remarks", *WantChina Times*, 16 February 2014. Retrieved 15 February 2014.
34. "Dragon Breathes Fire Over S. China Sea, Worries US", *Free Press Journal*, Mumbai, India, 28 February 2015. Retrieved 27 March 2015.
"US freedom of navigation operations challenge China's maritime security", *Want China Times*, Taiwan, 28 March 2015. Retrieved 27 March 2015.
Alexander, David (25 March 2015), "U.S. military challenged maritime claims of 19 countries in 2014", United States: *Reuters*, Retrieved 27 March 2015.
35. "Beijing Slams Washington's Plans for 'Incursion' Into South China Sea", sputniknews.com. Retrieved 10 October 2015.
36. "After Months of Waiting, US Finally Begins Freedom of Navigation Patrols Near China's Man-Made Islands", *The Diplomat*, 27 October 2015.
37. Blanchard, Ben; Shalal, Andrea (28 October 2015), "Angry China shadows U.S. warship near man-made islands", *Reuters*. Retrieved 26 November 2015.
38. "US B-52 bombers flew near disputed islands in South China Sea, says Pentagon", *The Guardian*, 12 November 2015.
39. See United States and the United Nations Convention on the Law of the Sea#History
40. Beckman, Robert (2013), "The UN Convention on the Law of the Sea and the Maritime Disputes in the South China Sea", *The American Journal of International Law*. American Society of International Law, 107 (1): 142–163. JSTOR 10.5305/amerjintelaw.107.1.0142.
41. Malik, Mohan, "Historical Fiction: China's South China Sea Claims," *World Affairs*. Retrieved 24 February 2016.
42. Taoka, Shunji (21 September 2015), Translated by Rumi Sakamoto, "'China Threat Theory' Drives Japanese War Legislation", *The Asia-Pacific Journal*: Japan Focus, 13 (38-5). Retrieved 26 September 2015.
43. http://www.bbc.com/news/world-asia-pacific-13748349
44. http://thediplomat.com/2016/11/why-dutertes-deals-with-china-may-be-security-concerns/
45. http://www.reuters.com/article/us-china-philippines-idUSKCN12K0AS
46. http://www.cfr.org/asia-and-pacific/armed-clash-south-china-sea/p27883
47. http://edition.cnn.com/2016/09/12/asia/china-russia-south-china-sea-exercises/
48. https://en.wikipedia.org/wiki/2001_Sino-Russian_Treaty_of_Friendship
49. http://rcif.com/russia-china-trade.htm
50. https://www.theguardian.com/world/live/2017/apr/07/us-syria-response-donald-trump-assad-pentagon-liveh
51. https://www.bloomberg.com/news/articles/2017-04-14/russia-says-evidence-growing-syria-chemical-attack-was-staged
52. https://www.theguardian.com/world/live/2017/apr/07/us-syria-response-donald-trump-assad-pentagon-live?page=with:block-58e7c34ce4b05b487c0e03f1#block-58e7c34ce4b05b487c0e03f1
53. https://thewire.in/109617/moscow-six-party-talks-afghanistan-commit-red-lines-taliban-engagement/

54. http://web.viu.ca/lina/FNCE%20429/Foreign%20exchange%20market/Exchange%20rate%20and%20monetary%20policy%20in%20China.pdf
55. Scott Grannis (16 September 2010), "Here's How Chinese Currency "Manipulation" Actually Helps America", Business Insider.
56. "Foreign Holdings of Treasuries as of May, 2011", http://www.treasury.gov/resource-center/data-chart-center/tic/Documents/mfh.txt
57. Barboza, David (2011-08-06), "China Condemns U.S. "Addiction to Debts"," *The New York Times*, http://www.nytimes.com/2011/08/07/business/global/china-a-big-creditor-says-us-has-only-itself-to-blame.html
58. Foster, Peter (2009-03-13), "Chinese premier Wen Jiabao worried about US debt", *The Daily Telegraph*, London.
"Update: China calls for global cooperation on debt risks", *Reuters*, 2011-08-05.
59. Kurt Brouwer, "China & the U.S. debt addiction", Marketwatch, http://blogs.marketwatch.com/fundmastery/2011/08/06/china-the-u-s-debt-addiction /http://www.vancouversun.com/business/China+Good+days+over/5215085/story.html
60. Jamieson, Alastair (2011-08-06), "China Calls for New Global Reserve Currency", *The Daily Telegraph*, London. Pierson, David (2011-08-06), "China Chastises U.S. Over Debt", *Los Angeles Times*. Fred E. Jandt (2012), An Introduction to Intercultural Communication: Identities in a Global Community, SAGE, p. 103.
61. *The Times of India*, September 10, 2013
62. Militaries of China, Vietnam to enhance cooperation—China Military—Huang Panyue, *Xinhua*, 14 January 2017. http://english.chinamil.com.cn/view/2017-01/14/content_7452098.htm
63. "China Returns U.S. Navy Drone Seized in South China Sea: The Two-Way", NPR http://www.npr.org/sections/thetwo-way/2016/12/20/506256081/china-returns-u-s-navy-drone-seized-in-south-china-sea
64. "Trump hails 'tremendous' progress in talks with China's Xi", *BBC News*, 7 April 2017 US & Canada, http://www.bbc.com/news/world-us-canada-39517569
65. 2017 Shayrat missile strike – Wikipediahttps://en.wikipedia.org/wiki/2017_Shayrat_missile_strike

4

Dispute over South China Sea: Potentials for Military Escalations

Vandana Mishra and Kamalakant Pathak

ABSTRACT

South China Sea (SCS) conflict since July 2016 has been in international media spotlight frequently. The dispute is fast turning into a hotbed of international politics. Some experts have opined it a dispute with potentials to become a flashpoint of another world war. China's assertions and expansionist approach towards SCS has invited protests by small and big countries alike. War of words among major powers of the world is in full swing and sounding sensational. Different countries are having different set of interests and problems in the dispute that has ensued. Increasing number of stakeholders has made it a multifaceted and complex issue in the aftermath of the rulings of Permanent Court of Arbitration (PCA). Authenticity of status of international law is at stake; a lot is being said about China's faith, trust and regards towards the instrumentality of International Law.

The conflict thus can be viewed from multiple dimensions such as geographical, political, economic and most important legal. The prospect of a huge stock of oil and natural gas in SCS has added another sensitive dimension alongside it being on the major sea lanes of communication. While China desires the whole region and is trying to increase its presence gradually, the other claimants are contesting China's claims of suzerainty over it. Increased US interventions have been escalating the possibility of military confrontation thereby magnifying the political risk in the region. China has been equally and emphatically responsive to such escalation. Accordingly, author intends to explore the following pertinent question through research: (i) underlying dynamics within the politics over SCS; (ii) legality of the claims of parties at conflict; (iii) legality of major power interventions; and (iv) potentials of military escalation in the wake of US power projections in the region.

Introduction

Changing trends in international relations has replaced the rigid compartmentalization of issues to a point where political, economic and geographical issues converge and intersect. So, vibrant and effective foreign policy discourses should take into account all the dimensions. Since the landscape of international politics has never been a level playing field for all the actors some states are always at an advantageous position. It has rightly been said by Lord Palmerstone that in International relations there is no permanent friend and there is no permanent enemy but only permanent interests. This compels us to view the relations from a realistic framework where some states shapes their foreign policies setting aside all the rules, laws and conventions. This is true especially when we talk about the so called great powers. However, presently the structure of international relations has undergone a tremendous change. The interdependent, complicated and competitive multipolar structures suggest that no state can be left alone to pursue its selfish and narrow interest unilaterally. The same applies to China in the case of South China Sea (SCS). SCS according to many experts of international politics has been fast changing into a flashpoint of international conflict among the several stakeholders. As in international politics perceptions are more widely prevalent than reality; the geopolitics of SCS is no different to this rule. SCS has come to the fore in almost all discourses of international relations and is being debated and discussed in view of the claims and counterclaims of states that are involved in it. The dominant argument has been that given the changing geopolitics of the SCS there are greater probabilities that it would lead to military escalation between China and the United States. Therefore, the authors endeavour to explore the grounds on which such claims are being made and the level of its authenticity.

South China Sea: An Introduction

SCS is a semi-enclosed sea in western Pacific Ocean covering an area of almost 3.5 million square kilometres. It lies south of China; to the west of Philippines; the east of Vietnam; and the north of Malaysia, Brunei, Singapore and Indonesia. The SCS is a crucial shipping lane, a rich fishing ground, home to a highly biodiverse coral reef ecosystem, and is also believed to hold substantial oil and gas resource. China, Vietnam, the Philippines, Taiwan, Malaysia and Brunei all have competing claims in SCS. Although largely uninhabited, the Paracels and the Spratly may have reserves of natural resources. There has been little detailed exploration of the area, so estimates are largely extrapolated from the mineral wealth of neighbouring areas.[1] The sea is also a major fishing ground that supplies the livelihoods to people across the region. The southern portion of the SCS is also the location of the Spratly Islands, a constellation of small islands and coral reefs, existing just above or below water, that comprise the peaks of undersea mountains rising from the deep ocean floor; The Spratly Islands are the site of long-standing territorial disputes among some of the littoral states of the SCS.

Changing Geopolitics of South China Sea

The geopolitics of South China Sea is changing at a rapid pace. It has given rise to a number of stakeholders. The underlying causes of the friction in the SCS are Structural and Strategic. It is a dispute over territory and sovereignty over ocean areas, and the group of two island chains which are being claimed in whole or in part by a number of countries:

- Spratly Islands[2]
- Scarborough Shoal[3]

Alongside the fully fledged islands, there are dozens of rocky outcrops, atolls, sandbanks and reefs, such as the Scarborough Shoal. China's sweeping claims of sovereignty over the sea—and the sea's alleged 11 trillion barrels of untapped oil and 190 trillion cubic feet of natural gas—have antagonized competing claimants Malaysia, Vietnam, Brunei, Taiwan, Indonesia, and the Philippines.[4] It is even more than the world's largest deposits. The water also accounts for 10 per cent of the global fisheries.[5] One third of the world shipping trade passes through its waters including 80 per cent of the oil imports.

Territorial Claims to the South China Sea[6]

Chinese Claims

- China claims by far the largest portion of territory—an area defined by the 'Nine-dash line' which stretches hundreds of miles south and east from its most southerly province of Hainan.

- It says that its right to the area goes back centuries to when the Paracel and Spratly island chains were regarded as integral parts of the Chinese nation, and in 1947 it issued a map detailing its claims. It showed the two island groups falling entirely within its territory.
- Those claims are mirrored by Taiwan.

There are two parts to the China's claims: It is not clear whether China claims only land territory within the nine-dash line, or all the territorial waters within the line as well.

The Republic of China mapped 291 islands, reefs, and banks in the SCS and put them under the nine-dash line in 1947. After its defeat at the hands of the Communists, the nationalist government transplanted itself in Taiwan.

Vietnam's Claims

- Vietnam hotly disputes China's historical account, saying China had never claimed sovereignty over the islands before the 1940s. Vietnam says it has actively ruled over both the Paracels[7] and the Spratlys since 17th Century—and has the documents to prove it.[8]

Philippines' Claims

- Philippines invoke the geographical proximity to the Spratly Islands as the main basis of its claim for part of the grouping.
- Both Philippines and China lay claim to the Scarborough Shoal (known as Huangyan Island in China)—a little more than 100 miles (160 km) from the Philippines and 500 miles from China.

Malaysia's and Brunei's Claims

- Malaysia and Brunei lay claim to territory in the SCS saying that they fall within their EEZ, as defined by UNCLOS.
- Brunei does not claim any of the disputed islands, but Malaysia claims small number of islands in the Spratlys.

The most serious trouble in recent decades has flared between Vietnam and China, and there have also been stand-offs between the Philippines and China. Some of the incidents include:

- In 1974, the Chinese seized the Paracels from Vietnam, killing more than 70 Vietnamese troops.

- In 1988, the two sides clashed in the Spartlys, with Vietnam again coming off worse, losing about 60 sailors.
- In 2012, China and the Philippines engaged in a lengthy maritime standoff, accusing each other of intrusions in the Scarborough Shoal.
- Unverified claims that the Chinese navy sabotaged two Vietnamese exploration operations in late 2012 led to large anti-China protests on Vietnam's streets.
- In January 2013, the Philippines said it was taking China to a tribunal under the auspices of the UNCLOS, to challenge its claims.
- In May 2014, the introduction by China of a drilling rig into waters near Paracel Islands led to multiple collisions between Vietnamese and Chinese ships.

Therefore, at the heart of changing geopolitics of the region are the claims and counterclaims of the stakeholders, i.e. the nation-states littoral to the sea. This has given rise to a situation of conflict among them with consequences in terms of great power interventions. The United States is the most involved nation-state which is trying to contain China over the last couple of decades, and is thus using SCS as a pretext. The US is working in tandem with Vietnam and is supplying arms to Hanoi. The US provoked and prepared the Philippines to take the matter to the Permanent Court of Arbitration (PCA) under the previous regime. The US is also working towards the realization of its 'Pivot to Asia' foreign policy choice to enhance its physical presence in the Asian region. The US is slowly and gradually cultivating India as well so that it can exploit Sino-Indian conflict to its own advantage and pit India against China over SCS.

Whereas on one hand maritime security has assumed an extremely important role on the international platform but it has become a hotbed of disputes among some of the coastal states. Moreover, the solution to the conflict seems complicated to decide as to who controls, how and which territory. Although there has never been a direct confrontation related to such issues but the possibilities of escalations cannot be ignored especially when we talk about the disputed territory of South China Sea. Whereas China claims most of the part there are other smaller nations with overlapping interests. The smaller nations as well as the major powers have the conflicting interests and a complicated web of power relations is formed when we talk about the interests of nations in South China Sea because of its economic significance and trade routes. However, China seems to be all set to act assertively with both military and economic aims.

China's Claims and Assertions

It is engaged in ambitious and aggressive bid to enhance its naval strategies. China has exhibited its assertiveness in a number of activities. In the 1950s itself it had occupied half of the Paracel islands which was also claimed by South Vietnam and gradually occupied the entire Paracel islands. Then, it advanced towards Spratly, mischief reef and southern South China Sea. Recently it also gained control over the Scarborough shoal. It is a rich fishing ground and has also started large scale reclamation and infrastructure building. It has also built air strips, military. In this way it is fanning the flame of discontent in the other claimants and has aggravated the dispute by building on island on mischief reef. It has also violated the Philippines' sovereign rights within its EEZ including fisheries and petroleum exploitation. The firing of water cannon by Chinese government vessel to drive away Filipino fishermen in the disputed shoal has also aggravated the dispute. There are also some cases of harassment by Chinese vessels. Even the Indian navy warships have been warned by Chinese aircraft to move out. It also aspires to establish mobile nuclear power plants in the SCS. Once the electricity and power is strengthened it will speed up the commercial developments in the region. Its activities have inflicted severe damage to the fragile ecosystem and serious harm to the endangered species. In this way it is gradually developing its defensive maritime capability building immense pressure on the other nations. China is also trying to develop its military capabilities and has stationed the naval forces in the woody island. It also seeks to acquire aircraft carrier and other capabilities; airstrip is also under construction in one of the Beijing occupied islands. Although the direct confrontation is not visible in the territory, significant developments regarding the military capability cannot be undermined. A recent government publication 'military secrets' declared that it is a top priority for China to have air support for the possible battle in the Spratly. Thus, it can be predicted that it will use military presence in the future. China is trying to deter other states from strengthening their claim and carrying out the development projects and is using various diplomatic and military means. China began claiming the Spratly Islands and Paracel islands in 1951 itself.[9] According to a report in the *New York Times*, China would not tolerate any interference in the South China Sea now part of China's core interest of sovereignty. In April 2001, in the EP3 surveillance aircraft incident, a Chinese pilot was killed; American flight crew was gravely endangered.[10] In March 2009, in another incident, the US hydrography vessel was surrounded and harassed by Chinese vessels. In 2011, incidents occurred between Chinese vessels and survey ships from the Philippines and Vietnam. Such kind of dangerous military activities speak volumes about the increasing capabilities and audacity of China. China's submarine strategy also came to the forefront when Chinese submarine collided with the US destroyer and the claims of the Philippines can be traced to the mutual defence treaty. The security alliances of the weaker states with the major powers also provide the chances of escalation. US also deployed the US Carl Wilson aircraft carrier as the part of routine maritime operations.

In the past decades, the states have been using land, sea, space or both to enhance their dominance in either trade or resources and various scholars have elaborated the power and influence of all the three spaces of dominance. However, the rising dispute over the South China Sea indicates re-emergence of sea power dominance in international sphere and has grabbed the worldwide attention because the resources it harbours are major driving force for all the nations. And many nations also operate through these international waters. The region also has proved to be extremely rich in fishing as well as resources such as oil and natural gas. The region has sparked intense tension and debates on the global platform because of its economic richness. The Spratly and Paracel islands are claimed by China as their integral parts. The activities of China have seriously threatened the sea lanes of communication. And it has also built airstrips on Spratly Island. It has militarized the woody island by deploying fighter jets, cruise missiles and has also warned the neighbours against drilling of oil and gas.

Claims of United States

The US has always made its presence felt in different regions of the world through its economic or military power projection. In the name of promoting the global order, it has always promoted its own security. The military activities and operations in the territory claimed by the US have provoked armed Chinese response. The US holds that nothing in the UNCLOS or State practice negates the right of military forces of all nations to conduct military activities in EEZs without coastal state notice or consent whereas China insists that any kind of such activities requires the permission of the coastal state which otherwise leads to violation of domestic and international law.

Instances of Sino-US Skirmishes

China routinely intercepts US reconnaissance flights conducted in its EEZ and periodically does so in aggressive ways that increase the risk of an accident similar to the April 2001 collision of the US EP-3 reconnaissance plane and a Chinese F-8 fighter jet near Hainan Island. A comparable maritime incident could be triggered by Chinese vessels harassing a US Navy surveillance ship operating in its EEZ, such as occurred in the 2009 incidents involving the USNS *Impeccable* and USNS *Victorious*.[11]

The US has also deployed destroyer ships to promote freedom of passage and to secure the sea lanes of communication. The large growth of Chinese submarines has also increased the danger of an incident, such as when a Chinese submarine collided with a US destroyer's towed sonar array in June 2009.

Since neither the US reconnaissance aircraft nor the Ocean surveillance vessels are armed, the United States might respond to dangerous behaviour by Chinese planes or ships by dispatching armed escorts. A miscalculation or misunderstanding could then result in a deadly exchange of fire, leading to further military escalation and precipitating a major political crisis.

Rising US-China mistrust and intensifying bilateral strategic competition would make managing such a crisis more difficult. China and the Philippines are facing conflict due to the natural gas deposits, especially in the disputed area of Reed Bank, located eighty nautical miles from Palawan. Oil survey ships operating in Reed Bank under contract have increasingly been harassed by Chinese vessels. As reported in the newspapers, the UK-based Forum Energy plans to start drilling for gas in Reed Bank this year, which could provoke an aggressive Chinese response.

On 20 May 2015, US navy P-8A surveillance and submarine hunting aircraft flew over islands and reefs where China was conducting construction activities. It also repeatedly carried out freedom of navigation operations in Spratly islands. Washington has also admitted that it conducted two FONOP in the South China Sea. On 27 October 2015, the US navy sent the US Lassesn, a guided missile destroyer to the waters within 12 nautical miles of Subi reef among the Nansha Islands. On 30 January, 2016, the USS Curtis Wilbur, another guided missile destroyer intruded in 12 nautical miles territorial waters of Zhongjian islands and Paracel islands. The US military has also sent strategic weapons including B 52 bomber and USS John Stennis aircraft carrier strike groups to perform patrol mission in the SCS region to show off the strong US presence in the region.[12] In this way the US has already fanned the flame of discontent by sending the naval vessels into the region. The involvement of the US speaks volumes about its concern for its allies such as the Philippines but there are several other intentions and well carved strategies behind in this region. Such an action of America is not something new on the international platform because history is full of such incidents where America has projected its economic and military power in the disputed regions of the world.

Oil politics has already escalated tensions in many regions of the world and will continue in the near future. The US has inherent interest in maintaining sea power. It has always followed unilateralist foreign policy. It cannot allow the shared domain to be used unilaterally. No matter how many bases are built it has shown its preparedness to counter and confront China. If it continues its overarching maritime claims in the sea, it will work towards maintaining the freedom of navigation, which is the mainstay of the US argument and stand on SCS. Obama administration has also conducted periodic air and naval patrols to assert the rights of free navigation in the South China Sea which were challenged by Chinese warships.

Possibilities of Military Escalation

- Whereas on one hand, China believes that any kind of military or intelligence gathering activities cannot be conducted within its EEZ. On the other hand, the US believes in the freedom of navigation without any notification to the claimants. Even the sea lines of communication, which are extremely important means of communications, are also threatened.
- China routinely intercepts the US reconnaissance flights conducted in its EEZ and periodically does so in aggressive ways that increases the risk of an accident similar to the April 2001 collision of the US EP-3 reconnaissance plane and a Chinese F-8 fighter jet near Hainan Island. A comparable maritime incident could be triggered by Chinese vessels harassing a US Navy surveillance ship operating in its EEZ, such as occurred in the 2009 incidents involving the USNS *Impeccable* and USNS *Victorious.*[13]

- The Chinese People's Liberation Army Navy (PLAN) currently operates one of the largest submarine fleets in the world.[14] Gradually China's military is developing ships, submarines, aircrafts, intelligence systems and foreign bases in a bid to become a global military power.[15] In June 2009, a Chinese submarine collided with a US destroyer's towed sonar array.[16] Thus, all these incidents show that military escalations cannot be ignored at any point of time. Managing the conflict becomes all the more difficult in the wake of growing mistrust between the two major powers.
- The other possibilities of escalation arise from the relationship of China and the US with the other claimants. There is serious conflict between China and Philippines over the natural gas deposits in Reed Bank. The oil survey ships have been constantly harassed by Chinese vessels. In 2011, two Chinese patrol vessels were reported to have accosted a seismic survey vessel contracted by Forum energy, operating in Reed bank.[17] Forum Energy is only one of fifteen exploration contracts that Manila intends to offer over the next few years for offshore exploration near Palawan Island. This issue can also escalate into a serious conflict if China intervened. Again in 2012, two Chinese maritime surveillance ships blocked a Philippine navy ship from arresting Chinese fisherman operating in Scarborough shoal. The Philippines and Vietnam, therefore, have called upon the international community to condemn the China's dominance over the South China Sea. Since the US had signed a mutual defence treaty with Philippines in 1951, there is greater chance of US full scale involvement. The Treaty states, "Each Party recognises that an armed attack in the Pacific Area on either of the Parties would be dangerous to its own peace and safety and declares that it would act to meet the common dangers in accordance with its constitutional processes."
- A fishing boat operated by the Vietnamese was pursued and sunk by two Chinese vessels off the coast of Quang Ngai. They were intercepted, harassed and sunk by two Chinese ships in waters of the Paracel archipelago.[18]
- Vietnam also seized a Chinese ship and detained its captain and two sailors, and also accused the crew of illegally intruding on its waters.[19]
- Vietnamese fishermen have also accused Chinese authorities for harassing and attacking them.[20]

- In 2011, Hanoi accused China of deliberately severing the cables of an oil and gas survey vessel in two separate instances.
- In 2015, Chinese and Vietnamese ships collided as Beijing tried to set up an oil rig at the South China Sea.[21]
- China also deployed surface to air missile launchers on Woody island, part of the Paracel chain that is also claimed by Vietnam and Taiwan.[22]
- China has also stepped up a programme in which dredged sand is used to reclaim small islands or coral reefs to make military bases in disputed waters. This has also led to the destruction of coral reefs.[23]
- In another possible scenario, an attack by China on vessels or rigs operated by an American company exploring or drilling for hydrocarbons could quickly involve the United States, especially if American lives were endangered or lost.[24]
- Vietnam state owned energy group, Petro Vietnam signed an agreement with Exxon Mobil to develop Vietnam's biggest gas project for energy generation. Exxon Mobil has plans to conduct drilling for natural gas.[25]
- In the short term, however, the likelihood of this third contingency occurring is relatively low given the recent thaw in Sino-Vietnamese relations.
- In October 2011, China and Vietnam signed an agreement detailing principles for resolving maritime issues but the effectiveness of the agreement still remains doubtful.

Conclusion

Experts of international politics and regional geopolitics are closely watching the developments over and in SCS. They are, however, divided in their perceptions with the dominant view that it may lead to a full-scale war between the two countries in near future. Their arguments are based on day-to-day development and assertions of both the countries against each other. They have also been taking into account the way both the countries are trying to woo the littoral states against their adversaries. However, a micro-level analysis of the facts and circumstances is suggestive enough of the fact that minor skirmishes shall continue to happen between the two powers of the world; but it will hardly escalate into a full-scale war in the given regional theatre. Firstly, both the parties have strengthened their military power over a long period of time with massive investments. They are also leading economic giants of the world. They understand that given their nuclear status any escalation will jeopardise their long-term economic interests; will cripple their military might and will lead only to catastrophe. It has rightly been said that nuclear war cannot lead to winning and losing of any state, rather it will only lead to devastation.

Secondly, the number of instances in the aftermath of Trump's assumption of power reveals that even US is only resorting to browbeating and is not interested in a full-scale conflict. The way Trump backtracked on his own stand of negating 40 year old "One China Policy" speaks volumes about his intentions. The US seems to be interested more in ensuring 'freedom of navigation' at sea rather than challenging the very sovereignty claim of China over the sea.

Thirdly, the US claim of 'freedom of navigation' at sea will protect its economic interests and will protect the sea lanes of communication through which major transportation of energy resources takes place.

Fourthly, the US is interested not to give a free hand to China in any matter that pertains to the international community. This may lead to undermining of US power projection within the comity of nations. Hence, the US will continue to challenge the Chinese assertions both directly and indirectly. The US prompting of the Philippines to take the matter to PCA is one such example of US indirect interventions in the dispute. The US is also trying to arm Vietnam and other neighbours. This again could be read as US indirect ways of challenging the Chinese unilateralism in the SCS.

Fifthly, the US is trying to prevent any militarization of the SCS zone, in view of the fact that it will undermine the US power projections within the Asia-pacific region. Therefore, preventing Chinese militarization efforts will continue to be the main plank of US assertions against China. A demilitarized SCS is in the larger economic interests and strategic interests of the US.

Finally, Asia is unipolar with China as the sole super power of the continent. It is not in the interests of the US. It is in line with such understandings that the US crafted its foreign policy of 'pivot to Asia'. Therefore, US assertions are mainly directed towards achieving the objectives of its own foreign policy choice of enhancing its presence in the region.

Therefore, given the fact that there is primacy of economic diplomacy over military diplomacy in the world today, both the US and China would be least interested to escalate their on-going conflict into a full-scale war.

NOTES AND REFERENCES

1. "Why is south china sea contentious?" *BBC*, July12, 2016. See http://www.bbc.com/news/world-asia-pacific-13748349
2. Spratly Islands are a disputed group of 14 islands, islets, and cays and more than 100 reefs, sometimes grouped in submerged old atolls, in the SCS. The archipelago lies off the coasts of the Philippines, Malaysia, and southern Vietnam. The islands contain approximately 2 square kilometre (490 acres) of land area spread over a vast area of more than 425,000 square kilometre (164,000 sq. miles). The islands have no indigenous inhabitants, but offer rich fishing grounds and may contain significant oil and natural gas reserves and as such are important to the claimants in their attempts to establish international boundaries. Some of the islands have civilian settlements, but of the approximately 45 islands, cays, reefs and shoals that are occupied, all contain structures that are occupied by military forces from Malaysia, Taiwan, China, the Philippines and Vietnam. Additionally, Brunei has claimed an EEZ in the south eastern part of the Spratlys, which includes the Louisa Reef.
3. It forms a triangle-shaped chain of reefs and rocks with a perimeter of 46 km (29 miles). It covers an area, including an inner lagoon of 150 square kilometre (58 sq. mi). It is 198 km west of Subic Way. It is a disputed territory claimed by the People's Republic of China, the Republic of China (Taiwan), and the Philippines. The Shoal's status is often discussed in conjunction with other territorial disputes in the SCS such as those involving the Spratly Islands. Since the 2012 Scarborough Shoal standoff, access to the Shoal had been restricted by the People's Republic of China (PRC). However, in 2016, following meetings between the Philippine President Duterte and his Chinese counterparts, China allowed Filipino fishermen to once again access the shoals for fishing.
4. "Territorial Disputes in The South China Sea", *Council on Foreign Relations*, May 12, 2017.
5. Max Fisher, "South China Sea: Explaining the Dispute", *The New York Times,* July14, 2016.
6. Most of the claim has been taken from BBC News. "Why is south china sea contentious?" *BBC*, July12, 2016. See http://www.bbc.com/news/world-asia-pacific-13748349
7. Paracel islands is a group of islands, reefs, banks and other maritime features in the SCS. It is controlled and occupied by the PRC, ROC (Taiwan), and also claimed by Vietnam. The archipelago includes about 130 small coral islands and reefs, most grouped into the northeast Amphitrite Group or the Western Crescent Group. They are distributed over a maritime area of around 15,000 square kilometres (5800 sq mi), with land area of 7.75 square kilometres (2.99 sq mi). It is home to Dragon Hole, the deepest, underwater sinkhole in the world.
8. "Why is south china sea contentious?" *BBC*, July 12, 2016. See http://www.bbc.com/news/world-asia-pacific-13748349
9. Taylor Fravel, "China's Strategy in South China Sea", *ISEAS-Yusof Ishak Institute,* Vol.33, No.3, December 2011, pp. 292-319.
10. Lyle Goldstein, "China's naval strategy in South China Sea, abundance of noise and smoke but little fire", special focus: The South China Sea Dispute, Vol.33, No.3, December 2011. pp. 320-347.
11. Bonnie S. Glaser, "Armed Clash in the South China Sea", *Centre for Strategic and International Studies.*
12. Hu Bo, "What's Behind US Military Moves in South China Sea", *Diplomat*, April 01, 2016.
13. Bonnie S. Glaser, "Armed Clash in the South China Sea", *Centre for Strategic and International Studies.*

14. "China's Submarine Capabilities", July 15, 2016. See http://www.nti.org/analysis/articles/china-submarine-capabilities/
15. Bill Gertz, "China's Millitary Capabilities Are Growing at a Shocking Speed", November 7, 2016. Seenationalinterest.org/.../report-chinas-military-capabilities-are-growing-shocking-1831...
16. "Sub collides with sonar array towed by US navy ship", *CNN*, June 12, 2009. See http://edition.cnn.com/2009/US/06/12/china.submarine/
17. Christopher Lane, "Reed Bank: South China Sea flashpoint", June 3, 2014. See http://www.atimes.com/atimes/Southeast_Asia/SEA-01-030614.html
18. Ankit Panda, "China steps up harassment of Vietnamese fisherman", *Diplomat*, July 13, 2015.
19. "Vietnam Seizes Chinese vessel in South China Sea" April 4, 2016. See https://www.theguardian.com/world/2016/apr/04/vietnam-seizes-chinese-vessel-detains-crew
20. Ibid.
21. Ibid.
22. Ibid.
23. Ibid.
24. Ibid.
25. "Tillerson, Exxon Mobil and South China Sea", January 17, 2016. See http://www.workers.org/2017/01/17/tillerson-exxon-mobil-and-the-south-china-sea/#.WRm05OuGPIU

5

China and the "Tragedy of the Commons" in the South China Sea

Krishnamurthy B

ABSTRACT

Global Commons (GCs) refer to the maritime, air, space and cyber space domains that comprise the circulatory system of our globalized world and also to the collection of resources and institutions that are part of the often intangible patrimony of humankind. They are concerned with environment, outer space, cyber space, worldwide web, internet, and the waters of the Oceans. They are also related to the unexplored continents like Arctic and Antarctic, which may well become both habitable and exploitable as a result of the trends in global warming. GCs hold together the international order based on near-uncontested access, the rule of law and freedom of manoeuvre and are expected to increasingly become a new theatre for global competition that may result in future conflicts and catastrophes.

GCs are beyond national jurisdiction of any specific country and are to be treated as the 'common heritage of mankind'. It remains the avowed duty of the international organizations like the UN and its agencies to protect and police them. The need of the hour is to contribute to the stewardship and preservation of the GCs through the creation and sustenance of Global Public Goods (GPGs)—international law, established norms as well as the rules and regulations of the road to guide and control the global political and economic order. There is an urgent need to protect and nurture GCs through the establishment of a rule-based system and to do away with one based on arbitrary uses of power and exertions of ownership.

China is challenging the concept of GCs and threatens them in the South

China Sea (SCS), an area of 3.5 million sq km or 1.35 million sq miles. It asserts that its territorial seas extend into much of the SCS and as such, it has the right to control navigation and research activities, not just fishing and seabed resources within its Exclusive Economic Zone. China is for limited access for others and exclusive access for itself in that region. Besides, China continues to cause environmental damages by building a series of artificial islands in the disputed sea by piling sand atop reefs and then adding airstrips and military installations, thereby destroying them. China's asymmetric anti-access and area-denial strategy and especially its assertive incrementalism in the SCS has international legal risks, since international law is built on norms. Unlike other claimants of the SCS, China backs up its claims with military force.

The neighbours of China dispute its exclusive claim on SCS and the living and non-living resources that it possesses, and have taken the case to the arbitration court at The Hague, which had rejected China's claims in the SCS and slammed it for causing serious environmental damages there. In retaliation, China rejected the ruling in a government White Paper. To signal the US and others that it has a strong ally in Russia, China plans to have a joint naval exercise in SCS along with Russia.

The present paper attempts to study and analyse the concepts of GCs and GPGs as well as China's claims and activities in the SCS. It also makes an earnest effort to argue that there is an urgent need to strengthen the hands of the UN in protecting the GCs through the formulation and strict implementation of the GPGs.

Introduction

Global Common Pool Resources or precisely, Global Commons (GCs)[1] denote the maritime, air, space and cyber space domains that comprise the circulatory system of our globalised world and also the resources, facilities, services and institutions that are part of the often intangible patrimony of humankind. They include such diverse and distinct factors as the global climate, the stratospheric ozone layer, outer space, high-seas fisheries, international waters, biodiversity, unpatented scientific discoveries and innovations and migratory wildlife. They are concerned with World Wide Web. They are also related to the unexplored continents like Arctic and Antarctic, which may well become both habitable and exploitable as a result of the evolving trends such as climate change and global warming. GCs constitute the connective tissue of the present day international system as global security and prosperity are contingent on the free flow of goods shipped by air or sea, as well as information transmitted beneath the ocean or through the space.[2]

International law identifies four GCs—the High Seas, the Atmosphere, the Antarctica and the Outer Space. These resource domains are guided by the principle of the common heritage of mankind and are treated as resources of interest or value to the welfare of the community of nations. Some such resources like tropical rain forests and biodiversity have lately been included among the traditional set of GCs. Some people define the GCs even more broadly, including science, education, information and peace.[3]

It is noteworthy that GCs constitute and cover a larger area of the Planet Earth than the territories controlled by sovereign states. For instance, the high seas account for around 64 percent of the world's oceans and Antarctica, covering an area of 14 million sq km, occupies about 10 percent of the earth's total space. They hold together the international order based on uncontested and unfettered economic and political access, a system of free trade, the rule of law, and freedom of manoeuvre.

GCs are domains/areas that no particular state controls but on which each and every one rely. They are open access resources, access to which is free and unrestricted and are everybody's property, available for common use. Since "everybody's property practically turns out to be nobody's property", their open access and lack of established ownership naturally result in their being abused, misused, and over-used. In practice, they are subject to what Hardin called "the tragedy of the commons"[4] and are expected to increasingly become a new theatre for global competition that may result in future crises, conflicts and catastrophes.

GCs do not fall within the exclusive jurisdiction of any particular state/ government and are beyond the national jurisdiction and as such, are to be treated as the 'common heritage of mankind'. It remains the avowed responsibility of the international organizations like the UN and its agencies to protect and police them, through the formulation and strict implementation of Global Public Goods—international law, established norms as well as the rules and regulations of the road to guide and control the global political and economic order as well as the institutions and mechanisms to formulate and execute them.

Unfortunately, in the current international system, the GCs exist without effective institutional framework to govern and protect them, which makes the scholars and environmentalists, who are concerned with their protection and nurturing, to mourn that they, as such, rest on 'fragile foundations'. The

GCs were continuously exploited and challenged by strong and powerful countries, who believe in the dictum, might is right and weakness is sin. Changes to the current international order, caused by the advent of new actors, new technologies, and new challenges to human and environmental security, pose fresh risks and challenges to their future use by humanity as a whole. Freeman is quite right when she claims: "Despite their huge size and significance to global prosperity, power, and planetary health, if governance at the global level is defined as the exercise of authority by supranational institutions, then the GCs are ungoverned."[5] A thorough examination of the nature of the various international legal and regulatory regimes that have emerged to regulate aspects of the GCs, proves that they are "fractured and complex".[6]

The present paper elaborates on the richness of the global commons available at the South China Sea (SCS), an area of 3.5 million sq km or 1.35 million sq mi. That factor has attracted the rapacious activities of the regional powers, especially China, which resulted in the "tragedy of the commons" in its waters. The paper also earnestly argues that there is an urgent need to strengthen the hands of the UN in protecting the 'Global Commons' through the formulation and strict implementation of the 'Global Public Goods'. China's intent and actions to challenge the concept of GCs in the context of SCS is unacceptable and needs to be checked. Comprehensive and conclusive laws, norms, and rules and regulations are to be formulated, and China, India and other emerging powers are to be roped in to achieve this important task.

II

In the estimate of John McManus, Professor of Marine Biology and Fisheries, and Director of the National Center for Coral Reef Research at the University of Miami, the SCS is one of the world's most biologically diverse marine environments, boasting around 500 species of reef-building coral. Its waters abound with at least one-tenth of the global fish stock, quite valuable in the present context of the growing demand for seafood. The SCS has long been a rich fishing ground for the regional cultures and civilizations.

It is likely that hundreds of thousands of species still remain undiscovered in the reefs of the SCS. Scientists believe that some of these species could transform medicine, as in the case of aspirin, a life-changing drug that was originally derived from plants. The Spratly Islands, a group of islets, reefs and shoals, and its surroundings are deservedly termed as a treasure trove of biological resources, hosting part of Southeast Asia's most productive coral reef ecosystems in which fish breed and replenish abundantly.[7] The Hague arbitral tribunal, which went into the merits of the Chinese claim on SCS in 2016 and tried to sort out the problem, called the SCS as home to "highly productive fisheries and extensive coral reef ecosystems, which are among the most bio-diverse in the world."[8]

Of late, China, the region's greatest power, staked its claim over nearly the entire SCS, the geographic commons of Southeast Asia's navigable rim land, through a U-shaped, nine-dash line printed on its maps, on the ground that it remained its territory from time immemorial and its "traditional fishing grounds."[9] The Chinese government claims most of its outcroppings as its historic birthright, so-called "integral" or "inherent" territory. Beijing uses the nine-dash line to claim sovereignty over around 90 per cent of the contested waters in the SCS, though this area extends as far as 1,243 miles away from the Chinese mainland. "Nansha is our national land, sacred and inviolable," remains the Chinese slogan, while claiming sovereignty over the Spratly Islands, Nansha in Mandarin.[10]

China is also challenging the existing delineation of the high-seas commons and threatens them in the SCS. It asserts that its territorial seas extend into much of the SCS and as such, it has the right to control navigation and research activities, not just fishing and seabed resources within its Exclusive Economic Zone (EEZ). China advocates limited access for others, while claiming exclusive access for itself. It has also challenged mainstream interpretations of UNCLOS in objecting to the activities of extra-regional powers, and insists that naval exercises, reconnaissance as well as surveillance activities undertaken without prior notification and without permission of the coastal state violate Chinese domestic law and international law.[11]

The Chinese fisher-folk, especially from Tanmen village on Hainan Island, go far and wide in the SCS and beyond in search of *Tridacnagigas* (giant clam, an edible shellfish), corals and other marine species such as Hawksbill sea turtles. By dragging small boat propellers across a reef these fishermen break up the coral bed and uncover the mollusks and in the process, have caused severe damage to more than 100 sq km in 40 coral reefs in the SCS. The Chinese appetite for endangered giant clam shells, which are carved like elephant ivory for interior decor and jewelry, has denuded swaths of the SCS.[12] In attempting to exclusively secure and control natural resources, China is destroying the most fragile and sensitive marine resource base of the SCS. Tanmen fishermen's growing presence and activities in the SCS are encouraged by the Chinese government so as to strengthen their sovereign claims over SCS and its resources. Since 2012, the rise of the giant clam shell handicraft industry has completely transformed this old fishing town and more and more fishermen have turned from traditional fishing to harvesting giant clams and sea turtles, which offer them much higher incomes. By 2015, Tanmen's giant clam industry was supporting nearly 100,000 people.[13]

Because of overharvesting, however, it is increasingly difficult for the Tanmen fishermen to collect enough giant clams and other marine species from the inshore waters of China to meet the booming demand. Consequently, there is a heavy price rise of raw giant clam over the past five years. Driven by huge potential returns, the Tanmen fishermen are going on expanding their area of operations, not only in waters adjacent to the reefs controlled by other South China Sea claimants within the nine dash line, but also in the EEZs belonging to the neighbouring countries and beyond. It has become quite common for Tanmen fishermen to travel across China's self-claimed nine-dash line to harvest the giant clams, corals and sea turtles.[14] The destruction caused by industrial-scale giant-clam harvesting significantly damaged the marine environment of the SCS and surrounding waters, and heralds the further degradation and depletion of their living resources, thereby diminishing not only the Chinese share but of their neighbours as well. Edgardo Gomez, Professor Emeritus and National Scientist at the Marine Science Institute, University of the Philippines, one of the most-respected marine scientists of the region and pioneer in the scientific cooperation activities in the 1990s, claims that giant clams have been "virtually wiped out" in the South China Sea, which was once a "marine paradise".[15]

China is also challenging the concept of GCs by causing a terrible environmental damage by its land reclamation programme in the SCS. The Chinese construct artificial islands in the SCS, employing dredgers to churn up coral reef and to asphyxiate and smoother them with sand and gravel so as to create land. Since 2014, China has transformed seven mostly underwater reefs into artificial islands, including ones with runways long enough to entertain military jets. The worst issue with the island-building is that the effect is going to be permanent, since a portion of coral reef that has been buried under tons of sand and gravel, can never ever recover.[16]

China has reclaimed an extensive area in the Spratly Islands and Tanmen fishermen have been used to deliver supplies and building materials to the Spratly outposts.[17] A 2016 report from the Pentagon alleges that China had managed to reclaim 3,200 acres of artificial land in the island chain by the end of 2015.[18] China is constructing harbours, runways, helipads, and radar facilities, and installing missile defence systems in these reclaimed lands. Three of these large reefs—Mischief, Subi, and Fiery Cross—have large anti-aircraft guns, close-in weapons systems and hangars capable of holding up to 24 fighter jets and several larger planes. Moreover, China is getting harbours constructed at these reefs at which largest naval vessels can dock.[19] Woody Island in the northeast of the island chain has perhaps the largest Chinese military presence in the SCS. In addition to 1,400 military personnel, it also has an airstrip that can take care of fighter jets, up to 20 aircraft hangars, helipads, radar facilities, and surface-to-air missiles with a range of 124 miles. Woody Island has been designated the official administrative capital of the region containing the island chains that China claims as its territory—Paracel, Spratly, and the area encompassing Scarborough Shoal.

Environmentalists point out that at least another 20 shallow reefs are in imminent danger from the resulting huge plumes of sand and silt, which kill nearly all animal life in nearby waters and permanent and unrecoverable damage is being done in the waters of the SCS and Beijing's island-building campaign means permanent ecocide in that region. John McManus maintains that China's process for constructing its islands has "nothing to do with the natural reef island building process." Between the dredging and island building, he accuses that China "kills basically everything".[20] Again, McManus points out that while construction itself is a problem, it pales in comparison with the environmental destruction damage done by the illegal harvesting of giant clams. According to his figures, while the Chinese dredging and island building activities have damaged or destroyed 55 sq km of reef, the destructive methods of giant clam fishermen have destroyed 104 sq km of once-living coral. He sarcastically remarks that the Chinese claim that they construct islands only on "dead coral" is correct to the extent that the coral had already been destroyed by giant clam fishermen based in Tanmen. China's marine scientists too have called attention to the decline of sensitive coral reefs in the SCS by as much as 80 per cent due to ravenous economic exploitation and with reclamation activities the remaining 20 per cent stand to be lost forever.[21]

It is sad to note that the biophysical impacts of the radical transformation of major coral atolls in the region's marine ecosystem extend well beyond their artificial foundations into the waters of surrounding littoral states as well. Gomez laments the destruction of 311 hectares of precious reefs and in his estimate the resultant economic losses are to the tune of at least $110 million annually. He also warns that it would result in the reduction in fish catch in the decades to come. He points out that the ecological footprint of China's reclamation spans more than the ground on which the new islands stand now, but on the surroundings as well.

It is also felt that settlement on the new islands will bring ruin through accompanying day-to-day activities which will bring in additional problems—sewage, garbage, anchoring, and marine debris. People will require a continuous supply of food which will call for perpetual exploitation of nearby waters. Chinese fishing has already caused the destruction of its southern coastal reefs and decline of coastal fish stocks; no doubt it will also cause the rapid decline of the distant fishing grounds. Batongbacal is quite correct while he points out that the island-building spree and fishing fleet mobilization result not only in the deliberate destruction of vital and productive commons—they also impair the long-term sustainability of the marine environment of all the littoral States around the SCS.[22]

III

The Chinese misadventure in the waters of the SCS and its challenging the international law, established norms and rules and regulations were questioned and condemned not only by the regional powers, but also by the international community, which urges Beijing to abide by the provisions of the United Nations Convention on the Law of the Sea (UNCLOS), which sets maritime zones of control based on coastlines. It also expects China to respect the international law, which discourages and bars claimant states from disturbing the *status quo* by unilaterally and permanently altering the disputed features, with the intention of scaffolding and reinforcing its tall claims. Regional and global powers, including Singapore, Japan and the United States are particularly concerned over freedom of navigation and over-flight in the SCS.

China's demarcation and exclusive claim of nearly all of the SCS and the living and non-living resources that it possesses as its own through maps marked with the so called nine-dash line that overlaps with the EEZs of Vietnam, the

Philippines, Malaysia, Taiwan, Brunei and Indonesia, was quite naturally disputed by the latter. As such the waters of the SCS have emerged as a potential flashpoint between these claimants. While China argues that the nine-dash line represents its historic maritime agreements, all others involved have disputed its over-arching claim. Against the Chinese argument that their island-building is "reasonable, understandable, and legal", these neighbours point out that the large-scale and irreparable damage wrought contravenes the fundamental principle of the international law that states' activities should not cause trans-boundary harm to other states. The Philippines used to be particularly sensitive to these developments since its coastal communities are highly environmental conscious and are totally depending on fishing for subsistence. The Chinese efforts to reclaim land, at the seven features in the Spratlys, directly threaten Vietnam's national interests. Moreover, the resource exploitation by the Chinese near the Paracels is a serious concern for the Vietnamese government and people.[23] Vietnam and the Philippines were seriously worried over the impact of China's reclamation activities on their maritime claims in the area.

On the occasion of Association of Southeast Asian Nations (ASEAN) Summit meetings, regional leaders constantly reaffirmed the regional body's commitment to maintain peace, stability, security and freedom of navigation in and over-flight over the SCS and expressed their concern over China's reclamation activities which have eroded trust and confidence among the regional powers and undermine peace, security and stability in the SCS.

Scholars and environmentalists have suggested that the ASEAN members should seriously consider multilateral peacekeeping patrols in the SCS, if needed with the active involvement of even extra-regional powers such as the US. There is also a proposal for a multilateral agreement to protect the marine environment, with the Antarctic Treaty as a possible model.[24] Putting pressure on China and preventing it from doing damage is advocated as a panacea.

As a last resort, the Philippines had taken the dispute to the Permanent Court of Arbitration at The Hague challenging China's claims and actions in the SCS region. However, the latter refused to participate in any capacity in the case. When the tribunal had asked China to provide its environmental assessment studies, which are required as per Article 206 of UNCLOS, China failed to comply. Besides, it had indicated that it will not honour the international court's ruling in case it goes against it. On July 12, 2016, a five-judge panel of arbitral tribunal issued its ruling in the Philippines vs. China case. The verdict not only unanimously rejected the legitimacy of the "historic rights" of almost all of China's maritime claims in SCS, but also slammed it for causing serious environmental damages in its waters. The Court also noted that none of the "scientific assessments" referenced by numerous Chinese officials have been made public. The arbitral tribunal also fixed the responsibility for the poaching and thereby causing devastation of coral reefs on the Chinese government. The tribunal was blunt while pointing out that the Chinese authorities were well aware of the fact that the Chinese fishermen have indiscriminately harvested endangered sea turtles, coral, and giant clams in the SCS and unabashedly inflicted severe damage on the coral reef environment and had not fulfilled their obligations to prevent such activities. The tribunal even suggested that the fishermen were deliberately allowed to harvest the clams on features, which would soon become devoid of life, and would justify the Chinese reclamation claims and it pointed out that "[C]ontroversial land-filling operations by China at Fiery Cross, Subi and Mischief reefs in 2014 and 2015 were immediately preceded by waves of chopper boats cutting their arc patterns across wide areas of the reefs". The tribunal condemned that "China had caused severe harm to the coral reef environment," specifically in reference to "China's recent large-scale land reclamation and construction of artificial islands" and ruled that China "violated its obligation to preserve and protect fragile ecosystems and the habitat of depleted, threatened, or endangered species" and "inflicted irreparable harm to the marine environment."[25]

However, since President Rodrigo Duterte came to power in the Philippines, the relations between his country and China improved a lot. Duterte was ready for a policy of compromise than of confrontation and under his government, both the countries continue to try to develop cordial relations. China succeeded in blunting the opposition of the Philippines government and successfully brought it to its side on the issue of territorial dispute involving the SCS. The Chinese Foreign Minister Wang Yi declared in June 2017 that relations between China and the Philippines have entered a "golden period of fast development".[26] As a result, in the August 2017 ASEAN meeting, while the Philippines tried to placate Beijing, Vietnam resisted its efforts and attempted to persuade other ASEAN members to take a stronger stand against Chinese expansionism in the SCS.[27]

IV

The Chinese reaction to the accusation that it is damning the international law and especially, the UNCLOS and the concept of GCs are two-fold. On the one hand, it had taken half-hearted measures in its endeavours to protect GCs in the SCS region. Since the harvesting of wild giant clams and coral contravenes international conservation conventions and as the giant clam is protected by the Convention on International Trade in Endangered Species of Wild Fauna and Flora and is also listed as a first class protected animal in China, Tanmen fishermen's harvesting of giant clams and other endangered species was thwarted by the Chinese government at both local and central levels. Steps were taken to prevent fishermen from harvesting giant clams and other endangered marine species.[28] However, with the rising tensions of SCS and the Chinese President Xi Jinping's visit to Tanmen town in April 2013, the Chinese authorities started turning a blind eye on Tanmen's booming giant clam industry.[29] Moreover, the Chinese fishermen were provided with subsidies, for everything from petrol and steel reinforcement for boats to an annual $4,600 in "danger pay," and a free satellite-navigation system, which would cost tens of thousands of dollars in the open market, to "summon the Chinese coast guard should foreign maritime forces intervene".[30]

On the face of a rapid depletion of giant clam stocks and growing awareness of the danger posed by their harvest to the marine environment in the SCS, the Chinese government began to crack down on the giant clam industry of Tanmen in 2015. In February 2015, the Policy Research Office of Hainan Provincial Government published a report urging local governments to tackle the illegal harvesting of giant clams. Accordingly, the local government of Tanmen issued an official notice banning the harvesting, transportation and sale of giant clams in early March. As a follow up, China's State Oceanic Administration stepped in to protect marine resources in the Spratly islands in July. Again, in September 2015, law enforcement agencies of Sansha city detained a fishing vessel that was harvesting giant clams near Woody Island.[31] Despite the ban on giant clam dozens of stores still line the streets of Tanmen, openly selling intricately carved giant-clam shells, proving that the ban was enforced half-heartedly and a sham in reality.

On the other hand, China tried to invoke intertemporal laws based on the deep historical record, such as archaeological findings on disputed reefs and islands to justify its activities. At best, China views "U.N.-backed codes of maritime governance as incompatible with domestic laws; at worst, it sees them as instruments of Western hegemony designed to undercut its expanding influence as a world power".[32] By this, China questions the legitimacy and impartiality of the international law, norms, rules and regulations, the Global public goods, set by the international organisation to protect and govern the GCs. China has also consistently opposed third party arbitration of the maritime disputes in the area, effectively nullifying international law—and arbitration bodies under its aegis—as a potential avenue for the resolution of the disputes. Acting on the same lines, China has contemptuously ignored the ruling of the Arbitrary Court and has rejected it in a government White Paper. Within weeks, China's Supreme People's Court issued a regulation stating a "clear legal basis for China to safeguard maritime order". On that basis, Beijing vowed to prosecute any foreigners found fishing or prospecting in disputed waters.[33]

Despite the Declaration on the Conduct of Parties of 2002, China continues its land reclamation spree with vigour, thereby swiftly and singularly establishing facts on the ground. It has left very little scope for a peaceful and diplomatic resolution of the maritime disputes with other regional claimants. Unwilling to be bound by any legalistic document, China has repeatedly dragged its foot on negotiating even just the guidelines of a Code of Conduct of Parties in the SCS.[34]

Though constantly advising patience to others, China has shown little patience for any kind of criticism from its Southeast Asian counterparts. In response to ASEAN's statement, of which reference has been made earlier, the Chinese Foreign Ministry spokesman accused the Philippines, without naming it directly, of hijacking ASEAN's agenda by "regionalizing" supposedly purely bilateral disputes, besides accusing some other ASEAN member countries for "carrying out reclamations on the Chinese islands such as the Spratlys."[35]

Moreover, by conducting patrols, deploying nuclear submarines, and establishing large-scale airstrips and garrisons in adjacent waters, China has transformed largely symbolic sovereignty spats into an increasingly militarized territorial showdown, while professing the "Year of China-ASEAN Maritime Cooperation" in 2015. By way of displaying its sovereign rights over the waters of the SCS, as well as to signal the US and others that it has a strong ally in Russia, China organised a joint naval exercise in SCS in the company of Russia.[36]

Yet another strategy followed by China is a blanket refusal of others' accusations of their industrial level fishing and land reclamation activities. The Chinese officials and scientists defend their activities and refute the allegations and have repeatedly described Beijing's building boom in the SCS region as "environmentally friendly". China's Foreign Ministry spokesperson claimed that China's island-building efforts in the Spratlys "strictly follow the principle of conducting green project and building ecological islands and reefs ... The impact on the ecological system of coral reefs is limited". He went on to say that "once China's construction activities are completed, ecological environmental protection on relevant islands and reefs will be notably enhanced and such action stands the test of time."[37] Chinese officials audaciously claim: "China's construction projects have gone through years of scientific assessments and rigorous tests, and are subject to strict standards and requirements of environmental protection," and such projects will not damage the ecological environment of the SCS and that China "cares about protecting the ecological environment of relevant islands, reefs, and waters more than any other country, organization, or people in the world".[38]

V

By deploying and operating its ravenous fishing fleet in the SCS, China has engaged in environmental aggression on a regional scale, and turned its land reclamation programme into a weapon of mass destruction of GCs in the region, to quench its greediness for territory and resources. Through its rapacious activities in collecting the resources of the SCS, which has resulted in "fisheries collapse", not only its neighbours but China too is going to be affected. It is indeed predicted that China, which consumes more fish than any other country in the world, is expected to suffer immensely, while causing such a fate on its neighbours as well.

China's asymmetric anti-access and area-denial strategy and especially, its assertive incrementalism needs to be checked. The arrogance that it displayed unabashedly against the Hague Tribunal ruling, has serious international legal risks, since international law which governs and regulates the use of GCs is built on norms and standards. The worst feature is that unlike other claimants of the SCS, China seems to be ever ready to steel up its claims with threat and use of force unreservedly.

The need of the hour is to contribute to the stewardship and preservation of the GCs through the creation and sustenance of global public goods—international law, established norms as well as the rules and regulations of the road to guide and control the global political and economic order. There is an urgent need to protect and nurture GCs through the establishment of a rule-based system and to do away with the one based on arbitrary uses of power and exertions of exclusive ownership. The hands of the UN are to be strengthened in protecting the 'Global Commons'. Comprehensive and conclusive laws, norms, and rules and regulations are to be formulated as well as indiscriminately implemented, and China, India and other emerging powers are to be roped into this important task of setting norms, rather than allowing them to continue to play the role of rebels against the established norms set by others.

NOTES AND REFERENCES

1. "Global Commons", available at http://www.unep.org/delc/GlobalCommons/tabid/54404/ (accessed on 26-1-2017)
2. Department of Defense, "Quadrennial Defense Review Report," United States Department of Defense, February 2010, available at http://www.defense.gov/Portals/1/features/defenseReviews/QDR/QDR_as_of_29JAN10_1600.pdf(accessed on 04-09-2017)
3. OHCHR, OHRLLS, UNDESA, UNEP, UNFPA, "UN System Task Team on the Post-2015 UN Development Agenda; Global Governance and Governance of the Global Commons in the Global Partnership or Development Beyond 2015," United Nations, January 2013, pp. 5–6, available at http://www.un.org/en/development/desa/policy/untaskteam_undf/thinkpieces/24_thinkpiece_global_governance.pdf (accessed on 04-09-2017)
4. Garret Hardin, "The Tragedy of the Commons", *Science,* 162, 1968, pp. 1143–248.
5. Carla P. Freeman, "The Fragile Global Commons in a World in Transition", *SAIS Review of International Affairs,* vol. 36, no. 1 (Winter–Spring 2016), pp. 17–18.
6. n. 3.
7. Jay Batongbacal, "Environmental Aggression in the South China Sea", May 7, 2015, available at https://amti.csis.org/environmental-aggression- in- the-south-china-sea/ (accessed on 18-5-2017)
8. Shannon Tiezzi, "South China Sea Ruling: China Caused 'Irreparable Harm' to Environment", July 15, 2016, available at http://thediplomat.com/2016/07/south-china-sea-ruling-china-caused-irreparable-harm-to-environment/ (accessed on 18-5-2017)
9. Hannah Beech, *The Environment Is the Silent Casualty of Beijing's Ambitions in the South China Sea*, June 1, 2016, available at, http://time.com/4353292/south-china-sea-environment-destruction-coral-giant-clams/ (accessed on 18-5-2017)
10. George Friedman, "3 maps explain China's real goal in the South China Sea", April 2, 2017, available at http://www.businessinsider.com/maps-explain-south-china-sea-2017-3?r=US&IR=T&IR=T(accessed on 18-5-2017)
11. Bonnie S. Glaser, *Armed Clash in the South China Sea, Contingency Planning Memorandum No. 14,* Council on Foreign Relations, Center for Preventive Action, April 2012, p. 1, available at, https://www.cfr.org/report/armed-clash-south-china-sea (accessed on 04-09-2017).

12. Beech, n. 9.
13. Zhang Hongzhou, "South China Sea: The Story of the Tanmen Fishermen", January 08, 2016, available at http://thediplomat.com/2016/01/south-china-sea-the-story-of-the-tanmen-fishermen/ (accessed on 18-5-2017).
14. *Ibid.*
15. Tiezzi, n. 8.
16. Beech, n. 9.
17. Hongzhou, n. 13.
18. Friedman, n. 10.
19. *Ibid.*
20. Tiezzi, n. 8.
21. Batongbacal, n. 7.
22. *Ibid.*
23. Bryan Lynn, Asia Arms Race Heats Up Over South China Sea, April 02, 2017, available at https://learningenglish.voanews.com/a/arms-race-heats-up-in-asia-amid-china-military-build-up-in-south-china-sea/3790851.html (accessed on 18-5-2017).
24. Tiezzi, n. 8.
25. *Ibid.*
26. http://www.philstar.com/headlines/2017/06/30/1714894/china-hails-golden-age-relations-philippines
27. *The Hindu* (Chennai), August 6, 2017.
28. Hongzhou, n. 13.
29. During his visit, President Xi exhorted the Tanmen Fishermen to establish the Chinese sovereignty over SCS through expanding their fishing activities far and wide. They were assured of state protection and financial aid, and in turn were expected to carry building materials for the Chinese land reclamation programme.
30. Beech, n. 9.
31. Hongzhou, n. 13.
32. *Ibid.*
33. Richard Javad Heydarian, South China Sea: Forging a Maritime Coalition of the Willing, May 7, 2015, available at https://amti.csis.org/south-china-sea-forging-a-maritime-coalition-of-the-willing/ (accessed on 18-5-2017)
34. *The Hindu*, August 7, 2017. Chinese Foreign Minister Wang Yi said in August 2017 that the start of consultation for a "code of conduct" in the disputed waters may be announced in the ASEAN annual summit meet in November 2017, if Beijing's conditions including non-interference by "outside parties" are met with. Chinese maintained that it is an Asian dispute and that it should be resolved only by the countries involved and there is no role for external powers.
35. Heydarian, n. 33.
36. *The Hindu* (Chennai), September 12, 2016.
37. Beech, n. 9.
38. Tiezzi, n. 8.

6

South China Sea: A Source of Conflict

Nandini J, Vamsi Krishna K and Dinesh Reddy M

ABSTRACT

South China Sea (SCS) which holds a host of natural resources has become a source of conflict now. As it has great potential with respect to maritime resources, strategic importance, and international trade, all countries which share boundaries with SCS are staking their claim. China, which is the world's second largest economy, is trying to exercise its domination over the SCS. Vietnam which is reasserting its claim over parts of SCS is supported by the US. Since 18th century the Philippines has been claiming its waters of SCS. The only features claimed by Malaysia that could generate maritime zones are the islands named Swallow Reef, Amboyna Cay, Braque Canada Reef, and Commodore Reef/Rizal Reef, and the rocks forming Erica Reef, Investigator Shoal, and Mariveles Reef. For Taiwan, the SCS is a peripheral theatre that cannot compare to the Taiwan Strait in terms of its supreme strategic value. Brunei and Indonesia also claim parts of the SCS. India, which is growing as a bright spot economy in Asia, has got its own interests in the SCS. This paper attempts to discuss the dimensions of territorial claims in the SCS by the countries concerned.

Introduction

The SCS is a marginal sea that is part of the Pacific Ocean, encompassing an area from the Karimata and Malacca Straits to the Strait of Taiwan of around 3500000 sq km. The sea carries tremendous strategic importance—one-third of world's shipping passes through it. It contains lucrative fisheries that are crucial for the food security of millions of South East Asia and huge oil and gas reserves are believed to lie beneath its sea bed. It is located South of China, East of Vietnam, West of Philippines and North of Indonesia.

The maritime disputes in the SCS have recently grown more complex and heated, given the issues at hand, the number of countries involved, and unwillingness among these countries to genuinely cooperate with each other to find peaceful zones in the region. All of them, save Indonesia, claim sovereignty over maritime features in the area. The conflict and tension on competing sovereignty claims over the SCS have grown considerably in the past five years. China has adopted an increasingly assertive posture towards its own claims by elevating it to a core interest,[1] strengthening its fishery law enforcement and building civilian and military facilities in the disputed islands and waters. China's rising military power and political influence in East Asia has generated anxiety and suspicion among some of its neighbours. In particular, its growing assertiveness over sovereignty and maritime rights in the SCS is viewed as a serious challenge to the status quo in the region.

History of SCS

The SCS extends from the southern tip of China and encompasses an area through which 40 percent of the world's trade passes. This area includes the Strait of Malacca, which is an important conduit for oil imports into the region. In addition to trade, the Sea is also home to rich fishing areas and potentially great undersea oil deposits. Five countries—Brunei, Malaysia, the Philippines, Vietnam and Taiwan—claim ownership over parts of the sea including portions that contain rocks or other small islands. China meanwhile claims almost the whole Sea and demonstrates its claim by referencing a nine-dashed line around the sea on its official maps of Chinese territory.[2]

Through the first half of the twentieth century, the Sea remained quiet as neighbouring states focused their attention on conflicts unfolding elsewhere. In fact, at the end of World War II, no claimant occupied a single island in the entire SCS. Then in 1946, China established itself on a few features in the Spratlys, and in early 1947, it also snapped up Woody Island, and part of the Paracel Islands chain, just two weeks before the French and the Vietnamese intended to make landfall. Denied their first pick, the French and Vietnamese settled for the nearby Pattle Island. But even at this stage, the SCS was not seen as a priority by any of the claimants. For that reason, after suffering their cataclysmic defeat at the hands of Mao's Communists, Chiang Kai-shek's forces retreated to Taiwan and abandoned their stations in the SCS. Even the French and Vietnamese could not be bothered to take advantage of the lapse in Chinese control, as they were preoccupied with the rapidly escalating war in Vietnam.

However, the next half century saw accelerating interest in the SCS. In 1955 and 1956, China and Taiwan established permanent presences on several key islands, while a Philippine citizen—Thomas Cloma—claimed much of the Spratly Island chain as his own.

By the early 1970s, the scramble was spurred by indications that oil lurked beneath the waters of the SCS. The Philippines was the first to move. China followed shortly thereafter with a carefully coordinated seaborne invasion of several islands. The Paracel China, it wrested Paracel islands from South Vietnam's control, killing several Vietnamese and sinking a corvette in the process. In response, both South and North Vietnam reinforced their remaining garrisons and seized several other unoccupied features.

Another decade of relative inaction was punctuated once again with violence in 1988, when Beijing moved into the Spratlys and set off another round of occupations by the claimants. Tensions crested when Beijing forcibly occupied Johnson Reef, killing several dozen Vietnamese sailors in the process.

The dispute seemed to take a turn for the better in 2002, when ASEAN and China came together to sign the Declaration on the Conduct of Parties in the SCS. The Declaration sought to establish a framework for the eventual negotiation of a Code of Conduct for the SCS. The parties promised "to exercise self-restraint in the conduct of activities that would complicate or escalate disputes and affect peace and stability, including among others, refraining from action of inhabiting on the presently uninhabited islands, reefs, shoals, cays, and other features and to handle their differences in a constructive manner."

In May 2009, Malaysia and Vietnam made a joint submission to the Commission on the Limits of the Continental Shelf setting out some of their claims. This initial submission unleashed a flurry of notes from the other claimants, who objected to the claims of Malaysia and Vietnam.

China responded to the joint submission by submitting a map containing the infamous "nine-dash" line. This could mean that China claims all the territorial features and all the waters enclosed by the nine-dash line, even those that exceed what's permitted under maritime law.

In 2012, Beijing bore out some of these concerns when it snatched Scarborough Shoal away from the Philippines. The two states had quarreled over allegations of illegal poaching by Chinese fishermen. After a two-month standoff, the parties agreed to withdraw from the Shoal. Manila did. Beijing did not. Since then, China has excluded Philippine boats from the Shoal's waters.

In response to this escalatory move, Manila filed an arbitration case against China on January 22, 2013, under the auspices of the U.N. Convention on the Law of the Sea (UNCLOS). The Philippine claims centre on maritime law issues, although China asserts that they cannot be resolved without deciding territorial issues first. For that reason, Beijing has refused to participate in the proceedings, although it has drafted and publicly released a position paper opposing the tribunal's jurisdiction. The Philippines has submitted its memorial as well as a response to China's position paper, and both nations are currently awaiting a decision from the tribunal as to its own jurisdiction.

China, however, has adopted an increasingly assertive posture in the region. In early May 2014, a Chinese state-owned oil company moved one of its rigs into waters claimed by Vietnam south of the Paracel Islands. This provocation touched off confrontation between Vietnamese and Chinese vessels around the rig, as well as rioting against foreign-owned businesses in parts of Vietnam. Faced with this pushback, China withdrew the rig in mid-July, a month ahead of schedule.

Very recently, Beijing has launched an accelerating land reclamation campaign across the SCS. In at least seven locations, Chinese vessels have poured tons of sand to expand the size of features occupied by China. Beijing has also begun construction of infrastructure on much of this reclaimed land, including an airstrip capable of receiving military aircraft. Although other claimants have reclaimed land in the past, China has reclaimed 2,000 acres of new land, more than "all other claimants combined over the history of their claims," according to the U.S. Department of Defense.

Since 1996, Vietnam and the Philippines, and to a lesser degree Malaysia and Brunei, have asserted claims within the area covered by the Chinese (PRC & ROC) nine-dash line. Since 1974, when the PRC troops confronted and expelled Vietnamese troops, most of the Paracel Islands have been occupied by the PRC.

Similarly, although there have been a small number of notable changes in influence or occupation, the occupation and/or control of most parts of the Spratly Islands has not changed significantly since the mid-1990s. Vietnamese troops control the greatest number of islands, reefs, etc., (approx. 29). Eight islands are controlled by the Philippines, five by Malaysia, one by Taiwan, and all of those mentioned have various degrees of "control" over other features. Although the Paracels are completely under PRC control, the PRC does not control any natural feature above sea level. The significance of this situation has changed dramatically since 2014 whence the PRC embarked on a truly remarkable program of land reclamation and artificial island building.[3]

In 2012, the Indian Ambassador to Vietnam, while expressing concern over rising tension in the area, said that 50 per cent of its trade passes through the area and called for peaceful resolution of the disputes in accordance with international law.

On 17 March 2016, in accordance with Memorandum Circular No. 94s. 2016, President Aquino created the National Task Force for the West Philippine Sea, to secure the State's sovereignty and national territory and preserve marine wealth in its waters and exclusive economic zone, reserving use and enjoyment of the West Philippine Sea exclusively for Filipino citizens.

Attributes of Conflict

Conflict had been a longstanding but after countries started exploration for resources it became a serious issue among international maritime issues. They are so many factors which added fuel to these flames namely, rich resource base, strategic importance, international trade.

Rich Resource Base: The SCS is an extremely significant body of water in a geopolitical sense. It is the second most used sea lane in the world, while in terms of world annual merchant fleet tonnage; over 50 per cent passes through the Strait of Malacca.

China announced in May 2017 a breakthrough for mining methane clathrates, when they extracted methane from hydrates in the SCS.[4]

The coastal waters of Southeast Asia and China along the SCS are remarkably productive and biologically diverse. Oil and gas resources beneath the seafloor are also believed to be extensive. Chinese estimates hinting at a new Saudi Arabia beneath the waves are probably overly optimistic, but hydrocarbon reserves are nevertheless considerable. With rising energy demand the SCS emerged as one of the world's most economically important waterways, providing transport, food and other vital resources for the densely populated region that touches its waters. The SCS is also one of the world's most contested places. Lying at the heart of Southeast Asia, the semi-enclosed sea is bordered by Brunei, China, Indonesia, Malaysia, the Philippines, Taiwan and Vietnam, all of which have some claim to the sea's vast marine and mineral resources. The SCS is vital for East Asian trade and for US trade across the Asia Pacific region. Ongoing disputes over territory and resources, likely to be aggravated by climate change, pose a threat to the US interests in the region. Interest in exploiting the fossil fuels of the region is growing. Renewable marine resources are already heavily exploited. The SCS provides up to 10 per cent of the global catch of fish. South East Asia relies more heavily on fish as a source of dietary protein and income generation than any other region. And with the rapidly growing middle class across East Asia, demand for fish protein has soared. This demand has led to more fishing ships than ever plying the waters of the SCS and increasing stress on the ecosystem. Overfishing is estimated to have depleted coastal fish stocks by 5-30 per cent. The sea's remarkable coral reefs, which provide food, jobs and protection against storms and floods, have also suffered unprecedented rates of destruction in recent decades. Losses of sea grass and wetlands as well as land-based pollution pose further threats to the rich marine environment. As degraded resources and rising demand force fishers to go ever further in search of fish, run-ins between fishing boats and maritime security forces have spiked, particularly in disputed areas. Southeast Asia is expected to suffer disproportionately from climate change. Global sea level rise will submerge the low-lying coastal areas surrounding the SCS and many of its islands. At the same time, rising temperatures and changes in rainfall may decrease agricultural production and increase a host of health threats. The impacts on agriculture and health would put considerable burden on communities, economic growth and government services

International Trade: The United Nations Conference on Trade and Development (UNCTAD) estimates that roughly 80 percent of global trade—both of which are significantly lower unadjusted estimates more accurately represents the value of SCS trade than the $5.3 trillion figure; this approach still overestimates the value of trade. It assumes that all maritime trade between any pair of countries which may use SCS waterways. For instance, this estimation includes all maritime exports from the United States to China even though some of this trade—especially a large portion of trade from the West Coast of the United States—does not enter the SCS.[5] Nearly 40 per cent of China's total trade in 2016 transited through the SCS.

Estimating more refined figures required isolating the share of maritime trade that likely transit through the SCS. This was accomplished by analyzing AIS data provided by Windward, a maritime data and analytics company, over a 60-day sample period.

This approach offers enhanced precision. For instance, the unadjusted calculation assumed that all of Japan's maritime exports to Indonesia traveled through the SCS. However, AIS data revealed that only 72.9 percent of trading vessels that departed Japanese territorial waters and headed towards Indonesia passed through the SCS. Similarly, only 16.2 percent of vessels traveling from Chinese territorial waters to the US traversed the SCS. These ratios were applied as modifiers to specific trading pairs, providing a final estimate.

Strategic Significance: SCS is also considered to be an area of strategic significance with respect to trade and also defence. China, in order to play dominant role in the SCS, has started construction of artificial islands and deployed defence and other forces to assert their sovereignty over SCS. Strait of Malacca which is route for sea trade to east had caught the attention of international community. In order to enhance the trade every country is reasserting it claims over its sea area of SCS. And also some western countries like America are also trying to make their presence felt in SCS by having its air and naval bases in neighbourhood countries. Claimants of SCS are reasserting their claims in order to protect economic interest, trade interest, sovereignty as well as strategic interest.

A critical and early Chinese test of the US resolve is likely to come in the SCS, where Washington has struggled to respond effectively to assertive Chinese behaviour. Enduring the US interests—freedom of navigation and over flight, support for the rules-based international order, and the peaceful resolution of disputes—are at risk in the region. The US goals to uphold regional alliances and partnerships, defend international rules and norms, and maintain a productive relationship with China remain valid. China has seized the initiative in the SCS, however, and the United States needs to revamp its strategy to reverse current trends and escape the trap of reactive and ineffectual policymaking. To this end, the new administration should perform an early, top-down, and thorough strategic review to enable greater consistency and effectiveness in America's South China Sea policy.

While geopolitics indicates geographical relations with politics, there is another importance which is strategic. The power politics, and military interests made SCS more important. In today's world the US leads, where China is a rising giant—economically and politically. US must have to keep an eye to SCS to check China. Besides, SCS is the route of US military supply to Middle East.

If we analyse the US interests in the SCS, we can identify two specific subjects here. First, US access of trade and military purpose and second, to check Chinese hegemony. When SCS covers $5.3 trillion shipped through it, $1.2 trillion of this was of the US. With 700 billion GDP and population of 525 million South East Asia is the 5th largest trading partner of US.

Claimants of South China Sea

There are seven countries involved in the dispute. Every country has made its own claims, some of which are supported with historical claims some others are not. Every country states that its claims are in compliance with international maritime laws. Due to strategic, and economic importance of the SCS enjoys no country is in a position to forbear its right. These issues are discussed in detail country by country.

China: The conflict and tension on competing sovereignty claims over the SCS has grown considerably in the past five years. China has adopted an increasingly assertive posture towards its own claims by elevating it to a core interest, strengthening its fishery law enforcement and building civilian and military facilities in the disputed islands and waters. China's rising military power and political influence in East Asia has generated anxiety and suspicion among some of its neighbours and in Washington. In particular, its growing assertiveness over sovereignty and maritime rights in the SCS is viewed as a serious challenge to the status quo in the region. This paper examines these issues and the claimant nation's strategic interests in the SCS to help better understand the changing strategic realities in East Asia and the nature of the disputes in the area. The SCS consists of over 200 tiny islands, reefs, shoals, atolls, and sandbanks grouped into three archipelagos—the Spratlys, the Paracels and the Pratas, Macclesfield Bank and Scarborough Shoal. The strategic importance of the SCS is mainly due to its geographical location as the area is gifted with the one of world's busiest and most strategic shipping lanes. More than 50 per cent of world trade passes through the Malacca strait, the Sunda Strait and Lombok Strait, obviously should reach their destinations via the SCS waters. More importantly, it also covers the most crucial energy routes through which oil and gas are transported to the East Asian countries such as China, Japan and South Korea from the Persian Gulf. Thus, the SCS enjoys geopolitical and geostrategic importance. In addition, it has huge proven oil and gas reserves. Hence, the sovereignty of the disputed islands not only involves the possession of territorial and maritime rights in the surrounding area but also the legal rights to exploit its resources, which represent extensive strategic and economic interests. From a strategic perspective, the geographical significance of the SCS is such that whoever has dominance over it will dominate East Asia in future. According to the existing literature and documents, China's sovereignty claims mainly rely on historical discovery, occupation and governance. Ancient maps and official records indicate that China's sovereignty over the SCS can be taken back to the Han (206-220 AD), Tang (618-906 AD), Song (960-1279 AD) and Ming (1368-1644 AD) dynasties. The Chinese ambassador (under the Qing dynasty, 1644-1912 AD) to Great Britain proclaimed his country's sovereignty over the Paracels in 1876 during the Opium Wars, while China deported a German survey team in the Spratlys in 1883. Based on modern international law, any state to claim sovereignty over any land that is discovered must provide evidence of permanent settlement, but China argues that symbolic sovereignty claims were already sufficient in the Great Age of Discovery and that the requirement of permanent settlement and actual possession were insisted only in the 18th century. In the 20th century, China effectively occupied two principal islands on the Paracels and the Spratlys—Yongxing and Taiping respectively—arguing that the effective occupation of two principal islands in the SCS also applied to the other uninhabitable islands (rocks and reefs). In support of its argument, China cited the case of Indonesia and Canada, whose unpopulated islands in no way affect their sovereignty. Hence, China has persistently insisted that its sovereign claims over the islands and its maritime rights in the SCS should not be influenced by an unreasonable requirement of permanent settlement.[6]

In the SCS, Beijing claims territorial sovereignty over two groups of islands and maritime rights over related waters. The contemporary basis for China's territorial claims is a statement that Chinese Premier Zhou Enlai issued in August 1951 during the Allied peace treaty negotiations with Japan. In the statement, Zhou declared China's sovereignty over the Paracel and Spratly Islands. In September 1958, China reaffirmed its claim to these islands when it asserted rights to territorial waters during the Jinmen crisis. The 1958 declaration marked the first time that China linked its claims to territorial sovereignty with the assertion of maritime rights, in this case, rights to territorial waters. From the mid-1970s to the present, official government statements have used roughly the same language to describe China's sovereignty claim. The claim is usually phrased as: "China has indisputable sovereignty over the Spratly Islands (or SCS islands) and adjacent waters. As the international maritime legal regime evolved, China began to codify its claims to maritime rights through the passage of domestic legislation. These laws harmonized China's legal system with the requirements of the UN Convention on the Law of the Sea (UNCLOS). In 1992, the National People's Congress (NPC) passed a Law on the Territorial Sea and the Contiguous Zone of the People's Republic of China, which reaffirmed the content of the 1958 declaration but contained more specific language. Following this law, China issued baselines for its territorial waters in 1996. In 1998, the NPC passed a Law on the Exclusive Economic Zone and the Continental Shelf of the People's Republic of China, in which it claimed additional maritime rights beyond those contained in the 1992 law. The EEZ law did not refer to the Paracels or the Spratlys, but, when combined with the 1992 law on territorial seas, it provides a basis for claiming maritime rights in the SCS. In April 2011, China affirmed this interpretation in a note verbal to the UN Commission on the Limits of the Continental Shelf (the Commission or CLCS) by stating that the Spratly Islands were fully entitled to territorial waters, an EEZ and a continental shelf.

Vietnam: No single strategy can describe how Vietnam is dealing with the SCS issue. Instead, Vietnam pursues a multitude of strategies that employ a wide range of mechanisms stretching from hard to soft power. At least seven distinct strategies can be identified with at the hard extreme of the spectrum; Vietnam tries to strengthen its presence and forces, both military and non-military, in the SCS. During the "scramble for the Spratlys" in 1988, when Beijing and Hanoi competed for foothold on the Spratly Islands, Vietnam set up permanent military garrisons on 11 land features in the archipelago, increasing its possessions here from 10 to 21 land features. From 1989 to 1991, Vietnam went out to occupy six underwater shoals on its continental shelf southwest of the Spratlys by putting permanent high-pillar structures here and manned them with garrisons. Slowly but surely, Vietnam continues to consolidate and increase its presence in these areas with more troops, facilities, equipment, and civilians. Since 2007, Vietnam started to populate the largest of its possessions in the Spratly Islands with permanent civilian habitants. Taking a leaf from China's playbook, Vietnam decided in 2012 to create a fisheries surveillance force as a third force, after the navy and the coast guard, to patrol its maritime waters, and in 2014, after the oilrig crisis, to lightly arm these vessels. To build a minimum deterrent force on the sea, Vietnam continued to modernize its navy and air force.[7]

The Philippines: Whereas recent adjustments to Malaysia's maritime claims involved only a small change to its continental shelf, the task is much more difficult for the Philippines. This is partly because Manila's former SCS claims, as depicted in the textbook map, were woefully out of step with accepted international law, and UNCLOS in particular. For years, the Philippines maintained the lines established by the Treaty of Paris and treated them as if they were a claim to territorial waters. As such a claim is possible only within 12 nautical miles of a country's shores the position was in desperate need of change. The same was true of the randomly drawn box surrounding the Kalayaan Islands Group in the Spratlys. Luckily, Manila recognized that the illegality of its own claims was undermining its position in the SCS by opening it to the same charges it was levelling against Beijing. To remedy this, it passed landmark baselines law in 2009. The law took two critical steps toward clarifying Philippine claims: It declared that Manila claims a 12-nautical mile territorial sea and an EEZ of upto 200 nautical miles from straight territorial baselines between coordinates enumerated in the law. It is worth noting that the Philippines' baselines, though not above reproach, have not drawn the charges of illegality that Vietnam's and China's have. The law did away with the "Kalayaanbox," declaring that, although Manila still lays claim to the islands and other features within it, it does so only via UNCLOS's "Regime of Islands". This means that the Philippines claim was concerned only with the waters generated by the land features within the Kalayaan Group, not all the waters in the former box. Manila has not defined which features are above water at high tide and therefore generate a 12-nautical-mile territorial sea or which, if any, also generate an EEZ and continental shelf by meeting the UNCLOS definition of an "island." As a result of the 2009 baselines law, the Philippines legal maritime claims in the SCS are now much clearer. A section of its southern boundary with Malaysia remains determined by the Treaty of Paris. But the vast majority of its SCS claims are now determined by the EEZs generated from its territorial baselines.[8]

Malaysia: The only features claimed by Malaysia that could generate maritime zones are the islands named Swallow Reef, Amboyna Cay, Barque Canada Reef, and Commodore Reef/Rizal Reef, and the rocks forming Erica Reef, Investigator Shoal, and Mariveles Reef. These islands are entitled to a territorial sea, EEZ, and continental shelf. The rocks are entitled only to a 12-mile territorial sea. In contrast, the 1979 Malaysian map showed a territorial sea around only Swallow Reef and Amboyna Cay, and not any of the other features. The other features listed above are either low-tide elevations lying more than 12 miles from an island or mainland or submerged at low tide. They have no maritime zone entitlements and are not subject to appropriation. The State, from whose continental shelf these features rise, has sovereign rights to them. Finally, based on the press statements accompanying notes, it appears that Malaysia's claim to Louisa Reef has been abandoned. There is uncertainty as to whether any Louisa Reef is above water at high tide. The 1979 Malaysian map did not show a territorial sea for Louisa Reef, suggesting that it was merely a low-tide elevation, which would not be subject to appropriation.

Brunei: It was hard to imagine any disputes flaring between Brunei Darussalam (or 'The Abode of Peace') and Beijing over territorial claims in the SCS. Brunei's claim originated in 1984 after it gained independence from Britain.

The same year, Brunei signed the 1982 United Nations Convention on the Law of the Sea (UNCLOS) and declared an Exclusive Economic Zone (EEZ) of 200 nautical miles. Brunei's claim to the SCS includes the maritime features of Bombay Castle, Louisa Reef, Owen Shoal, and Rifleman Bank of the Spratly Island chain.[9] Vietnam currently occupies Bombay Castle and Malaysia once operated a small navigational light beacon at Louisa Reef.

In contrast to the more vocal pronouncement in Manila and Hanoi, not much was heard concerning Brunei's claims, which are not formal and are more associated with maritime jurisdiction rather than sovereignty. In addition, Brunei is the only claimant of the six Southeast Asian nations (Brunei, Indonesia, Malaysia, the Philippines, Taiwan and Vietnam) which does not occupy any maritime features or maintain a military presence in the Spratly Island chain.

Yet, over the years there has been some assertion of its claim to the waters. Four years after the declaration of its EEZ in 1984, Brunei published a map revealing its jurisdiction over its continental shelf, although maps are now strictly confined to official use only. In 1992, Brunei took issue with Malaysia's claim over Louisa Reef and also launched a protest over China's decision to undertake research in nearby waters. In March 2003, Brunei and Malaysia attempted to resolve spats over oil and natural gas resources in Brunei's EEZ, which had seen both countries sending naval ships to drive each other away.

Taiwan: For Taiwan, the SCS is a peripheral theatre that cannot compare to the Taiwan Strait in terms of its supreme strategic value. Nonetheless, the Sea is an important factor to consider when evaluating Taiwan's national interests. Sea lines of communication connecting Taiwan to its markets and suppliers in Europe and the Middle East pass through the SCS, making it a key check point. Like all island nations, Taiwan is dependent upon free access to the sea for ensuring its existence, and survival is the paramount interest of any state matters for Taiwan's continuing struggle to survive as a free, sovereign, and independent state. Taiwan is a country that is not treated like a country. Recognizing this reality is essential because it colours every aspect of Taiwan's approach to international affairs, defence strategy, and security policy, often making what should be relatively simple issues impossibly complex. This problem is the direct result of the PRC's strenuous worldwide efforts to purge Taiwan's participation from the international community. Consequently, Taiwan does not have a seat at the United Nations and does not currently maintain diplomatic relations with the United States, Japan, or any of the world's other advanced economies. All felt compelled, or were forced, to cut their relations with Taiwan when they established relations with the PRC.[10]

Indonesia: Rich Natuna Islands, located in the SCS northwest of Borneo, tend to be subject to periodic hype from the international media. That's due to a couple of reasons. For one, though Indonesia is not officially a claimant in the SCS disputes, China's nine-dash line overlaps with the exclusive economic zone (EEZ) around the Natunas.

Moreover, with Indonesian President Joko "Jokowi" Widodo taking a tougher line on defending Indonesia's sovereignty and a number of recent run-ins between Indonesian and Chinese vessels near the Natunas, the issue has been dominating the headlines. Indeed, Jokowi himself made news in July when he made his first visit to Natuna aboard a warship in a far-from-subtle display of Indonesia's sovereignty over the area.

But, even apart from the China angle that is often hyped up, Indonesia's commitment to developing the rich resources in the Natunas also makes sense for economic reasons. Focusing on just the energy aspect alone (fisheries, too, is a priority) Indonesian government has said that there are seven oil and gas exploitation fields and ten exploration fields in Natunas. To get a sense of the potential, consider the fact that the East Natuna block on its own is said to have over 46 trillion cubic feet of gas, making it Asia's largest gas reserve.

India's Interest in South China Sea

The fundamental perspective of Indian interest in the SCS is underscored by the growing arc of Indian strategic interests in tune with its increasing trade and economic engagements. ASEAN and East Asia form the fastest growing component of India's economic interests and an area of acute economic and strategic interest. These linkages are likely to grow with India's growing trade with them which was expected to cross US$ 100 billion by 2015–16. This has led to strategically linking the ocean spaces of the Indian Ocean and Pacific Ocean; a term has been coined—the Indo-Pacific Ocean—to highlight seamless connectivity. It is, therefore, but natural that Indian interests will gravitate toward the security and stability of this expanded geo-economic and geo-political space at the confluence of the two major oceans. The extension of Indian strategic space into the Indo-Pacific Ocean will naturally have strategic consequences. China has reacted by asking India to stay away from the SCS while the Southeast Asian countries and Japan have welcomed the Indian presence. China, which looks upon the SCS as a springboard for its power projection in the Asia-Pacific, looks upon the Indian presence with the blinkered vision of China containment in concert with the democracies along the Asian Rim Land. It is indeed unfortunate that India's growing bilateral relations with Vietnam and with other Southeast Asian countries, in particular Indonesia, and growing strategic cooperation with Japan, are seen by the Chinese as an Indian attempt of strategic assertion in the Chinese backyard. The paranoia gets enhanced in the backdrop of US-India strategic partnership and American attempts at ensuring freedom of seas and asking China to resolve the issue bilaterally. As discussed earlier, India does not seek any confrontation with China nor is it trying to create any concert of democracies or any other mechanism that will restrain China or impinge on its interests. Just as the Chinese footprints in Myanmar, Nepal, Sri Lanka and Bangladesh are driven by trade and resource considerations apart from building strong bilateral ties, India too is attempting to build strong economic and strategic relations with the countries of ASEAN and East Asia to secure its markets and transportation linkages through the security of sea lanes. India has genuine economic interests in the region. During visit of the Vietnamese Prime Minister[11] to India in 2016, the two countries signed an oil and gas exploration agreement, in addition to significantly upgrading their military and trade relationship. In a rather trenchant editorial, China accused India of getting involved in the SCS dispute despite China urging India to stay out. It concluded that India has a vested interest in becoming involved as part of the larger strategy to contain China in the region. An influential Chinese Communist Party-run newspaper warned that "every means possible" should be used to stop India's Oil and Natural Gas Corporation (ONGC-Videsh) engaging in exploration projects in the SCS. It further warned India that its actions would push China to the limits, implying that India would bear the consequences of its action. There are mixed views on India's continued oil exploratory activity in the SCS. Some diplomats and analysts, generally concerned about China's rise, take the view that there is a need to pay close attention to the Chinese protest. They pointed out a range of possibilities that exist and a range of options that are available to the Chinese. The concern is what happens if China decides to take the conflict to the next level by triggering a confrontation in its own backyard, in terms of physical harassment.[12] They question what would be the reaction of the Indian government or for that matter Vietnam: will the Indian Navy be asked to react and in what manner? They also point out that China's propensity of upping the ante along the disputed India-China border is nuanced. Implicit in these arguments is a perspective that India has limited options and it would be prudent to give up its exploration rights or negotiate these with the Chinese, avoiding any confrontation. This is unnecessary passivism. While nobody wants to confront China, India needs to take all such steps in conjunction with Vietnam and other regional players to protect its own interests. While it is nobody's case to enter into confrontation with China, Beijing's India-centric jingoism also needs to be analyzed. Why is China adopting a coercive attitude against India while seeking mutual accommodation with ASEAN countries and even Vietnam and the Philippines? Under the circumstances, what are India's options? It needs to be categorically pointed out that India has interests in the region and these are purely economic and partly political. India's stakes in three blocks in Vietnam are as old as May 1988.

What is important and relevant is that all these years China did not formally raise any objection to any of the agreements or projects undertaken by India. It is only since it started claiming the area as being part of its core interest that China has become hypersensitive. India does not seek confrontation with China nor will it forsake its legitimate economic rights and agreements entered with a sovereign government. Second, it would be in the Indian interest to work with regional parties including ASEAN, China, Japan and even the US—to develop a framework for maritime cooperation. China must be encouraged to resolve the issue of its claims in the SCS in a spirit of mutual cooperation, regional harmony and peace. Unnecessary belligerence and assertiveness will only vitiate the atmosphere and harm its own long-term interests. If China insists upon coercing India, then India too can raise the issue of Chinese presence in Pakistan where the Chinese are involved in over forty-five projects for a cumulative investment of about $8–10 billion. Pakistan-Occupied Kashmir is Indian-claimed territory or, at worst, disputed. Moreover, China's projects like the up grading of Karakoram Highway and planned link to Gwadar in Pakistan are aspects which are of strategic concern to India, which New Delhi will be well within its rights to raise. The solution lies in resolving the issue in a spirit of mutual accommodation. Joint development of fossil and other resources will be for common good of the region, as against an attempt to corner them for use by one country flexing its military muscle.[13]

Conclusion

The essence of the Spratlys dispute lies in questions of territorial sovereignty, not law-of-the-sea issues. UNCLOS prescribes new legal rights and duties for Asian littoral states and other users of ocean space. In the SCS, the extension of 12 nm territorial sea and 200 nm EEZ has exacerbated conflicting claimed jurisdictions over non-living resources in overlapping Continental shelf zones. Moreover, various political antagonisms and disputed sovereignty claims over the Spratlys have seriously complicated the establishment of agreed-upon baselines for territorial waters. The complexities of overlapping claims and the long history of the dispute make determination of national sovereignty in the Spratlys extremely difficult. Obviously, if the issue of sovereignty can be resolved, then the maritime Jurisdictional principles codified in UNCLOS can be applied to the Spratlys. Such application would cede undersea resource rights to portions of the SCS to recognized legal owners. Yet, no claimant government is able to establish sufficiently substantial legal grounds to validate its claim. This situation, paradoxically, makes resort to binding arbitration or adjudication by claimant states, especially China, less likely since none is willing to risk an unfavourable outcome. The Spratlys dispute is sharpened by strategic and geopolitical considerations. China requires increasing energy resources to meet the growing needs of its rapid industrialization process, and its massive population exacerbates its energy problem, although as per 2008 data, the SCS has a mere 2 per cent of the world's proven oil reserves with projection of 2.4 million barrels per day of gas. ASEAN states are especially concerned because China historically has shown readiness to use military force to settle disputes within what it regards as its sphere of influence. China's build-up of naval forces is seen as expanding this sphere in the SCS through build-up of force projection capabilities. The Chinese moves at attaining blue-water naval capability are viewed by some as spawning a naval arms race among Asian states. As far as India is concerned, it has no strategic interests beyond economic engagement and security of its trade. It has entered into legal contracts with sovereign states, which are legally binding. It is important for China to recognize these facts and resolve any contentious issues in a spirit of mutual accommodation and cooperation, without being unduly jingoistic.

NOTES AND REFERENCES

1. Gregory B. Poling, 2013, *China Sea in focus clarifying limits of maritime dispute: Clarifying the Limits of Maritime Dispute*, Centre for Strategic and International Studies, Washington, https://csis-prod.s3.amazonaws.com/s3fs-public/legacy_files/files/publication/130717_Poling_SouthChinaSea_Web.pdf accessed on 31 August 2017.
2. Sean Mirksi, 2015, South China Sea dispute: A brief history, *Lawfare*, https://www.lawfareblog.com/southchina-sea-dispute-brief-history
3. Howard W French, 2015, *What's behind Beijing's drive to control the South China Sea?, The Guardian,* London https://www.theguardian.com/world/2015/jul/28/whats-behind-beijings-drive-control-south-china-sea-hainan, accessed on 05 September 2017
4. Wikipedia encyclopedia, Territorial *disputes in the South China Sea,* https://en.wikipedia.org/wiki/Territorial_disputes_in_the_South_China_Sea accessed on 05 September 2017.
5. Beina Xu, 2014, *South China Sea Tensions*, Council on Foreign Relations, China, https://www.cfr.org/backgrounder/south-china-sea-tensions accessed on 05 September 2017.
6. Jarrett step man, April 08 2017, *How China Plans to Dominate the South China Sea: Copy Great Britain, The National Interest,* accessed on 05 September 2017, http://nationalinterest.org/blog/the-buzz/how-china-plans-dominate-the-south-china-sea-copy-great-20080.
7. Stein tonnes on, 1999, *Vietnam's aim in South China Sea: National or Regional Security,*

Fourth Eurovient Conference in Passau, Germany,http://www.cliostein.com/documents/1999/99%20lec%20vietnams%20aim%20passau%20conference.pdfaccessed on 05 September 2017.

8. Mark E. Roson, 2014, *Philippines Claims in South China Sea A Legal Analysis, A* CNA Occasional Paper, U.S https://www.cna.org/cna_files/pdf/iop-2014-u-008435.pdfaccessed on 05 September 2017

9. J. Ashley Roach, 2014, A CNA Occasional Paper, Malaysia and Brunei: An Analysis of their Claims in the South China Sea, U.S, https://www.cna.org/cna_files/pdf/IOP-2014-U-009109.pdfaccessed on 05 September 2017.

10. Ian Easton, October 17, 2016, *Challenges Facing Taiwan in South China Sea*, Project 2049 Institute, America, http://www.project2049.net/documents/Challenges%20Facing_Taiwan%20in%20the_South%20China%20Sea.pdfaccessed on 05 September 2017.

11. R.S. Vasan, 2016, *India's Interest in South China Sea: Implications for Regional and Global Security and Stability,* Institute of South Asian Studies, Singapore, https://www.isas.nus.edu.sg/ISAS%20Reports/ISAS%20Insights%20No.%20334%20%20India%E2%80%99s%20Interests%20in%20South%20China%20Sea.%20Implications%20for%20Regional%20and%20Global%20Security%20and%20Stability.pdf, accessed on 05 September 2017.

12. Harsh V. Pant, December 18, 2012, *Understanding India's Interest in the South China Sea: Getting into the Seaweeds,* Center for Strategic and International studies, United States of America, https://www.csis.org/analysis/understanding-india%E2%80%99s-interest-south-china-sea-getting-seaweeds accessed on 05 September 2017.

13. Helen Clark, 2017, *Vietnam and India: Shared Interests in South China Sea* The Interpreter, Sydney, https://www.lowyinstitute.org/the-interpreter/vietnam-and-india-s-shared-interests-south-china-seaaccessed on 05 September 2017.

7

China's Constructive Engagement in South China Sea: A Liberalist Perspective

Rachit Kumar Murarka

ABSTRACT

Liberalism emphasises the mutual benefits of international cooperation, which is in contrast to the idea of realism. Realism focuses on security and warfare, and visualises international relations as a zero sum game. Usually, China has been analysed through the lens of realism, and it further accentuates when it comes to China's role in the South China Sea. Rarely, benefits of cooperation, which will occur to China and other States are debated. One can see the headlines in various print media like, 'What if China Shuts Down the South China Sea?', 'The End of a Stable Pacific', which only highlight the tension, overlooking the potential of mutual benefits. An estimated $5 trillion worth of goods are transported through the South China Sea. Approximately half of world's merchant ships pass through various choke points of the South China Sea, and many countries including China depend upon free navigation of the South China Sea for their energy needs. In the light of recent events, where President Trump has withdrawn USA from Trans Pacific Partnership (TPP), and in contrast, President Xi Jinping has defended the idea of Free Trade in World Economic Forum, Davos. China's constructive engagement in the South China Sea has unprecedented importance, to establish China as the champion of the Free Trade. A stable South China Sea is also significant for Regional Comprehensive Economic Partnership (RCEP) to materialise (India is one of the proposed members of RCEP). RCEP was proposed by China to counter the TPP. This paper would argue that China understands the importance of peaceful and stable South China Sea. This paper shows that mutual cooperation in South China is more beneficial to China through cost-benefit analysis, and the idea of free trade for which China has pledged its allegiance, than escalating tension in the region, which is portrayed generally by the realists.

Introduction

Robert Keohane and Joseph Nye Jr. have constructed the theory of complex interdependence. According to them the theory is helpful in explaining to what extent States have become dependent on each other. The theory came in response to the theory of realism which explains relations between States in terms of military power and power politics. The theory states that the essence of relations between States has changed, such as power politics and military power have assumed lesser role. On the other hand corporations, enterprises, and other non-state actors like NGOs have become more important and influential in interstate relationships. The theory rests on three factors; at the outset, multiple channels connect societies ranging from formal to informal, secondly, the agenda of interstate relations consists of multiple issues that are non-hierarchically organised, lastly, military force is irrelevant in areas in which complex interdependence prevails.[1] There is mutual benefit arising out of interdependence, as each part benefits from each other's actions, this doesn't leave much room for military intervention. Complex interdependence actually became a significant component of neoliberal idea, and has been widely used in international politics in an effort to understand interest of States to enter in cooperative arrangement and alliances with one another.[2] Contrary to the belief, this theory does not reject realism rather it raises the concern that at times there are certain situations where realists' assumptions and explanations are not adequate.[3]

South China Sea Dispute

Disputes regarding the establishment of sovereignty rights over small islands and demarcation of continental shelves are recent phenomena. Disputes and claims over land borders have much older history, but maritime demarcation is fairly recent human innovation.[4] Europeans introduced the practice of allocating regions above the sea level between States enjoying full sovereignty. However, parties involved in the South China Sea dispute use arguments based on ancient artefacts and documents to assert their claims.[5] The dispute in the South China Sea is over two groups of Islands: Paracels and the Spratlys.

Paracels is largely viewed as bilateral issue between Vietnam and China. The Spratly islands involve many States with overlapping claims. Some of the islands, reefs and rocks in this Island groups are currently occupied by Vietnam (22), China (14), and Philippines (11). Malaysia and Taiwan have also occupied some islands and reefs. Brunei has not occupied any feature but claims certain portion as its Exclusive Economic Zone (EEZ).[6] For the colonial European powers South China Sea was basically a trade route from the Straits of Malacca to China and Japan. With the United States and Japan annexation of the Philippines and Taiwan in 1898 and 1895 respectively, the South China Sea became a contested area, enmeshed in colonial power politics. However, the defeat of Japan in the second war speeds up the decolonisation process of the formal colonies of Japan. This leads to multiple sovereignty claims in the South China Sea islands.[7] China's difference of opinion in the South China Sea is largely over Paracels, which is a bilateral issue between China and Vietnam; regarding Spratly islands, China has disagreements with the Philippines. With respect to the South China Sea disputes, China basically has disputes with Vietnam and the Philippines.

Conflict over the Hydrocarbon Resources

Observing the South China Sea conflict from the lens of realism reinforces the belief that, right over exploration and exploitation of hydrocarbon resource as the possible source of South China Sea conflict. There are precedents like Iraq-Kuwait war over oil, Coup d'état in Chile over nationalisation of copper mines, and toppling of Mossadegh government in Iran over nationalisation of oil, that further uphold the belief that control over resources is the source of the conflict.

Realists like Morgenthau stressed territorial distribution as a principal way to maintain the balance of power.[8] Morgenthau has placed natural resources and geography as the features related with issues of territory and considered them as most important elements of national power.[9] "Realist thinking overlapped with conceptions of the state and territoriality developed by early 20th century scholars of geopolitics".[10] This overlapping of concepts necessitates maintaining control over territory in order to advance interests of State in the realm of security and economy. For realists control over territory is a zero-sum game. Territorial conflicts appear to be Pareto Optimal, where someone's gain is loss of other. Pareto Optimal solution is characterised by the conflict, selfishness and punishing the opponents attitude. Idea of Pareto Optimality strengthens the confidence of realists that territorial conquest is must for the gain of resources, and the control over the resources can only sustain balance of power.

This idea of control over resources has fuelled the narrative that domination over the oil and natural gas is the reason behind conflict in this region. The narrative is often expressed in 'militarised contest' for control and access of plentiful resources that is supposed to lie underneath the seabed.[11] The resource conflict account upturns fundamental relationship between territorial disputes and development of hydrocarbon resources. Struggle over offshore hydrocarbon resources is an element of the territorial dispute between China and other States rather than the 'proximate cause' of the dispute.[12]

EIA (Energy Information Administration) estimates oil reserve and gas to be approximately 11 billion barrels (bbl) and around 190 trillion cubic feet (Tcf) respectively in the South China Sea.[13] However, Wood Mackenzie (energy consultant) estimates are very low compared to EIA calculation. Wood Mackenzie has estimated only 2.5 billion barrels of oil in the region. EIA estimates are an addition of both proved and probable reserve.[14]

However, it must be taken into consideration that reserves are considered as gas or oil assets if they are located in places that are fairly well known, and must have been discovered by exploratory drilling. Reserves must also meet one more criterion that they should be extractable at net profit at market price with existing technology, ideally in a political stable area. Resources are different from reserves. Resources are the deposits that do not meet the any one of the criteria for reserves. There are different classifications of reserves which are based on the degree of probability.[15] According to the United States Geological Survey (USGS) report of 2010, there is 95 per cent probability that there is at least 764 million barrel of oil in the South China Sea Platform, at least there is 50 per cent chance of approximately 2192 million barrel of oil, and there is 5 per cent probability (very low probability) of roughly 5000 million barrels of oil.[16]

The report of USGS demonstrates the insignificant amount of oil with high probability in the South China Sea Platform. Comparing this data with current market trends does not substantiate the claim that control of hydrocarbons is the proximate cause of war. After September 2014, prices of oil nosedived; oil which was hovering well above $100 per barrel is now less than $50.[17] According to the leaked paper to the *Wall Street Journal*, OPEC (Organisation of Petroleum Exporting Countries) in its most 'optimistic scenario', anticipated that price will not touch triple digit till 2025. In fact the OPEC projected that price would not exceed $76 a barrel till 2025.[18] The low marginal production cost of OPEC countries which can be as low as $3 a barrel for the Saudi Arabia,[19] and the high cost associated with offshore exploration would make investment in hydrocarbons in the South China Sea economically unviable. Moreover, there are significant technical challenges to development of exploration rigs, which includes, water depth, typhoon prone zone, and very strong bottom-water drive.[20]

Critical enquiry into the question of resource control, concerning the South China Sea reveals that the narrative around resource conflict is inflated. Domination over resources is the chief source of the dispute, but reducing the South China Sea conflict just as struggle to control resources depicts a distorted account of conflict.

China-US Relationship

In the context of South China Sea dispute, China-US relationship is given less importance than the narrative of struggle to control resources. China's steady growth, over three decades had transformed its 'geopolitical standing in East Asia'.[21] This rise of China and changed geopolitical scenario had an impact on the United States, which is the dominant power in the East Asia since the surrender of Japan, which ended the World War II. The United States has close ties with ASEAN (Association of South East Nation), Japan, and South Korea. Because of its ties, the United States has operated in the 'seas opposite China' for long to ensure freedom of navigation.[22] The United States recognised China in 1979, before that the United States continued to recognise Nationalist Chinese government by Chiang Kai-shek on the Island of Taiwan.[23] After the recognition of China, the United States dealt coastal issues as per the framework of UNCLOS (The United Nations Convention on the Laws of the Sea), but the United States has not ratified the UNCLOS. The United States somehow uphold some of the principles of UNCLOS as the customary law, like passage of ships through territorial water of a coastal state, and freedom of navigation. Under these provisions the United States has conducted the "freedom of navigation patrols", this act of the United States challenges the sovereignty claim of China, which is one of the reasons of tension in the region. When China was ratifying the UNCLOS, it had cleared its position that a foreign state, need to give prior notification, for the passage of warships through its territorial water.[24] China emphasises, foreign warships must seek permission, before conducting any naval drills or operating in its EEZ (Exclusive Economic Zone). China's confrontation with the United States naval vessels has increased over the years. In year 2001, 2002, and 2009 China confronted with the United States vessels. However, the assertion of the United States to maintain the freedom of navigation is not altruistic. According to CSR (Congressional Research Service), basic aim of the United States is to check the rise of a regional hegemon, and as such development could threaten the United States core interest. The report further shows its apprehension towards growth in China's naval capabilities.[25] South China Sea is also important for the United States to carry on its operation in the West Asia. China is expanding its naval capabilities, and has built an aircraft carrier indigenously. While these developments are worrisome for the United States; China's goals are more defensive than offensive. China assesses the vulnerability of the United States ship operation too close to its territorial water. It is imperative for China to secure the 'sea lanes of communication', as these are important to ensure free trade without any external disturbance.[26]

Territorial water in the East Asia is the base for the United States Navy since the end of World War II; moreover, Japan, South Korea, and the Philippines are the allies of the United States. On the other hand, phenomenal rise of China, assuming the role of the United States to ensure freedom of navigation in the South China Sea has become the bone of contention. However, the economic relations between China and the United States, lessened the tension between these countries on the issue of the South China Sea.

Territorial Claims and Bilateral Trade

According to studies by scholars, most of the territorial claims do not lead to violent conflict between the States. Most of the territorial claims are decided or arrived at a solution via multilateral or bilateral negotiations.[27] Challenging the realist's notion that territorial claims are zero-sum game (only one party can control the claimed territory) Goertz and Diehl have demonstrated that majority of all territorial transfers over the last 165 years have been finalised peacefully.[28] Huth explains that since the World War II, less than one-third of all territorial claims have been disputed.[29] Realists failed to explain the decline in the use of force in case of territorial disputes. There is emerging scholarly agreement that violence is less and less used for resolving territorial disputes.[30] Many scholars attribute the drop in violence to increased interdependence, which includes bilateral trade. Rosecrance,[31] Strange and Stopford[32] have argued that trade has triumphed over territorial claims. Competition for the territorial claims has been replaced by the competition for the world market.

Basically China is in dispute with two countries in the region, Vietnam and the Philippines. As mentioned earlier, China and Vietnam have serious difference over Paracels, whereas China and the Philippines have conflicting stand on Spratly. Paracels is almost a bilateral issue between China and Vietnam. In the case of Spratly, many countries are involved, and they have issues with one another, but primarily China has problem with the Philippines.

China's Trade with Vietnam

China and Vietnam relations improved dramatically after 1991, and it practically benefitted both sides. In just a decade (1998-2008), China-Vietnam relations improved remarkably. From the insignificant trade volume of $3 million in 2000, the trade grew to more than $5 billion in 2003.[33] It is a phenomenal growth of 1600 times. This is one of the most robust trade growths, and it happened within a span of three years. In 2006, China surpassed Japan as Vietnam's largest trading partner, and Vietnam-China export-import turnover amounted to 12 per cent of Vietnam's export import turnover. In 2006, Vietnam's exports to China were worth of $3 billion. On the other hand, imports from China also rose steadily, from $1.6 billion in 2001 to $13.8 billion in 2008.[34] In 1995, there were 33 FDI (Foreign Direct Investment) projects of China in Vietnam with a total capital of $60 million. However, in 2004 the number of FDI projects augmented to 391 with a total capital of $401 million. Besides FDI, Chinese government has various forms of ODA (Official Development Assistance) in Vietnam. China has provided loans for the development of industrial complex, non-payment assistance, and non-payment loans.[35]

China and Philippines Relations

China's relations with the Philippines are different from those of Vietnam. In case of Vietnam, there was one prolonged conflict, and things were resolved in 1991. But, in the case of the Philippines and China relations, there are sporadic frictions. Trade robustness experienced in the case of Vietnam-China trading relations is not witnessed in the case of the Philippines. China's relations with the Philippines are also complex because of overwhelming influence of the United States in the Philippines. However, on the whole China-Philippines relations witnessed signing of 100 bilateral agreements from 1975-2000. Agreements were signed on areas including defence, aviation, energy cooperation, trade and investments, and people to people contacts. During 1975-2012, bilateral trade increased from $72.2 million to $36.37 billion.[36] During 1993-2002, the Philippines trade with China grew faster than the Philippines trade with rest of the world, with exports to China growing faster than imports from there.[37]

Even though internationalisation in today's world is real and substantial, national boundaries continue to have significant influence on international economic relations. There are evidences of home bias. Taking the case of the United States and Canada, McCallum has demonstrated that trade between Canadian provinces is 22 times more than the US-Canada trade.[38] Similarly Helliwell[39] demonstrates the similar effect in developing countries. Border effect is more acute in the developing countries. Simmons claims that firms face higher cost and risk in developing business in countries with which their country has a dispute.[40]

In the case of China and Vietnam trade it can be observed, though they became the biggest trade partner, the pattern of trade is uneven. China's export to Vietnam are much bigger than China's imports from Vietnam. Similarly, there are many FDI projects of China operating in Vietnam, but they are of lower value. FDI of China in Vietnam is very small compared to FDIs of other countries. Though China is the biggest trade partner of Vietnam, Chinese FDI represents just 1 per cent of FDI registered in the Vietnam.[41]

Similarly, in the case of the Philippines, though trade has expanded over the period, the relationship with the Philippines is largely characterised by power politics, and territorial water dispute. As opposed to Vietnam, the Philippines has surplus trade with China, which implies China's exports to the Philippines are smaller than China's imports from the Philippines. Yet the trade volume was affected by the dispute related to South China Sea. However, industrial equipment or industrial raw materials trade activities between the two countries were basically independent of conflicts impact.[42]

Road towards Peace and Cooperation

We need to think about international relations in a way that is neither subservient to realism zero-sum game approach to traditional concerns of state security, nor assumes that borders do not matter. Therefore, international boundaries should be visualised as "mixed motive games", characterised as having elements of "mutual dependence, conflict of partnership and competition."[43] This "mixed motive games" have a condition, which international relations scholars have associated with cooperation.[44]

The countries around the South China Sea have a long history of confrontation and very little experience of cooperation. The rapid economic development of countries around the South China Sea led to a struggle for the natural resources of the South China Sea. Consideration should also be given to increasing problem of pollution and the safety of navigation as well as to the protection of the marine environment and fragile marine ecosystem.[45]

China has assumed a bigger role in the region, and the cooperation between different States hinges on the behaviour of China. China with its colossal projects like Belt and Road Initiative, which includes Maritime Silk Road, need the cooperation of all the countries around South China Sea. The United States withdrawal from TPP[46] (Trans Pacific Partnership) and China's commitment to upholding the tenets of free trade calls for greater role of cooperation in the region.[47]

Despite many obstacles, ASEAN agreed to try to manage the potential conflicts in the South China Sea to convert them as much as possible into cooperation. In this direction, first Workshop was held in Bali in 1990. Many issues were discussed ranging from marine environment, navigation, and fishing. But, the 1990 workshop was held without the participation of China. However, in the second Bandung workshop of 1991 China joined the workshop. Various technical issues were discussed, including sovereignty rights over Paracels and Spratly islands. From 1991 every year joint workshops are taking place, which demonstrates that the States want to resolve the conflict through cooperation.

Similarly on the line of workshops, a lot of bilateral discussion and dialogues are taking place among parties. The bilateral dialogue between China and the Philippines in August 1995, produced eight point code of conduct between them. In a similar context in December 2000 Vietnam and China signed a bilateral agreement. The Fishing Agreement is unique as it establishes a "common fishing area" which is some kind of joint development project.

The problem of the South China Sea cannot be solved by resorting to violence. To fulfil its ambitious plans of Belt and Road initiative China needs to win the confidence of the littoral States. Similarly, for littoral States who cannot compete with the strength of Chinese military mechanism, cooperation is the only viable way. Cooperation alone can constructively address the problem of the South China Sea. Cooperation will not only addresses the sovereignty issues of the States, but it will also ensure the protection of fragile marine ecosystem and guarantee the freedom of navigation.

NOTES AND REFERENCES

1. Robert O. Keohane and Joseph S. Nye Jr (2012), "*Power and Interdependence*", 4th ed. Longman, New York.
2. Rana, Waheeda (2015), "Theory of Complex Interdependence: A Comparative Analysis of Realist and Neoliberal Thoughts", *International Journal of Business and Social Science*, Vol. 6 (2).
3. Ibid.
4. Tønnesson Stein (2001), "*An International History of the Dispute in the South China Sea*", East Asian Institute Working Paper No. 71
5. Ibid.
6. Djalal Hasjim, "The South China Sea: The Long Road Towards Peace and Cooperation", (eds) in Bateman, Sam and Emmers, Ralf (2009), *Security and International Politics in South China Sea: Towards a cooperative management regime*, Routledge New York.
7. Tønnesson Stein (2001), "*An International History of the Dispute in the South China Sea*", East Asian Institute Working Paper No. 71
8. Simmons, Beth A., "Trade and *Territorial Conflicts: International Borders as Institution*", p.6 https://wcfia.harvard.edu/files/wcfia/files/753_territoryandtradesimmons.pdf accessed on 28th April 2017.
9. Ibid.
10. Mackinder, Halford John. (1904), "The geographical pivot of history", *The Geographical Journal,* 23 (4): 421-444, quoted in, Simmons, Beth A., "Trade and *Territorial Conflicts: International Borders as Institution*", p.6 https://wcfia.harvard.edu/files/wcfia/files/753_territoryandtradesimmons.pdf accessed on 28th April 2017.
11. Maxie, Jeremy, "*The South China Sea Dispute Isn't About Oil, At Least Not How You Think*", posted on 25th April 2016 https://www.forbes.com/sites/jeremymaxie/2016/04/25/the-south-china-sea-dispute-isnt-about-oil-at-least-not-how-you-think/#76f4bac55c69 accessed on 26th April 2017.
12. Ibid.
13. EIA (Energy Information Administration) report, last updated on February 7 , 2013 https://www.eia.gov/beta/international/analysis_includes/regions_of_interest/South_China_Sea/south_china_sea.pdf accessed on 26th April 2017.
14. Ibid.
15. Daiss, Tim, "*Why The South China Sea Has More Oil Than You Think*", https://

www.forbes.com/sites/timdaiss/2016/05/22/why-the-south-china-sea-has-more-oil-than-you-think/#6c097ca3dd8f accessed on 26th April 2017.

16. USGS (United States Geological Survey) Assessment of Undiscovered Oil and Gas Resources of Southeast Asia, 2010 https://pubs.usgs.gov/fs/2010/3015/pdf/FS10-3015.pdf accessed on 27th April 2017.
17. What's behind the drop in oil price, https://www.weforum.org/agenda/2016/03/what-s-behind-the-drop-in-oil-prices/ accessed on 6th May 2017.
18. Crude Oil: Double bottom confirmed n a weekly time-frame, https://htotrading.wordpress.com/2015/05/22/ accessed on 8th May 2017.
19. https://knoema.com/vyronoe/cost-of-oil-production-by-country accessed on 11th May 2017
20. http://www.geo.fu-berlin.de/geol/fachrichtungen/geologie/mitarbeiter_neu/Professoren/cheubeck/pub_pdfs/Heubeck_et_al_2004_AAPG_Mem_81_Liuhua.pdf accessed on 11th May 2017.
21. Joshi, Manoj (2016), "The South China Sea Disputes: Territorial Claims, Geopolitics, and International Law", *ORF Occasional Papers*, http://www.orfonline.org/research/the-south-china-sea-disputes-territorial-claims-geopolitics-and-international-law/#_edn7 accessed on 24th April 2017.
22. Ibid.
23. http://www.history.com/this-day-in-history/united-states-announces-that-it-will-recognize-communist-china accessed on 24th April 2017
24. Joshi, Manoj (2016), "The South China Sea Disputes: Territorial Claims, Geopolitics, and International Law", *ORF Occasional Papers*, http://www.orfonline.org/research/the-south-china-sea-disputes-territorial-claims-geopolitics-and-international-law/#_edn7 accessed on 24th April 2017.
25. Ibid.
26. Ibid.
27. Hensel, Paul R., Sara McLaughlin, Mitchell et al. (2008), "Bones of Contention: Comparing Territorial, Maritime, and River Issues." *Journal of Conflict Resolution* 52 (1), February: 117-143.
28. Goertz, Gary, and Paul F. Diehl. 1992. Territorial Changes and International Conflict. New York: Routledge.
29. Huth, Paul K. (1996), "*Standing Your Ground*". Ann Arbor: University of Michigan Press, quoted in Simmons, Beth A., "Trade and *Territorial Conflicts: International Borders as Institution*", p. 7https://wcfia.harvard.edu/files/wcfia/files/753_territoryandtradesimmons.pdf accessed on 28th April 2017.
30. Ibid, p. 8.
31. Rosecrance, Richard N (1986), "*The Rise of the Trading State: Commerce and Conquest in the Modern World*", New York: Basic Books, quoted in Simmons, Beth A., "Trade and *Territorial Conflicts: International Borders as Institution*" p. 8.
32. Stopford, John, and Susan Strange (1991), "*Rival States, Rival Firms: Competition for World Market Shares*". Cambridge: Cambridge University Press, quoted in Beth A., "*Trade and Territorial Conflicts: International Borders as Institution*", pp. 8-9.
33. http://www.ide.go.jp/English/Publish/Download/Brc/pdf/01_vietnamandchina.pdf accessed on 7th May 2017.
34. Ibid.
35. Ibid.
36. Tuazon, Bobby M (2014), "*The Highs and Lows of Philippines-China Relations: Current Situation and Prospects*", paper from a Lecture for the Guangxi Academy of Social Sciences, Institute of Southeast Asian Studies, Nanning, p. 5.

37. Wang, Fang, "*South China Sea Territorial Disputes and Sino-Philippine Trade*", http://blog.chinadaily.com.cn/blog-1040969-30038.html accessed on 11th May 2017.
38. McCallum, John (1995), "National Borders Matter: Canada-U.S. Regional Trade Patterns", *The American Economic Review*, 85 (3), quoted in Simmons, Beth A., "*Trade and Territorial Conflicts: International Borders as Institution*", p. 9, https://wcfia.harvard.edu/files/wcfia/files/753_territoryandtradesimmons.pdf accessed on 28th April 2017.
39. Helliwell, John F (1998), "*How Much Do National Borders Matter?*",Washington D.C.: The Brookings Institution, quoted in, quoted in Simmons, Beth A., "Trade and *Territorial Conflicts: International Borders as Institution*", p. 9 https://wcfia.harvard.edu/files/wcfia/files/753_territoryandtradesimmons.pdf accessed on 28th April 2017.
40. Simmons, Beth A. (2005), "*Rules over Real Estate: Trade, Territorial Conflict, and International Borders as Institutions*", Journal of Conflict Resolution, Vol.49 (6), December, p. 829.
41. http://www.ide.go.jp/English/Publish/Download/Brc/pdf/01_vietnamandchina.pdf accessed on 7th May 2017.
42. Wang, Fang, "*South China Sea Territorial Disputes and Sino-Philippine Trade*", http://blog.chinadaily.com.cn/blog-1040969-30038.html accessed on 11th May 2017.
43. Simmons, Beth A., "Trade and *Territorial Conflicts: International Borders as Institution*", p. 10, https://wcfia.harvard.edu/files/wcfia/files/753_territoryandtradesimmons.pdf accessed on 28th April 2017.
44. Ibid.
45. Djalal Hasjim, "The South China Sea: The Long Road Towards Peace and Cooperation", eds, Bateman, Sam and Emmers, Ralf (2009), *Security and International Politics in South China Sea: Towards a cooperative management regime*, Routledge New York.
46. Edwards John, "*What's Next after the US withdrawal from the TPP*", http://www.aljazeera.com/indepth/opinion/2017/01/withdrawal-tpp-170126092759229.html posted on 26th January 2017, accessed on 12th May 2017.
47. President Xi's Speech to Davos https://www.weforum.org/agenda/2017/01/full-text-of-xi-jinping-keynote-at-the-world-economic-forum accessed on 12th May 2017.

8

China's Preoccupation in South China Sea and the International Response

Munmun Roy

ABSTRACT

The South China Sea (SCS) is significant not only to China and Southeast Asia but also to the nations which regularly utilize its Sea Lanes of Communication (SLOC) for their maritime trade. The SCS is considered to be one of the world's busiest international trade routes connecting the Western Pacific and Northeast Asia to the West Asia through the Indian Ocean. An attempt is made in the present paper to understand the response of the international community to the preoccupation of China in the SCS.

Introduction

The SCS is significant not only to China and Southeast Asia but also to the nations which regularly utilize its Sea Lanes of Communication (SLOC) for their maritime trade. The SCS is considered to be one of the world's busiest international trade routes connecting the Western Pacific and Northeast Asia to West Asia through the Indian Ocean. It is said that over US$ 5 trillion worth of global trade passes through the sea lanes of SCS every year and a majority of shipments contain energy and raw materials. More than half of the global total annual merchandise passes through the SCS. Further, the SCS is believed to hold vast hydro carbon energy sources—around 29 billion tons of petroleum reserves and 58 trillion cubic meters of natural gas reserves. The safety of the sea lanes and the freedom of navigation are therefore of paramount significance to all the nations which deal with maritime trade. Control of the SCS by any hostile or aggressive power will pose grave threat to the international trade and commerce.

The Nationalist government of the Republic of China claimed its sovereignty over the SCS in 1947 by publishing a map with a nine-dash line delineating China's maritime sovereignty in the SCS. This claim and the map continued after the Communist Party attained power in the mainland China in 1949. However, since 1949 till the early 1970s China did not carry out any activity in the SCS. It is only since the 1990s China initiated its assertion in the SCS leading to frictions with the nations of Southeast Asia, like Vietnam, Malaysia, Taiwan, Brunei, the Philippines, etc. The UNCLOS rules and guidelines did not seem to deter China to modify its stance on the SCS. In 2002, ASEAN and China issued a Declaration on the Conduct of Parties (DOC) in the SCS aimed at the cooperation on certain marine activities among the littoral states. For some time DOC seemed to work, but after China seized the Scarborough Shoal in 2012, the Philippines approached the Arbitral Tribunal. The Arbitral Tribunal announced its unanimous award vindicating the claims of the Philippines on the SCS. In the present paper an attempt is made to understand the international response to the SCS dispute in the emerging global order.

China is the principal player both in terms of aggression as well as usage in the SCS. China has always claimed its unique and sole rights on the small islets and reefs it occupied since 1970s. China indicated that it is prepared to confront not only the regional powers but also a super power like the US in the SCS dispute. The unanimous verdict of the International Arbitration at the Hague on July 12, 2016, has only angered China. China's position was very blunt. It stated that, 'the award is null and void and has no binding force. China neither accepts nor recognizes it.' It criticised the unilateral action of the Philippines which was a move taken in bad faith and designed to deny China's territorial sovereignty and maritime rights and interests in the SCS.

It is because of the Philippines that case was brought to the Hague Tribunal. Surprisingly the Philippines response was rather muted after its victory. The Philippines strongly affirmed its respect for this milestone decision as an important contribution to ongoing efforts in addressing disputes in the SCS. The new President of the Philippines Rodrigo Duterte's radical departure to go closer to China even after the Hague verdict in favour of the Philippines surprised the international community. It appears that China has been successful in its 'Cheque Book Diplomacy' in dealing with the Philippines in the SCS dispute.

As one of the SCS claimant countries, Vietnam has been watching the Philippines's case against China with great interest. Soon after the ruling was released, spokesperson for the Ministry of Foreign Affairs Le Hai Binh said Vietnam strongly supports the settlement of disputes by peaceful means.

Vietnam also reaffirmed its sovereignty over Paracel Islands (also claimed by China) and Spratly Islands (also claimed by China, Brunei, Taiwan, Malaysia and the Philippines), which it said was established in accordance with the 1982 United Nations Convention on the Law of the Sea. Vietnam has also emerged as the most vocal opponent of China's claims in the South China Sea, where more than $3 trillion worth of cargo passes every year. To China's annoyance, Vietnam held an ASEAN meeting in August 2017 for a communique expressing concern about island-building and criticised militarisation in the SCS.

Indonesia's interest in the SCS is limited to its own trade. It needs the UNCLOS and the freedom of navigation in the SCS. However, Indonesia does not want to be dragged directly in the power politics of China and the US. Indonesia urged all sides to show self-restraint and to refrain from any steps that could increase tensions in the region. Thailand, Malaysia, Singapore and Myanmar also expressed that the Tribunal issued its award and called on all parties to ensure the full and effective implementation of the Declaration on the Conduct of Parties in the SCS (DOC). Interestingly, Malaysia which has claims in the SCS dispute responded cautiously to the Hague verdict. It is but natural to the Southeast Asian nations to keep normal relations with China as they are dependent on China for their trade, investments and market.

Some of the nations, such as Myanmar, Laos and Cambodia, are strong traditional allies of China, have no strategic interest in the South China Sea. They strongly rely on China for both political and economic survival. Thailand has a continuing interest in working closely with China to build a canal through the Kra Isthmus in southern Thailand. This project is estimated to cost close to US$30 billion and the economic trade-off for Thailand will be extraordinary. If this canal is built it will allow ships to bypass the Strait of Malacca and will result in significant loss of maritime shipping revenue for Malaysia, Singapore and Indonesia. However, it would be in the strategic interests of these three nations to avoid confrontation with China in case it prioritises the financing and building of this canal with Thailand. (Wey 2016)

Although Japan is not directly involved in the SCS territorial dispute, Japan's energy security largely depends on the safety of the SLOCs in the SCS since 60 per cent of its energy imports pass through the SCS. Japan is also a leading importer of sea food from the Southeast Asian nations. Hence, for Japan the stability of the SCS region is very vital. Japan's main anxiety is that China's military buildup and reclamation activities in the SCS will result in the Chinese strategic control of SLOCs in the SCS. In such a scenario Japan would depend on China if it will allow the maritime traffic freely for Japan as well as other nations.

The ruling of the Arbitration Tribunal boosted Japan's confidence. Japan responded vehemently to the ruling and indicated that the ruling is final and legally binding on China. Japan's closest ally the US also influences the Japanese response to the situation in the SCS. Even before the Hague verdict, since 2015 the US encouraged Japan to develop and enhance its defence capabilities obviously against China and North Korea. (Jennings 2016; Fatton 2016.)

Australia has strategic interests in the SCS which Canberra has been expressing directly and indirectly. Ship-borne trade and security have been the real concerns of Australia since Australia's maritime trade routes with Northeast Asia must pass through the SCS. Australia has officially declared that since a major chunk of its trade passes through the SCS, strategic stability is very important to Australia (Kenny 2013). Not only the trade routes through the SCS, but also the safety of the Sea Lanes of Communication (SLOCs) has emerged as the requirement for Australia in the context of its increasing integration into Southeast Asia. With the increasing conflicts, claims and competition of major powers, Australia's security concerns seem to be linked with the stability in the Asia-Pacific (Homes 2013). Further, as one of the oldest and closest allies of the United States, Australia is obliged to maintain a strategic interest in the SCS. Hence, Although Australia, does not take a position on the competing claims on the SCS, Canberra clearly announced its legitimate interest in the maintenance of peace and stability, respect for law, unimpeded trade and freedom of navigation (Turnbull 2016; Hill 2015).

New Zealand's Foreign Minister Murray McCully's issued a statement, in response to the finding by the Permanent Court of Arbitration at The Hague.

'Maintaining peace and stability in the SCS is vital to the ongoing prosperity of the wider Asia-Pacific region. It is in all parties' interests to ensure the United Nations Convention on the Law of the Sea is respected. We hope that the tribunal's ruling can provide a platform for resolving the longstanding and complex issues in the SCS and we urge all parties to work towards this end'. (Small 2016)

It is extremely difficult for New Zealand to balance the military links with the United States and the strong trade and other common interests with Australia versus the burgeoning importance of China as an export destination. However, New Zealand's will always be inclined to fall in behind decisions under international law made by international bodies. As a small nation, especially faced with a proxy war between the world's two big battalions, New Zealand's careful articulation is but natural.

India is not involved in the SCS dispute, but consistently maintained that UNCLOS and freedom of navigation should always be respected. In terms of trade India has stakes in the SCS. The Indian government's official reaction was prompt and measured. The Ministry of External Affairs (MEA) issued a statement on the day of the award that called on all parties to show the "utmost respect" for the UNCLOS. It said, 'India supports freedom of navigation and over-flight, and unimpeded commerce, based on the principles of international law, as reflected notably in the UNCLOS'. Emphasizing India's specific national interest in the issue, it added: 'States should resolve disputes through peaceful means without threat or use of force and exercise self-restraint in the conduct of activities that could complicate or escalate disputes affecting peace and stability' (Malik 2016). India does not attempt to show any aggression in the SCS although it partners with the powers like USA, Japan, Vietnam, Malaysia, etc in joint military and naval exercises indicating its concerns over the Chinese aggression in the SCS.

USA is not a disputant in the SCS, although it has been challenging China in terms of freedom of navigation. The US, traditionally has been obliged to its allies like Taiwan and the Philippines to provide security in times of aggression by any hostile power. USA has been the only outside power which has so strongly opposed the Chinese claims of sovereignty in the SCS that it indicated its willingness even for a military confrontation with China. As a 'global police man', USA symbolically asserted its domination in the SCS dispute.

Although the United States has never acceded to UNCLOS, it accepts the UN convention as customary international law. The State Department points out that the court's decision is legally binding on both China and the Philippines. 'When joining the Law of the Sea Convention, parties agree to the Convention's compulsory dispute settlement process to resolve disputes', the statement said. 'In today's decision and in its decision from October of last year, the Tribunal unanimously found that the Philippines was acting within its rights under the Convention in initiating this arbitration' (Gady 2016).

The United States also reiterated its support for efforts to resolve the dispute through peaceful means, including through arbitration. Washington expressed hope that China and the Philippines would comply with the decision and urged all claimants to avoid provocative statements or actions. A statement from John Kirby, assistant secretary and department spokesperson of the Bureau of Public Affairs, said, 'We encourage claimants to clarify their maritime claims in accordance with international law—as reflected in the Law of the Sea Convention—and to work together to manage and resolve their disputes'.

Russia, in the recent times, has been moving towards China owing not only to Russia's increasing dependence on China in trade and economic matters and also due to Russia's assertion as Euro-Asian power. In so far as the SCS is concerned, Russia is not directly involved in the SCS dispute. However, since both China and Vietnam are strategic partners of Russia, Russia is not in a position to take sides in the SCS dispute. Russia's position seems to be that it does not intend to take sides in the conflict but Russia also is opposed to extra-regional involvement in the dispute. Indirectly, Russia seems to suggest an amicable settlement among the claimants in the SCS dispute, without the involvement of the US. At the same time, Russia also indicated its support for compliance with international law including UNCLOS and the 2002 Declaration of Conduct, after the judgment of the Permanent Court of Arbitration (PCA) in July 2016 (Tsvestov 2016).

The response of Russia to the SCS dispute may be interpreted in different ways. Since Russia is not a power in the Pacific/Asia-Pacific region, it has no stakes in the dispute. However, symbolically, Russia cannot afford to antagonize China when its economic dependence on China has only grown. Russia has also to take into account its own prestige as a global power as well as one among the P-5 in the United Nations. Any signal of disinterest in the SCS would damage Russia's image as a competing super power.

Association of Southeast Asian Nations (ASEAN) seems to be unable to cooperate on many common security issues. ASEAN was formed to soothe regional competitions and apprehensions among its pioneer members, particularly Indonesia, Malaysia, the Philippines and Singapore. ASEAN originally operated as a platform to discuss cooperation in socio-economic activities and adheres to the principle of non-interference in each other's internal affairs.

The ASEAN members that have an interest in the SCS, are perpetually locked in rivalry and competition among themselves in overlapping claims. Almost all of the ASEAN members are also entangled in border and territorial disputes among themselves. However, ASEAN has struggled to issue a strong and coherent response. The difficulty of ASEAN can be understood because half of ASEAN's members, namely Malaysia, Philippines, Vietnam, Brunei and Indonesia are involved in overlapping claims in the SCS. In 49th ASEAN Foreign Ministers' Meeting in Laos in 2016, ASEAN released a joint communique that was seen as 'too soft' on China. The communique failed to explicitly denounce China's assertive actions in the SCS. With so many conflicting interests and rivalries between ASEAN members ASEAN has been unable to produce a strong joint statement condemning China's actions in the SCS. Hence, the mixed and at times muted response of ASEAN seems to continue. (Wey 2016).

The European Union (EU) issued a statement on noting China's legal defeat over the SCS but avoided direct reference to Beijing, reflecting discord among EU governments over how strongly to respond to the court ruling. The European Union is neutral in China's dispute with its Asian neighbours in the SCS. However, Britain (now exiting EU), France and Germany want to make clear that Beijing must uphold international law as it seeks a bigger global role. It is becoming difficult for the European Union to speak with one voice as some smaller governments, including Hungary and Greece, rely on Chinese investment and are unwilling to criticize Beijing despite its militarization of SCS islands. In the statement of all 28 EU governments, the bloc acknowledged July 12, 2016, ruling in The Hague and said it was 'committed to maintaining a legal order of the seas and oceans'. After three days of difficult talks in Brussels to reach a common position, the European Union said all sides should resolve the maritime dispute 'through peaceful means, to clarify their claims and pursue them in respect and in accordance with international law' (Emmott 2016).

In the African continent the responses of over ten countries were rather muted. In the last two decades, China has invested in Africa in several projects besides providing aid to several African states. China has become the largest investor and market for the vast mineral and energy reserves in the African continent resulting in a considerable clout over Africa.

Erastus Mwencha, Deputy Chairperson of the African Union Commission, expressed support to China's position on the issue of SCS, calling on all directly related countries of the issue to give dialogue and consultation an opportunity to peacefully solve related disputes in accordance with the international law.

Tanzanian Foreign Minister Augustine Mahiga stated that Tanzania supports countries in the SCS region in peacefully settling the issue through dialogues and consultations. The statement also hoped that related institutions can keep to the rules of UNCLOS made in 1982 and respect the right of sovereign states and contracting countries to the Convention to independently choose the way for dispute settlement.

Oryem Okello, Minister of State for foreign affairs of Uganda, expressed support to directly related countries of the issue of SCS to peacefully settle territorial and maritime disputes in accordance with bilateral agreements and consensus in the region through friendly consultations or negotiations. He said that he could not understand the behaviour of the Philippines to unilaterally file the arbitration. Gambia, which resumed diplomatic relations with China recently, released a statement, firmly supporting the position of the Chinese government of not accepting or participating in the arbitration procedure unilaterally filed by the Philippines. The Kenyan government issued a statement calling on all related countries to peacefully solve the SCS disputes through consultations and negotiations in accordance with the Declaration on the Conduct of Parties in the SCS. The government of Kenya respects the opting-out statement China has made according to Article 298 of UNCLOS, pointing out that the international community should continue to play a constructive role to support efforts of countries in the region to safeguard peace and stability of the region. (Miaogeng 2016).

Conclusions

The preoccupation of China in the SCS has been posing a threat to the peace and stability in the Asia-Pacific Region for the past two decades. It was hoped that the Hague judgment would settle the dispute not only between China and the Philippines but also would serve as a precedent to any future maritime disputes among nations. Unfortunately, the rigid stance of China in defying the Hague verdict has complicated the peace and stability in the Asia-Pacific. Initially, the SCS dispute began as a sub-regional or regional in nature. However, when the issues of freedom of navigation and trade in conjunction with the vast energy resources as well as its transport became vital the SCS has become a stake for several nations, notably the US. The ramifications of the SCS have influenced even the countries which do not have a stake or even direct participation in the SCS oceans. Thus, even the countries in the African Union or the European Union itself have responded to the SCS dispute. The international response to the Chinese preoccupation in the SCS is a testimony to the fact that, in the 21st century, a regional dispute like this can have a global impact which is indicated by the response of the international community. Another dimension of the SCS dispute, which stands out in the emerging global order, is that China is clearly challenging the domination of USA, especially in the Asia-Pacific region. With its huge investments and aid China has been dominating in Asia, Africa and to a lesser extent in South America. The impending domination of China in the emerging global order is exemplified by the balanced response of the most influential regional organization, the EU. Nations seem to have realized the fact that it is very difficult to ignore China in the current international arena. At the same time, the nations and the regional organizations would not want to risk their relations between the competing global powers, viz. USA and China.

NOTES AND REFERENCES

Adam Leong Kok Wey (2016), 'Is the South China Sea fracturing ASEAN', August 25, 2016. http://www.eastasiaforum.org/2016/08/25/is-the-south-china-sea-fracturing-asean/

Anton Tsvestov (2016), 'Did Russia Just Ask China to 'Buzz off' on the South China Sea?', *The Diplomat*, July 16, 2016

Cameron Hill (2015), 'Australia and the South China Sea: Debates and Dilemmas', *Foreign Affairs*, Defence and Security, Parliament of Australia, http://www.aph.gov.au/About_Parliament_Departments/ Parliamentary_Library/pubs/BriefingBook45p/SouthChinaSea)

Franz-Stefan Gady (2016), 'South China Sea Verdict: US Reactions', *The Diplomat*, July 13, 2016.

http://www.eu-asiacentre.eu/news_details.php?news_id=185

https://thewire.in/170549/vietnam-calls-for-unified-southeast-asian-response-south-china-sea-dispute/

http://www.philstar.com/headlines/2016/07/13/1602416/world-leaders-react-south-china-sea-ruling.July 13, 2016

James R Homes (2013), 'The Geopolitics of Australia', October 9, 2013, *The Diplomat*.

Lionel Fatton (2016), 'Japan's New Security Policy: Towards Regional Involvement at Sea?', *Strategic Security Analysis*, April 2016.

Lu Miaogeng (2016), 'African Countries Express Support to China's Position On South China', June 22, 2016. http://allafrica.com/stories/201606220195.html

Malcom Turnbull (Prime Minister, Australia) (2016), https://www.pm.gov.au/media/2016-07-13/press-conference-foreign-minister, July 13, 2016.

Mark Kenny, 'Tony Abbott warns of conflict risk in South China Sea', *The Sydney Morning Herald*, October 10, 2013.

Mohan Malik (2016), 'India's Response to the South China Sea Verdict, July 22, 2016. https://www.the-american-interest.com/2016/07/22/indias-response-to-the-south-china-sea-verdict/

Ralph Jennings (2016), 'Japan is becoming player in South China Sea Sovereignty Dispute', *Voanews*, March 20, 2016.

Robin Emmott (2016), 'EU's statement on South China Sea reflects divisions', July 15, 2016. http://www.reuters.com/article/us-southchinasea-ruling-eu/eus-statement-on-south-china-sea-reflects-divisions-idUSKCN0ZV1TS

Vernon Small (2016), 'NZ reaction to South China Sea ruling treads gently over China's loss', July 14 2016, http://www.stuff.co.nz/national/politics/opinion/82052423/nz-reaction-to-south-china-sea-ruling-treads-gently-over-chinas-loss

9

South China Sea Affair: Makings of a New Munich Pact

Mithlesh Jayas Mukherji

ABSTRACT

In recent years there has been increasing focus by international experts on the South China Sea (SCS) and the Syrian Conflict. Both these events have had similar echoes in the past. The Syrian conflict bears similarity to the Spanish Civil war while the repeated assertions by the Chinese to their "*historical*" claims to the SCS and its *nine-dashed line* bear striking resemblance to the German claims for 'Lebensraum" over parts of Poland/Czechoslovakia/ Lithuania/Denmark/Austria.

The Chinese claims and actions in setting up artificial islands in the SCS are an attempt at creating sovereign territory in international waters and converting large portions of these into national waters by defining these waters as parts of the island shelf. In this endeavour, it has been opposed locally by Vietnam and the Philippines with support from the US, Japan and Australia. Curiously, even after a favourable International Court ruling, the new government in the Philippines has decided on bilateral negotiations with the Chinese thereby legitimizing Chinese actions in the SCS. These events create a potential for future conflict like the Munich Pact led to the Second World War. Chinese confidence, if their initials steps are successful, would rise and so would the scope and quantum of their future claims. Any step later, then would mean perhaps forcibly evicting the Chinese from claimed areas which could lead to Regional or even Global conflict. It would be better, therefore, for the other powers now to motivate the Chinese to observe the UNCLOS and by following a "carrot-and-stick" policy (better economic deals or partnerships vis-à-vis economic conflict or cancellation of deals involving China or even building up surrounding powers such as India, Vietnam or Japan) China could be goaded to accepting international laws.

Introduction

A study of the SCS dispute should include a look into the factors which caused the Second World War, the most devastating modern war. The Munich Pact of 1938 has often been pointed out to be one of the prime reasons for the start of the Second World War. This pact between Britain and France on one side and Nazi Germany on the other side institutionalized the appeasement policy then being followed by the Western Powers towards Nazi Germany. The Pact recognized Nazi claims over Czech ruled Sudetenland and other German populated areas over the protestations of the involved Eastern and Central European countries; effectively abandoning these to German expansionism. The Western Powers at the time aimed at promoting German expansion to its south East towards the Carpathians and into Soviet Russia in an attempt to cause friction between Germany and the Soviet Union. They also aimed at preserving Polish independence and its expansion into the Baltics and Byelorussia. These aims were however belied by Hitler's moves into Central Europe and into Poland thereby precipitating the Second World War. Thus, by acceding to threats by a bully, the League of Nations caused its own fall as well as laid the ground for a widespread war. It has been estimated that Hitler had aimed for European war against Britain and France after 1945; he had planned to grab the smaller states by bullying the powers before 1942 and then invade Soviet Russia after 1943; by when his militarisation of the German armed forces would have been complete. However, the lack of resistance to his expansion and occupation of Czechoslovakia (1938), Rhineland (1936), Saar (1935), Austria (1938), Memel (1939) and Danzig (1939) stoked his greed and motivated him to plan his invasion of Poland in 1939 and the Scandinavian countries in 1940 before turning on France.[1]

Thus, the failure by the responsible Powers to stand up to an expansionist Power has always led to the outbreak of widespread conflict rather than avoiding a conflict. This has been seen in the various Arab-Israeli wars, Iraq-Iran war as well as the First and Second World Wars. The dispute in the SCS has the potential to cause regional and global conflict if it is not managed intelligently. The expansionist Power in this case is China which claims almost the entire expanse of the SCS as its territorial waters.[2] This negates the principle of freedom of movement and trade in the high seas and if not responded to could trigger wider Chinese expansion into South East, East and South Asia.

The Importance of Claiming the South China Sea

The islands in the SCS over which China, the Philippines, Vietnam, Brunei, and Malaysia have competing claims are basically small rocky outposts jutting out from the sea with some of the bigger islands having reefs and atolls.[3] These islands, namely, the Paracel group and the Spratly islands, by themselves have no significant economic or military value. The dispute is over their location and in the sea bed below. The SCS is the main highway over which trade passes from the Indian Ocean into the Sea of Japan and the Pacific Ocean. It is the major route through which China, Japan, South Korea and Taiwan import oil as well as through which these countries trade most of goods to Asia and Africa.[4] About half of the world's entire merchant fleet tonnage passes through these waters.[5]

The SCS is important for China as well as Japan and South Korea as their trade routes run through the Indian Ocean and the Malacca Straits and into the SCS before coming out into the East China Sea and the Pacific.[6] China imports around 80% of its oil from the Persian Gulf which is shipped through this route.[7,8] In case of war with either the US or its allies or with India; these shipping routes would become vulnerable to blockade which could slow down Chinese mobilization. Hence, to protect its economic "*Chicken-neck*", in recent years China has been modernizing its navy and building up an expeditionary capability as far as the Indian Ocean.[9] This naval capability would best be deployed in a way that would allow it access to the southwest, making the Hainan area and the South China Sea most suitable. Moreover, the South China Sea will become a base for China's second-strike submarine-adapted nuclear capability intended to deter the United States from risking conventional conflict with China over Taiwan or any other issue. For strategic reasons, the Chinese navy seeks control over the area and acts to prevent the United States from establishing a presence there that could threaten it.

In addition to this massive volume of trade passing through this geographically enclosed area, the waters of the SCS abound in marine wealth. The SCS is one of the world's richest fishing regions, regarded by Chinese and Vietnamese fishermen as a traditional fishing zone. The University of British

Columbia's Fisheries Center estimated that catch statistics in the SCS have increased from 4.7 million tons in 1994 to 5.6 million tons in 2003, averaging about 5 million tons. With the advent of new techniques and new technology in deep sea fishing, mechanized trawling has almost depleted marine reserves in most continental shelves and fisherman have to move further out into the sea for better catches. The fish stocks have been overexploited and catch rates have been declining, resulting in smaller fish sizes and the gradual move from large, high-value fish to smaller, lower-value fish. This has led to fierce competition to exploit the fisheries in an area and the SCS with its rich reserves is subject to such fierce rivalries between Chinese, Vietnamese and Philippine fishermen. This competition for access to better fishing grounds in a background of overall declining fish stocks has been a reason for recent clashes occurring in the area with many of the host countries; especially China and Vietnam offering support from naval or coastguard vessels.[10]

In addition to fish and marine reserves, the sea bed in this area is estimated to hold significant reserves of natural gas which provides for valuable national security to countries like China and Vietnam and a source of additional income to countries like Brunei, Vietnam, Philippines and even Malaysia by way of exploration and export. The first commercial oil and gas extraction from this area started in March 1976 off the Philippine island of Palawan at Reed Bank and it involved a consortium of three Swedish and seven Philippine companies. Malaysia's Petronas presently is a major oil producer in the area and as per estimates in 2011, produced 500,000 barrels a day (bd) and 600 billion m^3 of natural gas. Petro-Vietnam in 2011 produced 300,000 bd of oil and 100 billion m^3 of natural gas.[11]

The South China Sea Dispute and Chinese Actions

The Chinese have based their claim over the whole of the SCS on the historical voyage of Admiral Zheng Hi and his famous treasure fleet which in the 15th century visited and received homage from the coastal states of the present Vietnam, Cambodia, Borneo, Indonesia and Malaysia and was thought even to have come up to the shores of Sri Lanka and the Kerala province of India. More recent historical claims of Chinese control over the SCS point to the Qing dynasty of China which had protested France's intrusion into the area over 1884-85.[12,13] But at that time, China's concern was the Paracels and not the Spratlys and contemporary evidence shows that the Chinese were limited in their claims for their southern borders as being the Paracels and not the Spratlys. Chinese interest in the Spratlys rose after the Nationalist (Kuomintang /KMT) takeover in 1911 and after French intrusion in the area in the 1930s. France intended to mine the guano deposits of the islands and was motivated to exclude the Japanese. In April 1930, France annexed the Spratlys and landed troops over the islands. China protested the French move into the Spratlys, and in April 1935, Chinese Land and Water Maps inspection committee under the KMT government drafted a map of the SCS which included a U-shaped line with eleven dashes which was later amended by the communist government into nine dashes giving rise to the "*Nine Dashed Line*" boundary. However, in 1939 Japanese invasion of the area ended all claims.[14]

In 1947, in the immediate aftermath of the Second World War and the defeat and the withdrawal of the Japanese from the area; the Chinese were the first to act and occupied the Woody Island in the Paracel island group before the French could come and who later settled for the nearby Pattle Island. Even though the San Francisco Conference in 1951 recognised Japanese withdrawal of all claims in the area did not appoint a successor state over the area because of competing Chinese and Vietnamese claims. This has opened a window for numerous competing claims by different countries. The Vietnamese claimed that according to the Geneva Agreement of 1954 which provided for the termination of French in Vietnam, they were the successor state and should be awarded the area. This was disputed by France which responded that the Geneva Agreement did not cover the Spratlys and was limited to only the Paracels of which the Chinese had already occupied the eastern part. The Philippines argued that the area had been occupied "*in toto*" by Japan during World War II and that their withdrawal left it free for all others. In fact, it occupied a part of the Spratlys in 1971 calling it the "Kalayaan Islands"; this action was contested and opposed by Malaysia which itself occupied another five islands by 1983. Till this time all of these actions taken by these States had been to occupy uninhabited islands unclaimed by any other country. By the mid-1970s, however, there were claims and counter-claims to almost all the islands with the Chinese and the Vietnamese claiming large areas of the open sea itself while the other claimants were limited to their continental shelves.[15]

Militarisation of this area started in 1974 with Chinese occupation of the entire Paracel Island group after evicting the Vietnamese forces in a short sharp engagement. Vietnam then was occupied fighting the Americans and in the process of unifying the country; and did not take any subsequent action against this Chinese aggression. The period between 1947 and 1997 was largely peaceful owing to Chinese preoccupation with their land borders and the mainly landward bend of their military strategy. Also Deng Xiaoping's focus from 1979 onwards was to improve the Chinese economic muscle and for this the Chinese were not prepared during this period from 1979 to 1996 to face-off the western Powers or their regional allies such as Malaysia or the Philippines.[16,17]

Further activities took place in the period 1979–87, when the Chinese repeatedly pressed their claims over the Spratly Islands. The Vietnamese, now free from their unification wars, opposed the Chinese, but the much smaller Vietnamese navy without any help from any other State or Power was hopelessly outclassed by the much larger PLA-N (Chinese Navy). Starting from small clashes in 1979–81; the South Fleet of the PLA-N strengthened itself and was able to carry out full area surveys by 1983; and build observation towers, troop shelters, radar sites and piers in these areas by 1993. There was a bigger clash with the Vietnamese navy in 1988 with the Vietnamese losing three ships and 73 sailors. The Philippines discovered that the Chinese had similarly occupied their claimed Mischief reef in the Spratly islands in 1993.[18]

The next important event which has influenced Chinese behaviour in this region occurred in 1995-96. In 1995, the Clinton administration allowed the Taiwanese premier to visit the US in spite of their "One-China" policy with the People's Republic of China (PRC). This angered the Chinese who fired missiles in the Taiwan Strait near a few uninhabited Taiwanese controlled islands; and moved troops to the Guangzhou coast. While this sabre rattling by the Chinese had been seen before and ignored by the Americans, this time the Clinton administration decided to show strength. Two carrier groups were ordered to steam through the Taiwan Straits between China and Taiwan to "cool off tempers" but actually to show the Chinese the dangers of facing up to US allies.[19]

This made the Chinese realize their vulnerability to US naval power and the weakness of their "*1st island chain for defence*" lying adjacent to the mainland. They found that the US could target deep inland from outside the territorial waters and that they needed strategic depth at sea also; particularly when the largest core of the Han Chinese areas lay adjacent to the coast. Since then the Chinese naval strategy has been to push the "*1st island chain*" as far as possible from the mainland; and with this aim, the Chinese have been trying to convert the SCS into a Chinese lake.[20] Since 1997, the Chinese have been making steady progress on this aim of pushing away the distance a US carrier group could come comfortably from the mainland. The massive upgradation of facilities at the Hainan Island and the completion of the Sanya naval base gives the PLAN easy entry and control over the SCS. Furthermore, airbases over the Woody Island enable the Chinese to attack easily the Vietnamese coast, Borneo or even the Philippines. Since 2012, the Chinese have been also engaged in artificial island building in the SCS; as well as have built newer air bases and missile launching sites.[21] The aim of these activities would be to present a de facto occupation of the SCS and also to prevent hostile forces from entering the region.

Strategic Implications of Chinese Actions for Involved Countries and Outside Powers

The Chinese actions of creating artificial islands, positioning air defence and cruise missiles as well as building air bases for advanced aircraft and its recent moves towards creating carrier groups have had the result of upsetting all security calculations in South East Asia and in the eastern Indian Ocean. A Chinese anti-carrier DF21D missile if fired from Hainan or Southern China would reach the Philippines, Indonesia or Malaysia. But if fired from the SCS islands, it could then easily cover the Andaman Islands, Bay of Bengal, India's eastern coast and the Australian north.[22,23] This would create difficulties for the US, India or Australia to project strength into Southeast Asia and definitely for the US to protect its treaty allies. This would result in the entire region falling under Chinese domination. This was why the Philippine President Benigno Aquino III in 2014, when requesting the US not to desert its Philippine ally, described the situation as a "*Munich Moment*" drawing parallels to the event described in the beginning of this article. In 1938, France did not want war and accepted Hitler's demand for Sudetenland leaving the Czechs defenseless. While the French thought that Hitler would be satisfied with the treaty at Munich, the effect was the opposite with World War II breaking out a year and half later.[24]

Implications for the Philippines, Vietnam and other ASEAN countries: The absolution of Chinese control over the SCS would not just mean loss of economic and trade independence for the ASEAN. A look at a map would show that Chinese hegemony over the SCS would endanger the coherence of the ASEAN itself. PLAN and PLAAF units would be interdicting the waterways between Vietnam, Borneo, the Philippines and Malaysia effectively inhibiting regional security.[25] If left unchallenged, one by one over a few years each of these then isolated States would have no choice but to accept Chinese military and trade dominance.

Implications for the US as well as its allies (Japan, Taiwan, Australia-New Zealand and South Korea): The loss of US influence in the SCS would be militarily not much of a loss to American security. But the loss to American influence, its alliance system and its trade with its East Asian allies would be immense.[26] Chinese control of the SCS would open the southern Taiwanese and Japanese flanks to infiltration by the Chinese. It would help the Chinese prevent formation of a coalition against them and prevent hostile states achieving a continuous front along its seaboard. Also loss of freedom in the SCS would mean higher trading costs as the merchant fleets of Japan and South Korea would have to sail around the Philippines and then the Sunda Straits to enter the Indian Ocean.[27] But, will America sit quietly as Britain and France did in 1938 while the strategic balance shifts? Washington's deployment of the USS Carl Vinson, with its full group of associated warships, was a clear signal that America would not sit by idly. The last time America showed such force in the South China Sea was in early 2016, when there were concerns of imminent Chinese reclamation activity on the Philippine claimed Scarborough Shoal. China's growing military prowess is putting pressure on America to develop a stronger naval presence in the region, with power projection capabilities at nearby bases, particularly at Subic and Oyster Bay in the Philippines.[28,29] Also America cannot be seen as giving up on its allies as such a move would cause a domino effect and undermine the US system of military alliances worldwide.[30]

Implications for India: Chinese control of the SCS would be another "*Tibet Moment*" for India with loss of strategic depth and the ability to outflank the Chinese if the situation arose. India would then be squarely boxed into South Asia and surrounded by Chinese client states. The PLAN would be sitting right at the doorstep of the Indian Ocean and with its larger numbers of submarines could seriously restrict the Indian navy's freedom of action. India would then be looking at Chinese military at its northeastern land border, south eastern sea border and after the CPEC at its northern and north western borders as well. India will have to develop military relations with Vietnam, Singapore, the Philippines and Taiwan as well as South Korea, Japan and Australia.[31] These major powers could create an arc to hem in Chinese influence in Southeast Asia. India can strengthen Vietnamese navy and air force as well as provide offensive missile technology. The main aim should be to make the Chinese not apprehensive about their security but at the same time drive home the point that any move towards affecting the security system in the region would extract high costs.

Conclusions

A look at a map of Southeast Asia and the South China Sea will show the centrality of control over the SCS for domination of the region. At present China controls the northern and north western part of this area; the US and its allies are to south/south east; India to the west and Vietnam in the north west. Chinese claims based on history cannot be accepted in the modern world as there were lots of overlapping empires. By the same logic Mongolia could claim more than 3/4 of China and Japan can claim nearly half of China. Chinese security concerns could be met by accepting Chinese control over the Paracels' which are much closer to Hainan; the area around the Spratlys' should be demilitarized and declared as an open trade zone. The claims of the ASEAN countries could be worked out on mutually agreeable templates. But, it would be essential to face up to Chinese claims at the present and not give in, as doing so would only encourage them to become more belligerent the next time. The US would have to stand by its allies in this tough situation; and while China has achieved a de facto control over parts of the Spratlys, the cost of maintaining their position could be increased for them. The other powers like India and Japan could help the ASEAN countries by building up their defence forces and providing weapons and operational training. It would be better for the Major Powers such as the US to motivate the Chinese to observe the UNCLOS and by following a "carrot-and-stick" policy (better economic deals or partnerships vis-à-vis economic conflict or cancellation of deals involving China or even building up surrounding powers such as India, Vietnam or Japan) China could be goaded into accepting international laws.

NOTES AND REFERENCES

1. Peter Beinart, China, the Philippines, and the Makings of a 'Munich' Moment The right way to use the most misunderstood analogy in U.S. foreign policy, https://

www.theatlantic.com/international/archive/2014/02/china-the-philippines-and-the-makings-of-a-munich-moment/283649/

2. Ibid
3. Leszek Buszynski, "The development of the South China Sea maritime dispute", Australian National University, http://geographymonkey.com/uploads/3/2/7/0/3270375/development_of_dispute.pdf
4. Sean Mirski. "The South China Sea Dispute: A Brief History". *Lawfare,* June 8, 2015.
5. Leszek Buszynski, no. 3.
6. Sean Mirski, no. 4.
7. Leszek Buszynski, no. 3.
8. Sean Mirski, no. 4.
9. Sean Mirski, no. 4.
10. Leszek Buszynski, no. 3.
11. Leszek Buszynski, no. 3.
12. Leszek Buszynski, no. 3.
13. William Johnson, "Everything you need to know about the South China Sea Conflict-in under five minutes", June 9, 2015. http://blogs.reuters.com/great-debate/2015/06/09.
14. Leszek Buszynski, no. 3.
15. Leszek Buszynski, no. 3.
16. Leszek Buszynski, no. 3. and Sean Mirski, no. 4.
17. William Johnson, no. 13.
18. Leszek Buszynski, no. 3, and Sean Mirski, no. 4.
19. Conn Hallinan, "How Trump Could Blunder into War with China", January 27, 2017. http://fpif.org/authors/connhallinan/.
20. Ibid
21. Sean Mirski, no. 4.
22. Conn Hallinan, no. 19.
23. Marian Fritz, "Showdown or Just Hot Air? The South Chinese Sea Conflict", December 2, 2015, http://www.europeanblog.de/tag/south-china-sea/
24. Peter Beinart, no. 1.
25. Marian Fritz, no. 23.
26. Richard Javad Heydarian, "Why Asia is Trembling over a U.S.-China South China Sea Showdown", The National Interest, April 14, 2017, http://nationalinterest.org/print/blog/the-buzz/why-asia-trembling-over-us-china-sea-showdown-19548.
27. Marian Fritz, no. 23.
28. Richard Javad Heydarian, no. 26.
29. Richard Javad Heydarian, "A Dangerous Showdown in the South China Sea", The National Interest, June 28, 2014, http://nationalinterest.org/feature/dangerous-showdown-theSouth-chinasea-10775?page=show
30. Ibid
31. Ibid

10

Australia and South China Sea Conundrum

Om Prakash Dahiya

ABSTRACT

Australia has significant interests in the South China Sea, both economically, in terms of freedom of trade and navigation, and geopolitically, as the United States is invested in upholding the rules-based order in the region. Australia has been conducting its own airborne surveillance operations in the South China Sea and Indian Ocean, called Operation Gateway, since 1980. These patrols are conducted by P-3 Orion maritime aircraft and some of them have been verbally challenged by China. While Australia has not conducted a surface Freedom of Navigation Operation (FONOP) an operation similar to those of the US Navy, it regularly conducts naval presence patrols, exercises and port calls throughout the region. As Washington's closest ally in the region, Australia may come under growing pressure from the United States to make its presence felt in the South China Sea beyond statements of diplomatic support for freedom of navigation.

The intentions behind China's activities in the South China Sea are the source of considerable debate in Australia, in the region, and around the world. However, despite heated discussion, it is difficult to say with certainty what China is aiming to achieve, or what the implications and unintended consequences might be. The rapidly changing strategic landscape in the South China Sea threatens to marginalise Australia unless it takes positive action to remain a relevant and influential player in the region's strategic calculus. Positive action includes taking a much more visible and unqualified stance against

Chinese territorial aggrandisement and invitations to regional powers to create a coordinated maritime domain security and surveillance regime.

The paper analyzes and focuses on the role of Australia in South China Sea as well as its impact on the Indo-Pacific strategic calculus.

Introduction

Australia has significant interests in the South China Sea, both economically, in terms of freedom of trade and navigation, and geopolitically, as the United States is invested in upholding the rules-based order in the region. Australia has been conducting its own airborne surveillance operations in the South China Sea and Indian Ocean, called Operation Gateway, since 1980. These patrols are conducted by P-3 Orion maritime aircraft and some of them have been verbally challenged by China.[1] While Australia has not conducted a surface Freedom of Navigation Operation (FONOP) an operation similar to those of the US Navy, it regularly conducts naval presence patrols, exercises and port calls throughout the region. As Washington's closest ally in the region, Australia may come under growing pressure from the United States to make its presence felt in the South China Sea beyond statements of diplomatic support for freedom of navigation.

The intentions behind China's activities in the South China Sea are the source of considerable debate in Australia, in the region, and around the world. However, despite heated discussion, it is difficult to say with certainty what China is aiming to achieve, or what the implications and unintended consequences might be. The rapidly changing strategic landscape in the South China Sea threatens to marginalise Australia unless it takes positive action to remain a relevant and influential player in the region's strategic calculus. Positive action includes taking a much more visible and unqualified stance against Chinese territorial aggrandisement and invitations to regional powers to create a coordinated maritime domain security and surveillance regime.

The South China Sea is one of the world's most important international waterways, carrying more than half the globe's merchant fleet tonnage. Its sea lines of communication carry most of the energy supplies for Japan, South Korea, and Taiwan, as well as a large proportion of China's trade. The South China Sea also serves as an important transit route and operational theatre for the militaries of the United States and many of its allies and regional friends.[2] Notably, it is the shortest and easiest route for military units, as well as commercial cargos moving between the Pacific and Indian Ocean regions. It is a strategic thoroughfare of global importance.

Image 1: South China Sea Maritime Traffic

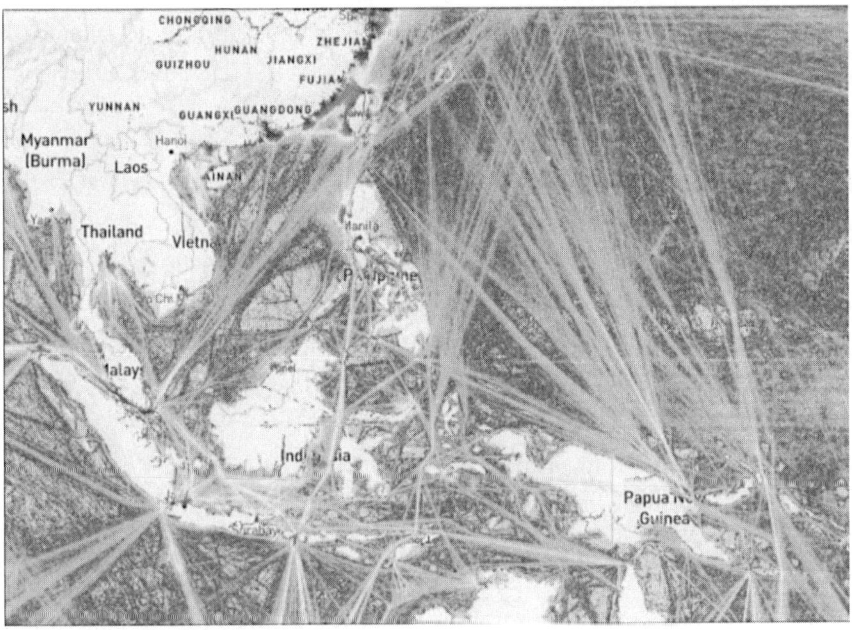

Source: http://www.marinetraffic.com/

The geology below the South China Sea floor is also reported to hold valuable reserves of oil and gas. Although estimates of the scale of these resources vary, they are thought to comprise at least 7 billion barrels of oil and 900 million cubic feet of natural gas.[3]

The South China Sea fishery is also of considerable importance. Although China's recent military and paramilitary activities and the intensity of commercial fishing have done serious damage to the local ecosystem, these waters remain an important source of protein for all of the littoral states. In the meantime, China's developing presence in the South China Sea reinforces Beijing's coercive power in the region.[4] Innocent passage, especially by commercial vessels, is being respected, at least in the short term. However, Beijing is making clear that the terms and conditions of foreign activity, even by other littoral states, will be determined and enforced by China. Relevant Chinese authorities have signaled that Beijing is considering the declaration of an Air Defence Identification Zone (ADIZ) over the entire South China Sea. Military facilities now nearing completion will permit Chinese forces to enforce any such declaration with fighter intercepts of non-complying aircraft.[5]

Although most international observers had few doubts that many of China's actions in the South China Sea were serious breaches of international law,[6] the ruling of the Permanent Court of Arbitration for UNCLOS made the extent of Beijing's transgressions clear in July 2016.

Australia-China Calculus

So far, the Australian leadership has been hesitant to address directly how to tackle and reverse Beijing's actions in the South China Sea. There has been no agreed assessment of the challenge posed by Beijing, no process for analysing alternative allied counter-strategies, and no clear program of measures selected for implementation. For Canberra, the South China Sea is far more important because of its intrinsic strategic value and because of its critical importance to their close partners in maritime ASEAN. For the littoral states of the South China Sea, the strategic balance and effective sovereignty of the region is critical for their future security and economic well-being. These differences in priority between Australia and their friends are placing strains on long-standing security relationships. The development of an effective response to China's creeping incrementalism in the South China Sea has been an intrinsically difficult challenge. Beijing has employed a very sophisticated strategy and operational concept that could be implemented without challenging the US alliance commitments to Australia or directly confronting the US or allied forces.[7]

The concerns of many Australian business people and policy makers have led them to avoid taking any measure that may disturb their business and broader economic relationships with China. These concerns have been most apparent in the Australia and other corporations that have invested heavily in developing close ties with Chinese enterprises. Chinese agencies have been active in fostering these worries, propagating false dilemmas, and exaggerating the potential consequences for regional economies of any actions taken to confront China's assertiveness.

China's economic leverage with the close Western allies is probably most pronounced in the case of Australia. However, the shape and trajectory of Australia's economic relationship with China is more complex than many analyses have portrayed. China is Australia's largest trading partner by a significant margin,[8] but, when it comes to sunk foreign investment, China is only number seven with a smaller stake in the country than either Singapore or the Netherlands. Moreover, the "quality" of Chinese investment in Australia is relatively low, directed mostly to resource extraction, infrastructure, and rural and urban property.[9]

Moreover, China's economic partnership with Australia may have peaked. The slowing of China's economy and the marked changes underway in China's economic structure are already reducing the market opportunities for many of Australia's traditional exports. Although the growth of China's middle class is generating new export opportunities in some sectors, most of these new product areas are the subject of intense international competition, and some are constrained by new layers of Chinese regulation.[10] The overall downward trend in Australia–China trade is clear from the latest statistics and will probably be maintained.[11] A key conclusion is that China will continue to be an important market for Australia, but its relative importance may decline during the coming decades.

For Australia, export opportunities are now growing more rapidly in other countries. The economic structures and development trajectories of these countries mean that they will probably be more important consumers of Australia's traditional exports in coming decades. Indeed, there is a possibility that India may be a more important market for Australia than China within twenty-five years.

Most Australians also understate the strategic value of Australia's exports to China. Australia is about to become the world's largest exporter of liquefied natural gas (LNG) and a key supplier of energy for electricity generation, especially for China's coastal provinces. Australia and Indonesia are the world's top two exporters of coal, which, again, is a critical import for China. Indonesian coal is primarily used for power generation and Australian for steel production. Australia is expected to control well over half of the world's production of lithium within five years, a resource that is critical for new-generation batteries and broader power storage applications. In addition, Australia has the world's largest proven uranium resources and is a trusted supplier of high-quality food and pharmaceutical products. Given the driving imperatives of the Chinese leadership, Beijing is likely to be cautious about seriously undermining its economic relationship with Australia, or its relationships with the other close Western allies, for that matter.

The bottom line is that pro-Chinese commentators in Australia and other countries continue to assert that cooperative relations with Beijing will be essential for their economic well-being.[12] The more nuanced reality is that, while Chinese attempts to coerce Australia through the manipulation of trade and investment regimes would have limited economic leverage, they have far greater psychological power in the absence of effective domestic counter measures.

A factor accounting for the Western allies' timidity over Chinese behaviour in the South China Sea is the success of Beijing's information operations in Western countries. These operations have been assisted by the Chinese acquisition of media enterprises in Western countries as well as the courting of key decision-makers, journalists, and academics, accomplished through fully paid visits to China; the contribution of very substantial funds to political parties; the establishment of pro-Beijing associations of many types, including Confucius Institutes in universities; the regular insertion of Chinese produced supplements in metropolitan newspapers; and the organization of periodic "patriotic" demonstrations, concerts, and other events by Chinese embassies, consulates, and other pro-Beijing entities. Cyber and intelligence operations have been used to reinforce key messages; recruit Chinese intelligence agents and "agents of influence"; and, periodically, to intimidate, coerce, and deter allied counter-actions.

These very active Chinese information, intelligence, and cyber operations have been reported extensively in the Australian media in recent months. For instance, Greg Sheridan, the Foreign Editor of *The Australian* wrote: "Early last year the Abbott government established a multi-agency effort to assess by exactly how much, and how effectively, the Chinese government in Beijing was gaining influence over Australian national policy.... The more they looked, the more they found. The government project disclosed the most sophisticated and sustained efforts in our history by the Chinese government and its agencies to penetrate and direct Australian elites in a way that favours Chinese state policy. From time to time, federal cabinet has been briefed on Chinese government moves to militarize the South China Sea and the like. It has also been briefed on Chinese government-sponsored net-works of influence and patronage within Australia. Chinese agents of influence have been identified... This is all made much more powerful, has a vast force multiplier effect, because it folds neatly into all the vast espionage, cyber intrusion, diplomatic, military, and other levers of power Beijing uses.... The ABC's Chris Uhlmann...disclosed the extent of funding from sources closely linked with the Chinese government of all major political parties in Australia. Between 2013 and 2015 this was more than $5.5 million."[13]

Peter Jennings, a leading strategic commentator, focused on other Chinese operations: "In February, President Xi Jinping visited the offices of China Central Television in Beijing, calling on it to "objectively, truly, and comprehensively introduce China's social and economic development to the world audience." A Party directive of this nature explains why, since late May, readers of Fairfax Media newspapers in Australia have been receiving lift-outs made up of editorial copy from the Communist Party newspaper, *The People's Daily*. Similar material is available in *The Washington Post*, Britain's *Daily Telegraph*, and France's *Le Figaro*. China also invests millions of dollars into hundreds of Confucius Institutes at universities around the world. There are ten such institutes in Australia with a remit to "forge strategic alliances with business, industry, government, and other institutions with an interest in closer and more productive ties with China."

In June 2014, Liu Yunshan, the head of the publicity department of the Communist Party Central Committee, described Confucius Institutes as a "spiritual high-speed rail link" between Chinese dreams and the rest of the world. More recently, Beijing has intensified attempts to align and influence its diaspora communities. In Australia, there is clearly Chinese pressure on community groups to lobby government to take a more quiescent policy line on Beijing's aggressive militarization of the South China Sea.[14]

Another contributing factor to the timid response is largely cultural. The experience of the last decade suggests that Western electorates are more fearful of triggering confrontation and the escalation of an argument than their Chinese counterparts. This thinking is reflected in a concentrated form in some Western bureaucracies by their deep risk aversion. If the Western interest is the avoidance of confrontation and the preservation of peace at any price, that price is likely to be extremely high. When confronted by an expansionist, non-democratic peer competitor, the repeated avoidance of confrontation results in the loss of important strategic positions and the evaporation of much international credibility.

Australia and the Allies

When Western leaders have focused on these issues in recent years, they have almost always emphasized three primary interests:

- First, the maintenance of free sea and air transit through the South China Sea;
- Second, an acknowledgement that the United States, Australia, and Japan have no territorial claims in the region and do not take a position on the territorial claims of other countries; and
- Third, the allies' strong interest in the claimants exercising restraint and peacefully resolving territorial disputes in the region in accordance with international law.

Australia's foundation statement on the South China Sea expressed very similar sentiments when it was released in May 2014. "Australia does not take a position on competing claims in the South China Sea, but has a legitimate interest in the maintenance of peace and stability, respect for international law, unimpeded trade, and freedom of navigation. Australia urges parties to exercise restraint, refrain from provocative actions that could escalate the situation, and take steps to ease tensions. We call on governments to clarify and pursue territorial claims and accompanying maritime rights in accordance with international law, including the Convention on the Law of the Sea (UNCLOS)."[15]

When the *Australian Defence White Paper* was released in February 2016, the strategic importance of maintaining the "rules-based global order" was mentioned no less than forty-eight times.[16] Then on the day after the release of the Permanent Court of Arbitration's decision, the Australian Prime Minister, Malcolm Turnbull, and the Foreign Minister, Julie Bishop, held a joint press conference in which Malcolm Turnbull said the following: "Now as Julie has said, and we have both said on many occasions, we have no position on the competing claims for sovereignty. We have no claims of our own. But we insist that it is absolutely vital that all countries abide by international law, settle disputes peacefully and in the context of this particular dispute, that has been the subject of the decision last night that both countries abide by the decision of the tribunal. It is an important test case for how the region can manage disputes peacefully. It is an opportunity for all parties in the region to come together and for claimants to re-engage in dialogue with each other based on greater clarity around maritime rights. So both of us have been urging claimants to refrain from coercive behaviour and any unilateral actions designed to change the status quo in the disputed areas. As I have said many times, every nation in our region has benefitted enormously from the many, many decades of relative peace and tranquillity in this region. It is vital that is maintained. There is so much at risk in the event of conflict, in the event of heightened tensions, so this is an important decision, it is one that has been made in accordance with international law and it should be respected by both parties and indeed by all parties and all claimants."[17]

The security, stability, and prosperity of the Western allies, their partners and friends are heavily dependent on maintenance of the rules-based global order. This order provides a clear framework that is fair, almost universally acknowledged, and highly predictable. It provides an environment within which individuals, corporations, and nations can plan, invest, and operate with confidence and minimal friction. It is an essential lubricant of the global economy and a pre-condition for sound international relations and global peace.

The Western allies have a particularly strong interest in seeing the United Nations Convention on the Law of the Sea maintained. This convention has been ratified by 169 countries and provides a clear and fair set of principles and processes for determining the maritime rights and responsibilities of member states. It also provides sound mechanisms for adjudicating maritime disputes. These provisions have been used to resolve many long-standing conflicts. Through these and associated means, UNCLOS is contributing significantly to international peace and security. For a major power signatory to the Convention to persist in operating with little regard to the Convention's rules and refuse to implement the lawful adjudication of maritime disputes is completely unacceptable.

The failure of the Western allies to act strongly to defend the rule of law in the South China Sea is effectively ceding key norms of international behaviour to the strong and powerful, rather than to the lawful. When a powerful authoritarian state is permitted to seize effective sovereignty over a substantial maritime region without being thwarted by strong counter-action, the constraints on further potentially more serious aggressive actions are greatly reduced. There is a serious risk that the Western allies will be seen in Beijing as paper tigers. Indeed, Australia has already been described in the Chinese press as a "paper cat".[18]

Other Southeast Asian countries are also moving to acknowledge Beijing's rising power, taking account of their strong economic ties with China and distancing themselves from what some consider to be American meddling in their internal affairs. This is the case with the authoritarian regimes in Cambodia and Laos as well as with the American treaty ally Thailand. The pro-Western government in Malaysia has also recently moved to purchase some military equipment from China for the first time.[19]

This fraying of pro-Western alliances and relationships highlights a risk that large parts of Southeast Asia may shift into China's strategic orbit. This would represent a fundamental change in the geo-strategic alignment in the Western Pacific and a serious deterioration in the strategic interests of Washington and other allied capitals.[20]

What Specific Types of Action Deserve Consideration?

There are eight primary categories of action that could play important roles in an allied strategy to counter China in the South China Sea.

1. **Diplomatic measures:** These are actions to assure, persuade or pressure opponents, neutrals, and partners to act in accordance with one's interests. Diplomatic measures may include the private or public communication of warnings, suggestions, proposals, and other messages. They include steps to broaden coalitions and the initiation of actions within international forums such as the G20 and the United Nations. They may be undertaken not only by members of foreign ministries, but also by government leaders, military personnel, and, indeed, by many members of allied societies.
2. **Geostrategic measures**: These are actions designed to change the geographic focus of a competition so as to gain relative advantage. Candidate geo-strategic measures to counter China could include steps to expand and strengthen the members of the alliance or, alternatively, to undermine an opponent's international supporters. They could also include steps to build strategic pressure on China in theatres far removed from the South China Sea in which Beijing is strategically vulnerable.
3. **Military measures:** These include discussions, information sharing, and equipment supply between relevant countries, as well as signalling intent via military movements and exercises, military staging, basing,

and other activities. Many potent military measures involve the introduction of new military capabilities, especially those that compel a competitor to respond and are difficult to counter. At the highest end of military measures are numerous types of combat operations that can be tailored to send a message, assure, warn, deter, defend, and inflict various types and levels of damage.

4. **Economic measures:** These employ financial, fiscal, or budgetary actions to protect economic interests or damage a competitor's economic interests. Economic actions include changes to rules governing international commerce, the processes of transferring technology or other intellectual property, the regulations governing the operations of foreign economic entities such as banks, and various kinds of economic and financial sanctions.
5. **Immigration measures:** These involve modifications to the laws, regulations, or rules by which foreign citizens enter a country, the permissible purposes for entry, the means and modes of legal entry, and the periods that foreign citizens are permitted to stay. Potential measures in this category could include limits on the numbers of particular categories of international visitors, reductions in permissible periods of stay, and constrained access to particular fields of study, etc.
6. **Information measures:** These are programs to communicate one's own interests and behaviours in a positive light while painting a competitor's actions and behaviours in a poor light. Target audiences may include one's own society, neutral communities, and categories of people within an opposing country. These programs can include sponsored academic research, all kinds of broadcast media, and carefully tailored programs to reach strategically important community groups.
7. **Counter-leadership measures:** These are programs specifically designed to cause problems for the competitor's leaders and their immediate supporters. They are frequently designed to foster dissent, undermine a leader's legitimacy, or impose other pressures on the competitor's key leaders.
8. **Legal measures:** These are steps that can be taken to hold competitors accountable for breaches of international law by seeking the adjudication of United Nations tribunals or other relevant authorities.

Various steps can be taken to draw the attention of the international community to legal transgressions and to pressure guilty parties to comply.

An effective campaign plan should combine a carefully chosen set of measures from the above categories into a "combined arms" operation. The intent should be to produce clearly defined effects in a phased manner over appropriate timescales. Some campaign elements will deliver desired effects immediately, but others may take time to develop into serious irritants that corrode the opposition's strategic position.[21]

Australia may be able to play a strong role in working with the maritime states of Southeast Asia to strengthen their security resilience. Canberra may also be well-placed to initiate some security enhancements in the Indian Ocean.

A successful allied counter-strategy would need to progress beyond the so-called "pivot" and "rebalancing" to a more thoroughgoing military engagement with the region that might be called the Regional Security Partnership Program.[22] The primary goals of such a program would be to demonstrate continuing allied military superiority in the theatre, deter further Chinese adventurism, and reinforce the confidence of regional allies and partners in the reliability of their Western partners so that they feel able to staunchly resist any attempted Chinese coercion.

There could be many elements of a successful Regional Security Partnership Program.

Amongst the most important should be the following:

- The creation of new mechanisms for close security consultation between the leaderships of the close allies (essentially the United States, Japan, and Australia) and their partners and friends in the Western Pacific. While there might be scope for periodic meetings of government leaders and defence ministers, the most effective mechanisms in this region may be bilateral and small-group forums that provide plenty of scope for regional leaders to float their own initiatives and guide their own local security development. The most effective approach is likely to be a security network that builds on existing frameworks (such as the Five Power Defence Arrangements linking Singapore, Malaysia, Australia, the United Kingdom, and New Zealand), rather than attempting to establish an Asian version of

NATO. There is, in consequence, a need for the United States and its close allies to permanently station and operate much stronger military forces in the Western Pacific.[23] The most likely places for hosting the increased American presence would be the U.S. Western Pacific territories, Australia, and Japan. However, there may be opportunities for American forces to also increase their footprints in Singapore, South Korea, and elsewhere. Australia could look to increase its long-running military operations in Malaysia and Singapore and possibly expand its cooperative defence activities with Indonesia, India, the Philippines, and elsewhere. Japan could also give some priority to assisting the Philippines, Vietnam, and potentially others.

Deploying additional military units to the Western Pacific would not only require welcoming local communities, suitable facilities, and advanced industrial support capabilities, but also large, sophisticated, and relatively unconstrained exercise and range areas. They would be essential both to maintain force readiness and tailor operational practices and tactics to suit local conditions. In this context, Australia could take the initiative to establish the Western Pacific Exercise and Range Complex. This would network and further develop Australia's already extensive exercise and range facilities, offering them for scheduled use by the close allies, and periodically other security partners, to strengthen national and multinational operational capabilities and foster interoperability.

- The United States, Japan, Australia, and South Korea could also offer regional partners opportunities to strengthen their indigenous defence industries by working more closely in numerous modes. There may be scope for joint design, development, and production programs; enhanced logistic cooperation; assistance with facilities development, etc. Closer cooperation in developing intelligence, surveillance, and cyber defences would also be desirable.

The rapidly changing strategic landscape in the South China Sea threatens to marginalise Australia unless the government takes positive action now to remain a relevant and influential player in the region's strategic calculus. Positive action includes taking a much more visible and unqualified stance against Chinese territorial aggrandisement and invitations to regional powers to create a coordinated maritime domain security and surveillance regime. Perhaps most importantly, Australia must direct the ADF to undertake concrete measures (including independent FONOPs) to demonstrate that despite political differences with the current and at least one potential future US administration, Australia can be relied upon to uphold the globally accepted set of norms embodied in the phrase 'rules based international order.'[24]

The passage by 'USS William P. Lawrence' on May 10, 2016, within 12 nautical miles of Fiery Cross Reef reinforced statements by the US government that it won't be deterred from sailing where international law allows. China's military overreaction similarly reinforced its determination to oppose any attempt to thwart its goal of exclusive regional domination. Quartz's Steve Mollman is just the latest commentator to predict that China's actions are part of a concerted plan to initiate a war with the US at a time and place of its choosing.[25]

As part of this plan, China has embarked upon a systematic campaign to intimidate other SCS nations into submission through a series of orchestrated confrontations with its maritime militias (disguised as fishing vessels),[26] backed up by a 'coast guard' whose vessels are far superior in range and weaponry to anything comparable among its near neighbours. By doing so, China seeks to neuter in advance any possible support for US provocations against China's continued pursuit of military domination of the South China Sea.[27]

President Xi's strategy aims to delegitimise US claims that it's acting on behalf of the international system. China refuses to acknowledge the utility and efficiency of multilateral negotiations and arbitration. Instead, it demands that each of its neighbours undertake bilateral negotiations.[28] In such a scenario, China's overwhelming economic penetration of nations like Vietnam, Cambodia, Indonesia, and Malaysia, acts as a surrogate for military threats (which are, in any event, thinly veiled).

Australia must counter that potentiality now. The threads are there; the only thing missing is the skilled weaver to craft a seamless cloak to bolster the security of the 'nearer region' and the Indo–Pacific in general. First, Australia must step up and offer to lead—or at least be a principal player—in the newly announced Indonesia–Malaysia–Philippines maritime security patrol program.[29] Although targeted solely at transnational crime (for now, anyway), with time and experience this could become the nucleus of a regional collective maritime security framework that could credibly deter or confront China's maritime militia and coast guard.

Second, Australia should market its next generation of Offshore Patrol Vessels (OPVs) to Indonesia, Malaysia, Vietnam, and the Philippines. If each of those nations commit to purchasing six to ten OPVs, that would more than double the number of ships to be built in Australian shipyards. Since defence jobs remain a critical component of the upcoming federal election, an early statement in support of such efforts would allay workforce and economists' fears of a jobless defence expansion.[30] That will require more finesse that the government has recently shown, but will be critical as doing so holds the potential for direct competition with Japan. The Abe government has actively sought to bolster the surface maritime security capabilities of both Vietnam and the Philippines. If Australia could broker US financial assistance to one or more potential purchasers, that would also contribute to enhancing Australia's reputation for proactive support of US policies vis-à-vis the South China Sea.

Alternatively, Australia could arrange for the transfer of the *Armidale class* OPVs to one or more regional partners once RAN's new OPVs enter service. Either eventuality helps build interoperability with important neighbours and enhances their own ability to fend off challenges by 'little green fishermen' from China—as well as reduce the threat of transnational crime.[31]

Finally, Australia must demonstrate a more robust commitment to the enforcement of globally accepted norms for interstate behaviour than has been the case up until now. The measures outlined in the opening paragraph above would be a good start. Restricting action to tepidly urging China to resolve its differences peaceably may reassure those who are more focused on economic than national security concerns, but does nothing to reassure neighbours and allies that Australia will match rhetoric with action should circumstances dictate.[32]

The time may soon arrive when Australia will no longer have the luxury of choosing how to respond. Better that the domestic and international groundwork is well laid now than to have to do so in the midst of an international crisis, when reasoned arguments often fall victim to fear and anger.

Conclusion

The South China Sea disputes have entered a dangerous new phase in the last several years. Alongside China's unprecedented construction and fortification of artificial features, incidents at sea involving clashes between various combinations of fishermen, coast guards and, occasionally, naval assets, are occurring on a routine basis. With the nationalist credentials of authoritarian and democratically elected claimant governments at stake, the potential for miscalculation and escalation (whether inadvertent or intended) is growing.

Australia's aspirations for a viable 'rules-based' strategic order in the Indo-Pacific are under significant pressure as regional powers contest the very nature and scope of these rules via the disputes. Key Australian interests and relationships are being tested. As Australia's largest trade partner since 2007, China's rise and pursuit of its 'legitimate interests' have been supported by successive Australian governments. A key question emerging from China's recent actions in the South China Sea is where do these 'legitimate interests' begin and end—do they include the establishment of 'spheres of influence', the revision of existing regional and global norms, and the right to resort to unilateral action to achieve these ends? From Beijing's perspective, these are all strategic behaviours that have been exhibited by previous great power aspirants, including the US.[33]

Whether coming to terms with China's rise should involve an element of genuine strategic 'accommodation', as opposed to simply 'engagement', is a question that Australian policymakers often appear reluctant to publicly canvass. In response to recent Chinese actions in the South China Sea, Australia's current strategy might be best described as one of 'dissuasion'—working with others to convince China of the costs of unilateral actions, while simultaneously using engagement to reinforce the benefits of the existing, US-led regional order. Even though the pay-offs thus far might appear slight, the alternatives are perhaps even less appealing.[34] Whether this calculus would hold in the face of even more forceful Chinese actions—such as Beijing proclaiming an Air Defence Identification Zone in the South China Sea—or provocative moves by other claimants, remains to be seen.

The longstanding alliance with the US is routinely invoked as the foundation of Australia's security. The South China Sea disputes have forced a sharper consideration of the benefits and risks of the alliance and the conditions under which these could manifest. This has been most prominent in debates surrounding whether Australia should replicate several recent 'Freedom of Navigation Operations' (FONOPs) undertaken by the US Navy through the contested waters; in particular, whether Canberra should authorise naval

FONOPs within the 12-nautical-mile limit of China's newly constructed artificial islands. China has recently intensified warnings of 'serious measures' should Australia seek to challenge Beijing's claims though naval operations.[35]

The FONOPs debate reflects a dilemma common to all alliances—the alternating anxiety between the fear of 'abandonment' by an ally in the event of a conflict, versus the fear of 'entrapment' in an ally's conflict that is contrary to one's own interests. Whilst some argue that Australia's interests demand FONOPs of the kind conducted by the US, others counter that such actions could draw the ire of China, with whom Australia also seeks to maintain a good relationship.[36] These anxieties persist. The result has been a form of 'strategic ambiguity' in which Australia has communicated its intention 'continue to traverse the water and the skies around the South China Sea in accordance with international laws' without saying whether it would breach the limit of any claimed Chinese boundaries. Again, whether this position could withstand a significant escalation of the conflict remains to be seen.[37]

Efforts by the Association of Southeast Asian Nations (ASEAN) to engage both China and the US in multilateral institution-building through venues such as the East Asia Summit are a key focus of Australia's diplomatic and strategic planning. However, the failure to produce a long-awaited 'code of conduct' for managing the disputes bodes poorly for multilateralism. Indeed, some contend that China has deliberately delayed the code in order to 'buy-off' non-claimants such as Cambodia and Laos through increased aid and investment while ramping up construction in disputed areas.

There is now a view that ASEAN is irrevocably split on the South China Sea disputes following several recent failures to agree on consensus language. In the face of these divisions, some ASEAN claimants have resorted to appeals to international arbitration (which China says it will not abide by), as well as more traditional power balancing strategies—upgrading alliances and military cooperation, and intensified acquisition of advanced maritime weaponry. Facing difficult choices in its relations with China and the US and the prospect of a divided ASEAN, Australia is likely to pursue complementary initiatives to advance its maritime security interests.[38] These could include intensified 'mini-lateral' cooperation with other non-claimant states such as India, Japan, Singapore and Indonesia, all of whom share misgivings about China's ambitions and actions. Indonesia will likely be a focus given Jakarta's increased concerns with recent Chinese incursions into its maritime domain.[39] Australia may also face continued calls to reconsider its approach to its maritime border issues with East Timor. In the meantime, the risk of conflict continues to rise.[40]

The first question is, for how long can Australia maintain its current, calibrated approach in the South China Sea? The answer to that depends to a large extent on the course of US– China relations in the year to come. Even if a decision in Canberra is to accept greater costs and risks in resisting China's advances in the South China Sea, a second question is: has Beijing's consolidation of control now reached an irreversible point?

NOTES AND REFERENCES

1. Shannon Tiezzi, "'Nearly All' Australian Patrols in South China Sea Are Challenged by China", *The Diplomat,* February 05, 2016. http://thediplomat.com/2016/02/nearly-all-australian-patrols-in-south-china-sea-are-challenged-by-china/
2. Colin Willett, Deputy Assistant Secretary of State for Multilateral Affairs, Bureau of East Asian and Pacific Affairs, U.S. Department of State, "South China Sea Maritime Disputes", http://docs.house.gov/meetings/AS/AS28/20160707/105160/HHRG-114-AS28-Wstate-WillettC-20160707.pdf
3. United States Geological Survey, "Assessment of Undiscovered Oil and Gas Resources of Southeast Asia, 2010", United States Department of the Interior, Fact Sheet 2010–3015, June 2010, available at https://pubs.usgs.gov/fs/2010/3015/pdf/FS10-3015.pdf
4. Ross Babbage, *Countering China's Adventurism in the South China Sea Strategy: Options for The Trump Administration,* A Joint Publication of the Center for Strategic and Budgetary Assessments and Strategic Forum, 2016
5. China's vice foreign minister Liu Zhenmin, reported in Neil Connor, "China Threatens to Impose Air Defence Zone on Disputed Area of South China Sea", *The Telegraph*, July 13, 2016, available at http://www.telegraph.co.uk/news/2016/07/13/china-declares-right-to-set-up-air-defence-zone-in-south-china-s/
6. Ross Babbage, "It Is High Time to Outmaneuver Beijing in the South China Sea", December 28, 2016, http://csbaonline.org/about/news/it-is-high-time-to-outmaneuver-beijing-in-the-south-china-sea
7. Andrew Greene, "US, Australia urged to get tough on Beijing over South China Sea", *ABC News online*, 17 Dec 2016, http://www.abc.net.au/news/2016-12-17/us-australia-urged-to-get-tough-over-south-china-sea/8128742
8. Anne Holmes, "Australia's economic relationships with China", Parliament of Australia Publishing, http://www.aph.gov.au/About_Parliament/Parliamentary_Departments/Parliamentary_Library/pubs/BriefingBook44p/China
9. Department of Foreign Affairs and Trade (DFAT), Australia, "Which Countries Invest in Australia?" updated October 2016, available at http://dfat.gov.au/trade/topics/investment/Pages/which-countries-invest-in-australia.aspx.
10. Ross Garnaut, "Australian Opportunities through the Chinese Structural Transformation", *Australian Economic Review,* Vol. 44, Issue 4, 30 Nov 2011.
11. DFAT, Australia, "Australia's Direction of Goods & Services Trade—Calendar Year (from 1987 to present)," updated October 2016, available at http://dfat.gov.au/trade/resources/trade-statistics/Pages/trade-time-series-data.aspx.

12. James Brown, "China-Australia relationship needs to broaden from trade", The Saturday Paper Edition No. 27, August 30 - September 5, 2014. https://www.thesaturdaypaper.com.au/opinion/topic/2014/08/30/china-australia-relationship-needs-broaden-trade/1409320800
13. Greg Sheridan, "Chinese Influence Runs Deep to Favour Official Beijing Policy", *The Australian*, September 10, 2016.
14. Peter Jennings, "Australia Needs to Limit Its Exposure to Corruptive Influences," *The Australian*, September 3, 2016.
15. DFAT, "Statement on Developments in the South China Sea", media release, May 14, 2014, available at http://dfat.gov.au/news/media-releases/Pages/statement-on-developments-in-the-south-china-sea.aspx.
16. Australian Government, Department of Defence, 2016 Defence White Paper (Canberra: Commonwealth of Australia, 2016), available at http://www.defence.gov.au/whitepaper/Docs/2016-Defence-White-Paper.pdf.
17. Prime Minister of Australia, "Press Conference with Foreign Minister", July 13, 2016, available at https://www.pm.gov.au/media/2016-07-13/press-conference-foreign-minister.
18. "'Paper cat' Australia will learn its lesson", *Global Times*, editorial, July 16, 2016, available at http://www.globaltimes.cn/content/997320.shtml.
19. Charles Clover, "China and Malaysia Sign Wide Ranging Naval Co-Operation Deal", *Financial Times*, November 1, 2016.
20. Ross Babbage, Game Plan: The Case for a New Australian Grand Strategy (Canberra: Connor Court for the Menzies Research Centre Ballarat, 2015), pp. 73–88.
21. Ross Babbage, *Countering China's Adventurism in the South China Sea Strategy: Options for The Trump Administration*, A Joint Publication of the Center for Strategic and Budgetary Assessments and Strategic Forum, 2016.
22. Ibid.
23. Michael McDevitt, "The South China Sea: Assessing U.S. Policy and Options for the Future", *A CNA Occasional Paper* (Arlington, VA: CNA Corporation, November 2014), iii.
24. Tom Hanson, "Australia in the South China Sea: time to act, not react", *The Strategist*, Australian Strategic Policy Institute, Canberra, 30 May 2016. https://www.aspistrategist.org.au/australia-south-china-sea-time-act-not-react/
25. Steve Mollman, "It is time to rename the South China Sea", *Quartz Online*, August 22, 2016. https://qz.com/763161/it-is-time-to-rename-the-south-china-sea/
26. Andrew S. Erickson & Conor M. Kennedy Tanmen Militia: China's 'Maritime Rights Protection' Vanguard, *The National Interest*, May 6, 2015. http://nationalinterest.org/feature/tanmen-militia-china%E2%80%99s-maritime-rights-protection-vanguard-12816
27. Linda Jakobson, China's Unpredictable Maritime Security Actors, Report, Lowy Institute for International Policy, December 2014.
28. "Xi Jinping: China to Further Friendly Relations with Neighbouring Countries," *Xinhua*, 26 October 2014, http://news.xinhuanet.com/english/china/2013-10/26/c_125601680.htm.
29. Ana Jacinta Olabre and Alexis Romero, "Philippines, Indonesia, Malaysia kick off joint patrols in Sulu Sea", *Philstar Global Online*, June 19, 2017. http://www.philstar.com/headlines/2017/06/19/1711573/philippines-indonesia-malaysia-kick-joint-patrols-sulu-sea
30. Nguyen Tien Thinh, "Australia in the South China Sea: time to act, not react", 30 May 2016, http://www.southchinaseastudies.org/en/component/content/article/151-newsflash/1599-australia-in-the-south-china-sea-time-to-act-not-react
31. Gareth Hutchens, "Australia should not join US in South China Sea operations, says retired

defence chief", *The Guardian*, Tuesday 21 February 2017. https://www.theguardian.com/world/2017/feb/21/australia-should-not-join-us-in-south-china-sea-operations-says-retired-defence-chief

32. Euan Graham, "National Interests and the Role of Major and Middle Powers in the South China Sea: Australia's Cautiously Calibrated Approach", National Asian Security Studies Program Issue Brief No. 4.4 December 2016.
33. Wang Jisi, "China's Search for a Grand Strategy," Foreign Affairs 90, no. 2 (March/April 2011).
34. Cameron Hill, Australia and the South China Sea: debates and dilemmas, Foreign Affairs, Defence and Security, Parliament of Australia, http://www.aph.gov.au/About_Parliament/Parliamentary_Departments/Parliamentary_Library/pubs/BriefingBook45p/SouthChinaSea
35. Patricia Lourdes Viray. "Australia reasserts stance vs South China Sea militarization", *Philstar Global*, March 16, 2017, http://www.philstar.com/headlines/2017/03/16/1681730/australia-reasserts-stance-vs-south-china-sea-militarization
36. Eliza Borrello, "Donald Trump, issues in South China Sea could cause problems for Australian fuel supply, experts say", *ABC News*, 3 March 2017, http://www.abc.net.au/news/2017-03-03/south-china-sea-donald-trump-australia-fuel/8321230
37. James Goldrick, "Why Australia must send its navy to assert the freedom to operate in the South China Sea", Lowy Institute for International Policy, 29 October 2015. https://www.lowyinstitute.org/the-interpreter/about-interpreter
38. Bob Carr, "Australia's pragmatic South China Sea policy best for our region", *The Australian*, March 18, 2017, http://www.theaustralian.com.au/news/inquirer/australias-pragmatic-south-china-sea-policy-best-for-our-region/news-story/f1991e69f3b4e1b35ca14c05ea99fd71
39. Koh Swee Lean Collin, "Challenging sovereignty at sea: What the South China Sea ruling means for Indonesia", *Asia and the Pacific Policy Society*, 26 July 2016, http://www.policyforum.net/challenging-sovereignty-sea/
40. Bonnie Glaser, "High stakes for Australia in limiting China's South China Sea incursions", *The Sydney Morning Herald*, 22 May 2015, http://www.smh.com.au/comment/high-stakes-for-australia-in-limiting-chinas-south-china-sea-incursions-20150521-gh6nwv.html

11

South China Sea Dispute: Implications for Maritime Security

Zheer Ahmed

ABSTRACT

Maritime security in the South China Sea (SCS) has emerged as one of the most imperative security concerns in the world politics and are increasing for several reasons: higher volumes of shipping traffic, protection of exclusive economic zone resources, piracy, terrorist threats, greater international scrutiny of ports and shipping, and the modernization of regional naval and coast guard forces. Maritime security in the SCS also becomes crucial as Coastal states and international user states have many overlapping interests in the SCS as coastal states are concerned for sea resources whereas international users concerns are for freedom of navigation. Moreover, both coastal states and international users have different views about the seriousness of the threats such as maritime terrorism, piracy and trafficking, etc. And both the actors (coastal as well as international users of the Sea) stand poles apart to draw one single line necessary to address maritime security in the Sea. Therefore, the dispute in SCS has been described as 'new central theatre of conflict' in the world politics. This article examines the convergent and divergent maritime security interests of coastal states (China, Vietnam, the Philippines, Indonesia, and Malaysia) and international user states (United States, Japan, Australia and India) in the South China Sea.

It finds that multiple stakeholders pursuing diverse interests have yet to close the gap between goals and means of achieving maritime security.

Introduction

South China Sea is located south of China, east of Vietnam and Cambodia, northwest of the Philippines, east of the Strait of Malacca and north of Bangka-Belitung islands and Borneo.[1] The SCS is a marginal sea that is part of the Pacific Ocean. It encompasses an area of 3,500,000 sq kms from the Karimata and Malacca Strait to the Strait of Taiwan. The SCS collectively is an archipelago comprising over 250 small islands in which the Spratly, the Paracels, the Pratas and Scarborough Shoal are the important ones. Though the sea is having large number of islands, it is mostly uninhabited. The navigational importance of the sea is that it covers one-third of the world's shipping sailing and it is also believed that it holds huge oil and gas reserves beneath its seabed. In addition, the SCS also forms a strategic waterway of global significance, providing the key maritime link between the Indian and Pacific Oceans. This makes the sea a subject of competing claims of sovereignty by several of its coastal countries.

There are two groups of stakeholders in the SCS: the claimant states include China, Vietnam, Malaysia, Taiwan, Philippines and Brunei and the non-claimant states are the United States, Japan, Australia and India. Political and military involvement of the claimant and non-claimant states to secure Territorial claims and international water ways respectively results into a dispute in the SCS. However, it is more a dispute over the SCS's territorial and maritime claims by the claimant states within the region. The dispute includes the islands, reefs, banks and other feature of SCS, including the Spratly islands and Paracel islands. The dispute gyrate from retaining or acquiring the rights to fishing areas, the exploitation of crude oil and natural gas in the seabed of various parts of the sea and extends to the strategic control of important shipping lanes.

Non-claimant states namely, the United States of America, Australia, Japan and India are concerned with issues over the navigational importance of the sea and, therefore are actively implicated for navigation of the sea in the SCS. To uphold free navigation in the SCS, non-claimant states conduct freedom of navigation operations to promote the SCS as international waters[2] as it is estimated that US$ 5 trillion worth of global trade passes through the SCS.[3]

Therefore, Maritime security concerns become momentous for the states whose foreign trade transportation is heavily dependent on SCS's navigation, such as the United States, Japan, Australia and India. For their own interests, maritime security in SCS has been defined differently by claimant and by non-claimant states. For claimant states militarizing the SCS is to define maritime security, whereas for non-claimants states it defines as freedom of navigation, absence of piracy and absence of maritime terrorism.

Maritime security in the SCS has emerged as one of the most imperative security concerns in world politics. In simple terms, maritime security is defined as an absence of any threat for the navigation in the sea lanes, absence from piracy threats and absence of maritime terrorism. However, claimant states define maritime security through militarization means and therefore yearning militarization to secure their maritime boundaries. In terms of piracy and maritime terrorism, Joint War Committee of the London marine insurance marked the SCS as "prone to hull war, strikes, terrorism and related perils with the areas such as Iraq, Lebanon and Somalia."[4] The committee indicates an absence of maritime security in the sea as it is highly prone to piracy and maritime terrorism, along with militarization.

Maritime security concerns in the SCS are increasing for several reasons: higher volumes of shipping traffic, protection of exclusive economic zone resources, piracy, terrorist threats, greater international scrutiny of ports and shipping, and the modernization of regional naval and coast guard forces. SCS coastal states link maritime security with state security and therefore give less attention to combat maritime terrorism and piracy and contemplate more on maintaining control over newly acquired ocean resources, protecting national security by militarizing the maritime boundary and protecting bureaucratic interests.[5] Moreover, there are other aspects as well to define maritime security in SCS; first is bilateral dispute between China and Vietnam over the sovereignty of Paracel Islands, which China has controlled completely since 1974.[6] Second is maritime rights of the coastal states especially claims to exclusive economic zones and continental shelves. And third is, freedom of navigation, including the security of sea lines of communication that pass through these waters and naval modernization by developing states in the region. Therefore, maritime security perhaps is the most essential aspect of SCS dispute for claimants as well as non-claimant states.

Maritime Security: Militarization of the South China Sea

A Case of China

There is no agreement among the claimant states in terms of a legitimate basis for a claim over the SCS. China along with Vietnam and Taiwan base its claim on historic rights of sovereignty.[7] To legitimize its claim, China, as a militarily advanced and superior to other coastal states, exercises its maritime naval power by demonstrating power projection capabilities.[8] Ken Booth argues that the roles of maritime forces fall into three categories viz. Military, Diplomatic and Policing.[9] Militarization of the SCS is a strong case in favour of Ken Booth's argument by the Chinese maritime forces. For it, SCS represented the threat of foreign encroachment on Chinese territory from small Southeast Asian states and moreover China's political and economic ties with the other claimants were also not as strong as those with other countries.[10] Therefore, militarization of the sea has been considered vitally important by China to attain its maritime security goals.

Militarization of the SCS by China began in the 1980s when it began to realize that future international conflict would be of limited nature with threat to Chinese periphery rather than the heartland. In 1985, Chinese People's Liberation Army's (hereafter PLA) Navy wing began to identify the need to shift from coastal defence to offshore defence. The adoption of this offshore defence strategy had important implications for the SCS as the Paracels and the Spratly Islands were now included in the area of operations. In 1992, Chinese president Jian Zemen made it clear that maritime rights in the SCS is a sovereign right of China and therefore the role would be modified to ensure national unification, safeguard territorial integrity, and protect maritime rights and interests.[11] With this plan the PLA established three ring combat strategy, e.g. inner ring within 150 nautical miles of the mainland, the navy would deploy a variety of small coastal defence vessels to protect this area. The centre ring between 150 and 300 nautical miles deploy larger vessels to engage and destroy an enemy fleet. Outer ring, beyond 300 nautical miles (from the Korean Strait in the north, Okinawa in the east and the Spratly Islands in the south), the navy would rely upon submarines and aircraft.[12] It has been argued that development more of advanced weaponry for Navy was to protect Chinese claims in SCS.[13]

Modernization program for developing more sophisticated land, air and naval forces was consciously adopted by the PLA in regard to defend its claims in the SCS. China's rapprochement with Russia in the 1990s has been seen in the context of Chinese needs of more advance technology to protect its interests in the SCS. Therefore, they bought 50 Su-27SK and 28 Su-27UBK fighter aircraft from Russia. It is also looking to purchase Russian A-50 *Mainstay* airborne early warning and control system (AWACS) aircraft. At the same time, however, China is also developing its own domestic military industry to develop an upgrade program for their JH-7 fighter bombers as well as J10 fighter jets. It is reliant on Russia for the manufacture and deeper maintenance of some key aircraft systems, such as the high performance jet engines used in the latest generation fighter aircraft. Nevertheless, China's naval forces are in the process of modernization, focusing on deploying vessels that have greater range, are more survivable, and carry more lethal weapons systems. For example, to reinforce its maritime security, the PLA have purchased four *Sovremenny* class guided-missile destroyers armed with SS-N-22 "Sunburn" anti-ship cruise missiles, the SA-N-7 "Gadfly" and SA-N-12 "Grizzly" surface-to-air missile system, a single *Luhai* class guided-missile destroyer armed with the C-802 ship-to-ship missile and they also integrated tactical data systems, an improved antisubmarine warfare suite that includes embarked helicopters, and diesel or gas turbine propulsion.

The Chinese are also building two new type of guided missile destroyer with fleet-air defence capabilities. Regarding submarine force, the PLA has developed two new classes of attack submarine Ming (type 035) and Song (Type 039). The PLA-N's five *Song* submarines are the most advanced domestically produced submarines in China and incorporate a streamlined hull and skewed propeller for better submerged performance. The PLA has also purchased four *Kilo* class attack submarines and has ordered an additional eight of the more advanced EKM636 for delivery in 2007. The Chinese are also producing a nuclear powered attack submarine which is expected to be capable of firing a land attack cruise missile. Therefore, considering Chinese advancement of its military capabilities in regards to protect its claims over the SCS put forward Chinese version of maritime security in the sea.[14]

However, Chinese power projection capabilities remain limited due to lack of amphibious ships, heavy cargo carrying aircraft and other logistical shortcomings. The PLA remains technologically underdeveloped and it suffers from a lack of integration in its command, control, and communication systems; targeting; air defence; and antisubmarine warfare capabilities.[15] China's cooperation with Russia is helpful to acquire effective and advance defence system. But these two countries have no capability to screen large areas of operations, especially while operating against land based airpower in the littoral waters of an adversary.[16] China also lacks quality over quantity in aircraft and submarines.[17] Further, China's lack of military capabilities for a 'Blue Water' Navy restricts pursuit of an expansionist maritime policy in the SCS.[18] Even today, the PLA lacks long range amphibious capability and has no effective logistical and infrastructure support to supply equipments to their forces. Moreover, the limited number of Sukhois in the Chinese inventory does not guarantee to control of the sky over the SCS. Therefore, Chinese efforts to control the SCS through military means have limited impact as it lacks advance military industry and PLA's dependence on foreign technology constraints its militarization efforts in the SCS.

The Case of Other Claimant States

Along with China, Taiwan and Vietnam base their claim over the SCS on historic right of sovereignty. The Philippines, Malaysia and Brunei assert their claim on the ground of proximity within their Exclusive Economic Zone. Indonesia claims its maritime rights from Natuna Island. Each claimant state of the SCS has a claim over Sea's resources. China's initiative of militarization to control the SCS and its claim of maritime rights in the name of maritime security gave other claimant states a reason to militarize the sea. In the name of maritime rights' protection these states heavily spend money to modernize their military which could be a means for maritime security of these states. Active participants in the game of militarization of the SCS are: Vietnam, Malaysia, Taiwan and the Philippines.

China's military power is restricted due to the distance its forces would have to travel to get to the Spratly Islands. Such restrictions, however, do not impinge other claimants' military options. In this context, although Vietnam does not possess a large naval force but the Paracel Islands which have been captured by China from it in 1974 were within its fighter jets (MiG-21 and Su-22) range.[19] While the majority of the Vietnamese fighters are no match for the Chinese Sukhois, the Vietnamese can deploy a far greater number of fighter and attack aircraft over a potential combat area.

Taiwan has a relatively modern naval force equipped with American, Israeli and domestically produced ships and weapon system. However, its power projection capabilities are severely limited due to its primary concern for defence against invasion from China. Because of these limited military capabilities, the force responsible for patrolling the SCS is not the Navy but rather the coastal police force, which is equipped with only lightly armed patrol vessels. Brunei, unlike Taiwan has extended its role in the SCS from coastal enforcement to protection of their offshore oil platforms and economic zones. Singapore though is not a claimant state in SCS dispute has developed a balance force equal to claimant states for the protection of its sea-lanes of communication.

Malaysia has focused its maritime capabilities on a limited number of surface warships, hence its air force comprises highly sophisticated aircraft such as, MIG-29 Air-to Air combat fighter and F/A-18s armed with Harpoon anti-ship missiles. Malaysia also has a maritime aerial surveillance capability to patrol a large portion of the SCS. Surveillance operations were also conducted by Royal Australian Air Force from the Butterworth air base on the Malaysian peninsula. Nevertheless, concerning Malaysian naval capabilities, these are restricted by a lack of funding for the Royal Malaysian Navy as well as the failure of the Malaysians to develop sufficient doctrinal approaches for an effective maritime capability.[20]

Indonesia has not been able to adequately modernize its maritime forces and its efforts to modernize its army have been cancelled due to Asian financial crisis. Even though, Indonesian military is weaker and it is not directly involved in the SCS dispute, there have been speculations that Chinese 'Historic Waters' dashed line overlaps with the Indonesian continental shelf boundary, which was delimited between Malaysia and Indonesia in 1969 and which contains large Natuna natural gas fields. However, Indonesian foreign minister Ali Alatas and Chinese foreign minister Qian Qichen washed-up the shadows and declared that China has recognized Indonesian sovereignty over the Natuna Island and Indonesia and China did not have overlapping claims.[21] Therefore, Indonesian role in maritime security discourse in the SCS dispute is comparatively secure as China acknowledged Indonesian claim over the Natuna Island.

The Philippines position in the SCS dispute is altogether different as in the SCS Arbitration Case, the tribunal ruled in favour of the Philippines. The tribunal ruled that China has no historical rights based on nine dash line map.[22] China responded to the tribunal decision by rejecting the ruling.

Rejection of the Tribunal's ruling by the most powerful claimant country in the SCS dispute is an act of provocation for the militarization of the sea by other claimant countries, especially the Philippines. Although, the Philippines does not possess any real capability to fight in the disputed area and largely relies on its Mutual Defense Treaty with the United States to protect its interests in the area. However, the treaty does not trust America to use force to defend the Philippines in any case.[23]

To counter China and protect its interest in the SCS on the one side and lessen its dependence on the United States on the other, the Philippines parliament passed a law that authorized the spending of US$ 2 billion to upgrade the armed forces. One law has also been passed for the development of Navy's fighting capabilities, including surface, amphibious, anti-air, and anti-submarine warfare capabilities. Another bill also passed in the Congress allotting US$ 6.3 billion to modernize its military. The Air Force was also allotted funds to purchase surveillance aircraft as well as multi-purpose fighter attack aircraft.[24]

Maritime Balance: External Actors in SCS Dispute

External actors in the SCS dispute such as USA, Japan, Australia and India play an important role to provide a maritime balance approach to secure maritime security for sea lines of communication and to counter maritime terrorism.

Role of USA and Japan

Both USA and Japan maintain strong interests in the military balance in the SCS. As for the United States, its policy related to the SCS dispute has been determined largely by two factors, maintaining freedom of navigation its global war on terror and since September 11, 2001. While the six aircraft carriers and 27 nuclear-powered submarines that form the core of the Pacific Fleet ensure that the US military capability is unsurpassed in the region, the United States has stated its neutrality with respect to the territorial dispute. In 1992, the US ambassador to the Philippines, Frank Wisner stated that the US would oppose the use of force and that it would not allow threats to the peace and stability of the area to go unchallenged.[25] Moreover, Joseph Nye, US assistant secretary of defence for international security (1995), also explained the three components of the US policy of 'active neutrality' in the SCS dispute: the US would remain neutral on the issue of territorial dispute, it would oppose the use of force in SCS and it would not allow any threats to peace and stability in the region to go unchecked.

The USA launched three maritime security initiatives to avoid militarization and achieve maritime balance in SCS. These are: Container Security Initiative (CSI), Proliferation Security Initiative (PSI) and Regional Maritime Security Initiative (RMSI). While the first two are global in scope, the third one directed specially at the SCS. CSI aims to counter the grave risks in the large number of shipping containers delivered to the US every year. The PSI aims to seize shipments of Weapons of mass destructions and missiles-related equipments and technologies by seas, land or air before they fall into the hands of terrorist's organizations or state sponsors. More than 75 countries around the world support the PSI. Despite considerable pressure on the US to fully participate in the PSI, key maritime players in SCS such as China, Indonesia and Malaysia have not joined it so far.[26] As key SCS maritime states rejected US initiative to secure maritime security the US goes with bilateral means in the SCS region with the maritime states. Therefore, from Singapore, the US Navy travelled to Malaysia, Brunei, Indonesia and the Philippines to conduct bilateral naval exercises.[27]

RMSI by the USA caused considerable consternation as it favoured troops presence in the SCS area. According to Admiral Fargo, then commander of the US-Pacific commands RMSI was meant for putting special operations forces on high speed vessels so that the US can use boats that might be incorporated with these vessels to conduct effective interdiction in these sea lines of communication where terrorists are known to move about the transit throughout the region.[28] China, Indonesia and Malaysia the key players in the militarization of the SCS, vehemently rejected the idea of US troops in the area, emphasizing their own capabilities in tackling the threat. However, it was made clear by the US that the primary focus of the plan would be intelligence sharing and not a US troop's presence.[29]

Though the Japanese self-defence forces are of a high standard with regard to their size and technological developments, Japan urged claimant states to seek multilateral approach for averting the militarization in the Sea. Significance of the SCS is very high as its sea lanes play vital role in Japan's foreign trade.[30] Almost all oil supplies from West Asia to Japan pass through the SCS or archipelagic sea lanes. In mercantile sphere, Japan stands fourth after the US,

China and the European Union to have trade with ASEAN countries.[31] Japan opposes militarization of the SCS though proposes to combat piracy and maritime terrorism threats. For this, Japan with the help of International Maritime Organization and International Maritime Bureau established the Asian Maritime Security Initiative in 2004. This security initiative provides regional technical assistance and information sharing among the member countries. The second initiative is Regional Cooperation Agreement on Anti-Piracy in Asia, which aims to prevent piracy and armed robbery against ships as well as strengthening cooperation among the member countries in the areas of information sharing, capacity building and operational matters.[32] Coastal states of the SCS rejected Japanese proposals to combat piracy and joint patrolling in the sea as they see it as a breach of their sovereignty and EEZ.

Role of Australia and India

Australia's seaborne trade is valued at more than A$180 billion annually. Almost all (99.5%) of its trade by weight and 73.5 per cent by value is seaborne.[33] Its top trading partners are the coastal states of the SCS, namely, China, Malaysia, Japan, South Korea, Singapore and Thailand. This economic factor makes freedom of navigation and sea lanes of communications in the SCS a high priority for Australia. In the defence context, Australia's 2000 Defense White Paper deals with the maritime security in the region. The paper says that Australia would be concerned against any threat to maritime security in the region whether from inside and from outside.[34]

Primary vehicle for Australia's multilateral security commitment in the region has been the Five Power Defense Arrangements (hereafter FPDA). Under FPDA, Australia, New Zealand and the United Kingdom provide defence to Malaysia and Singapore against external threat. In 2004 the focus of FPDA had shifted from conventional threat to non-conventional threats including terrorism and piracy. The first exercise which focused on maritime security took place in the SCS.

India's engagement with the Southeast Asia began in the 1990s with the inauguration of India's 'Look East Policy' in 1991. India has pursued its 'Look East' policy whose twin objectives were to promote bilateral ties with the individual states and partnership status with ASEAN. India established its presence in the SCS in the early days of its 'Look East' policy by conducting its first-ever joint naval exercises with Indonesia and Malaysia in 1991 and

Singapore in 1993. In 2001, India held separate bilateral exercises in the SCS with the navies of Vietnam and South Korea. Indian Navy now conducts exercises regularly with Singapore. India's defence ties with the coastal states of the SCS are also being strengthened.

India's current maritime doctrine states that 'the Indian maritime vision for the first quarter of 21st century must look at the arc of Persian Gulf to the SCS as a legitimate area of interest.[35] India's involvement in the SCS dispute is purely dictated by national interests as India has never been a part of the dispute in the SCS area. It has no territorial claims as well. Unlike Japan, USA and Australia, India does not have any strategic ambitions in the region except India's current involvement in the SCS to secure freedom of maritime navigation in the international waterways. Therefore, the SCS could be a region where India could balance China as a rising threat to India. However, as the major trade partner of China and ASEAN, India has an economic incentive to keep SCS lane of communications open for international shipping. Now, India is also embarking on second phase of its 'Look East' policy, which has been renamed as 'Act East' policy now, so as to expand its scope to include Australia, China, Japan and South Korea. India's new 'Act East' policy would be more emphasizing on security cooperation, including joint operations to protect sea lanes and pooling the resources against the common threats.

Conclusion

The number of regional maritime security problems in the SCS is increasing. There are trans-boundary 'regional and global' maritime problems, such as congested navigation, illegal or excessive fishing, piracy and terrorist threats which cannot be dealt with effectively by any one nation-state alone and therefore require a collective action. Maritime security in the SCS has been seen through the lens of cost and benefit method in which cost outweigh the benefits. Therefore, there is little progress in the sphere of maritime security in the SCS. Along with excessive cost and less benefit in the SCS, there have been other reasons also which define the limitations of maritime security in the SCS. First, international users themselves have divergent priorities and activities in SCS. For example, the US policy in the SCS has been driven primarily by its global war on terrorism and therefore it proposed maritime counter terror measures such as CSI, PSI and RMSI. Japan is mainly interested in anti-piracy measures whereas Australia's efforts are more in soft cooperation category. India's involvement in the SCS is limited and considered passive in maritime security discourse. Second, limited progress has taken place because many coastal states give high priority to protecting national sovereignty and control over their newly acquired ocean resources rather than collective anti-piracy and counter-terrorism efforts. Third, mutual suspicions about the military and intelligence gathering activities among the coastal states are becoming more intensive, intrusive, controversial and dangerous.[36] Finally, another reason is the lack of reciprocity and transparency associated with the CSI and PSI. The CSI for instance is directed exclusively towards safeguarding US-bound Cargo. It does not address Asia bound trade or intra-Asian trade. The PSI limits the right of commercial vessels operating internationally to remain free from arbitrary search and seizure. Thus claimant and non-claimant states are pursuing different interests in the diverse ways to achieve maritime security in the SCS, which resulted in the absence of maritime security in the SCS.

NOTES AND REFERENCES

1. "Limits of Oceans and Sea" (3rd edition), International Hydrographic Organization, 1953, Retrieved 7 February 2010: 30.
2. Schwarz and Sciutto (2016), "US Protests after Chinese Military Jet Lands on the South China Sea", *CNN Politics,* April 19, 2016.
3. Fensom, Anthony (2016), "$5 Trillion Meltdown: What if China Shuts Down the South China Sea?", *The National Interes*t, 16 July 2016.
4. International Chamber of Shipping (2005), "Hull War Risk Listed Areas", ICS, 17 August 2005: London, International Chamber of Shipping.
5. Chung Christopher and Rosenberg, David (2008), "Maritime Security in South China Sea: Coordinating Coastal and User State Priorities", *Ocean Development and International Law*, 39(1): 60.
6. M. Taylor Fravel (2008), *Strong Borders, Secure Nation: Cooperation and Conflict in China's Territorial Disputes,* Princeton, NJ: Princeton University Press, pp. 272–287.
7. Craig A. Snyder (1997), "Building Multilateral Cooperative Security", *Asian Perspective,* 21(1) Spring-Summer:5-6.
8. Dick Sherwood (1999), "Implications for Naval Roles", in Doug MacKinnon and Dick Sherwood, eds., *Policing Australia's Offshore Zones Problems and Prospects,* Wollongong Paper on Maritime Policy No. 9, Wollongong, NSW: Centre for Maritime Policy, University of Wollongong: 129.
9. Booth, Ken (1977), *Navies and Foreign Policy*, London: Croom Helm, 1977, 15–25.
10. John W. Garver (1992), "China's Push Through the South China Sea: The Interaction of Bureaucratic and National Interests", *The China Quarterly* (December 1992): 1021-22.
11. Dick Sherwood (2000), "Oceans Governance and its Impact on Maritime Strategy", in David Wilson and Dick Sherwood, eds., *Oceans Governance and Maritime Strategy*, St. Leonard's, NSW: Allen and Unwin: 28.
12. Jiang Zemen quoted in Wen-Chung Liao, *China's Blue Waters Strategy*: 13-14.

13. Mike Yeong (1992), "China's New Assertiveness", *Business Times* (Singapore), 27 August 1992.
14. SIPRI Yearbook 2002: 420–21.
15. Brown Harold (2003), *Chinese Military Power*, Mourice R. Greenberg Centre for Geoeconomic Studies, Council for Foreign Relation: 28.
16. Ibid: 47.
17. Gary Klintworth (1996), *Asia Pacific Security: Less Uncertainty, New Opportunities*, Melbourne: Addison Wesley Longman: 221.
18. Michael G. Gallager (1994), "China's Illusory Threat to the South China Sea", *International Security*, 19(1): 193.
19. IISS, Military Balance: 174-75.
20. Mak N. Joon (2001), "Maritime War in the 21st Century? War? What War?", in David Wilson Eds. *Maritime War in the 21st Century*, No. 8, National Library Australia: 58.
21. "Indonesia Satisfied by China's Natuna Explanation", *Reuters World Service*, 21 July 1995.
22. PCA press release: "the South China Sea Arbitration" (Republic of the Philippines v. The People's Republic of China, 12 July 2016.
23. "US Refuses to Include Spratlys in Defence Treaty with Manila", *Agence France Presse*, 10 December 1996.
24. "Ramos Signs Military Modernization Law," *Agence France Presse*, 23 February 1995.
25. IISS, *Military Balance, 2003–4*: 26.
26. Australian Government, Department of Foreign Affairs and Trade (2006), Proliferation Security Initiative, [online: Web], accessed on 28 March 2017, URL://http.www.dfat.gov.au/globalissue/psi/indes.htmal.
27. Eric G. John (2005), "the United States and Southeast Asia: Developments, Trends and Policy Choices", statement before the House International Relations Committee Relations, Subcommittee on Asia and the Pacific, Washington D.C., 21 September 2005 [Online: Web]. Accessed on 30 March 2017, URL;//www.state.hov/p/eap/rls/rm/2005/53683.htm
28. "Crack US Troops May be Used to Flush Out Terrorists in Key Southeast Asian Waterways", *Channel New Asia*, 5 April 2004
29. John D. Anusiewicz (2004), "Officials Clarify Maritime Initiative and Amid Controversy", *American Forces Press Services*, 4 June 2004.
30. Japan Ministry of Foreign Affairs (1997), Press Conference by the Press Secretary [online: web] Accessed on 23 March 2017 URL://httpwww.mofa.go.jp/announce/press/1997/5/530.html#3.
31. ASEAN-Japan Centre, Statistics, [Online: Web]. Accessed on 3 April 2017, URL: www.asean.or.jp.
32. Regional Cooperation on Anti-Piracy in Asia [Online: Web], Accessed on 3 April 29, 2017, URL: www.recaap.org.
33. Government of Australia, Department of Transport and Regional Services, Office of Transport Security (2004), *Maritime Risk Context Statement*, Canberra: Department of Transport and Regional Services: 4.
34. Commonwealth of Australia, Department of Defense (2000), *Defense 2000: Our Future Defense Force*, Canberra: Department of Defense: 31.
35. Integrated Headquarters, Ministry of Defense (Navy), *Indian Maritime Doctrine*, INBR , New Delhi: Integrated Headquarters, Ministry of Defense: 56.
36. Mark J. Valencia (2005), "Introduction: Military and Intelligence Gathering Activities in the Exclusive Economics Zones: Consensus and Disagreements II", *Marine Policy*, 29(2005): 97-99.

BIBLIOGRAPHY

ASEAN-JAPAN Centre, Statistics, [Online: Web], Accessed on 3 April 2017, URL: www.asean.or.jp.

Australian Government, Department of Foreign Affairs and Trade (2006), Proliferation Security Initiative, [online: Web], accessed on 28 March 2017, URL://http.www.dfat.gov.au/globalissue/psi/indes.htmal.

Booth, Ken (1977), *Navies and Foreign Policy*, London: Croom Helm, 1977: 15-25.

Brown Harold (2003), Chinese Military Power, Mourice R. Greenberg Centre for Geoeconomic Studies, Council for Foreign Relation: 28.

Chung Christopher and Rosenberg, David (2008), "Maritime Security in South China Sea: Coordinating Coastal and User State Priorities", *Ocean Development and International Law*, 39(1): 60.

Commonwealth of Australia, Department of Defense (2000), *Defense 2000: Our Future Defense Force*, Canberra: Department of Defense: 31.

"Cracks US Troops May be Used to Flush Out Terrorists in Key Southeast Asian Waterways", *Channel New Asia*, 5 April 2004

Craig A. Snyder (1997), "Building Multilateral Cooperative Security", *Asian Perspective,* 21(1), Spring-Summer: 5-6.

Dick Sherwood (1999), "Implications for Naval Roles", in Doug MacKinnon and Dick Sherwood, eds., *Policing Australia's Offshore Zones Problems and Prospects,* Wollongong Paper on Maritime Policy No. 9, Wollongong, NSW: Centre for Maritime Policy, University of Wollongong: 1 2 9 .

____ (2000) "Oceans Governance and its Impact on Maritime Strategy", in David Wilson and Dick Sherwood, eds., *Oceans Governance and Maritime Strategy*, St. Leonard's, NSW: Allen and Unwin: 28.

Eric G. John (2005), "the United States and Southeast Asia: Developments, Trends and Policy Choices", statement before the House International Relations Committee Relations, Subcommittee on Asia and the Pacific, Washington D.C., 21 September 2005, [Online: Web] Accessed on 30 March 2017, URL: //www.state.hov/p/eap/rls/rm/2005/53683.htm

Fensom, Anthony (2016), $5 Trillion Meltdown: What if China Shuts Down the South China Sea?, *The National Interest*, 16 July 2016.

Gary Klintworth (1996), *Asia Pacific Security: Less Uncertainty, New Opportunities*, Melbourne: Addison Wesley Longman: 221.

Government of Australia, Department of Transport and Regional Services, Office of Transport Security (2004), *Maritime Risk Context Statement*, Canberra: Department of Transport and Regional Services: 4.

"Indonesia Satisfied by China's Natuna Explanation", *Reuters World Service*, 21 July 1995.

IISS (2003-04), Military Balance: 174-75.

Integrated Headquarters, Ministry of Defense (Navy), Indian Maritime Doctrine, INBR, New Delhi: Integrated Headquarters, Ministry of Defense: 56

International Chamber of Shipping (2005), Hull War Risk Listed Areas, ICS, 17 August 2005: London, International Chamber of Shipping.

Japan Ministry of Foreign Affairs (1997), Press Conference by the Press Secretary, [online: web] Accessed on 23 March 2017 URL://httpwww.mofa.go.jp/announce/press/1997/5/530.html#3.

Jiang Zemen quoted in Wen-Chung Liao, *China's Blue Waters Strategy*: 13-14.

John D. Anusiewicz (2004), "Officials Clarify Maritime Initiative and Amid Controversy", *American Forces Press Services*, 4 June 2004.

John W. Garver (1992), "China's Push Through the South China Sea: The Interaction of Bureaucratic and National Interests," *The China Quarterly* (December 1992): 1021-22.

"Limits of Oceans and Sea" (3rd edition), International Hydrographic Organization, 1953, Retrieved 7 February 2010: 30.

M. Taylor Fravel (2008), *Strong Borders, Secure Nation: Cooperation and Conflict in China's Territorial Disputes*, Princeton, NJ: Princeton University Press: 272-287.

Mak N. Joon (2001), "Maritime War in the 21st Century? War? What War?," in David Wilson Eds. *Maritime War in the 21st Century*, No. 8, National Library Australia: 58.

Mark J. Valencia (2005), "Introduction: Military and Intelligence Gathering Activities in the Exclusive Economics Zones: Consensus and Disagreements II", *Marine Policy*, 29 (2005): 97-99.

Michael G. Gallager (1994), "China's Illusory Threat to the South China Sea", *International Security*, 19(1): 193.

Mike Yeong (1992), "China's New Assertiveness", *Business Times* (Singapore), 27 August 1992.

PCA press release: the South China Sea Arbitration (Republic of Philippines v. The People's Republic of China, 12 July 2016

"Ramos Signs Military Modernization Law", *Agence France Presse*, 23 February 1995.

Regional Cooperation on Anti-Piracy in Asia, [Online: Web], Accessed on 3 April 29, 2017, URL: www.recaap.org.

Schwarz and Sciutto (2016), US Protests after Chinese Military Jet Lands on the South China Sea, *CNN Politics*, April 19, 2016.

SIPRI Yearbook 2002.

US Refuses to Include Spratlys in Defence Treaty with Manila," *Agence France Presse*, 10 December 1996.

12

Freedom of the Seas, International Law and the South China Sea Dispute

Amritha V. Shenoy

ABSTRACT

Freedom of the seas is a heated debate in international law since the advent of Europeans in Asia. Asians supported the freedom since ancient times as is evident from history that India, China, South East Asian countries and others conducted free trade with each other. For facilitating this trade, they did not impose restrictions on their power over sea. The freedom was exploited by the Europeans on their advent in Asia. Later, they tried to restrict the freedom by monopolising trade with their rival European traders. For instance, the Portuguese tried restricting the Dutch and the Dutch tried restricting the British, so on and so forth. A heated debate of the times is observed in the writings of Grotius and Freitas. After decolonisation, the Asian scholars reminded the freedom of the seas as existed in ancient times. Despite delimitation of the seas, high seas was declared as the common heritage of mankind in the UNCLOS. The South China Sea dispute is between small States and a great power China. Other States like the USA, India, etc., are asserting the freedom of the seas in the South China Sea region beyond the maritime territories of the States. The Philippines approached the Permanent Court of Arbitration for achieving its demands. International law fora today are important means for small States to achieve their rights provided under international law. The Court said that under UNCLOS China has delimitation of seas but at the same time it should not go beyond its rights to grab other States' rights. The paper will discuss the historical aspect of freedom of the seas, its inculcation in UNCLOS and its reassertion by the PCA in South China Sea Dispute. It will also highlight the importance of international dispute settlement fora for redressal of grievances of small States when the great powers are fledging their power on them.

Freedom of the Seas in Asia

Seafaring is a known feature of ancient Asia. India and China were famous in the ancient world for seafaring and international trade. Indus Valley civilisation has left traces of seafaring and shipbuilding. In the Vedic epoch in India, references are seen in the Vedas on ships and sea faring. It cannot be concluded that seafaring was a regular feature of the Vedic period, but, we cannot deny its existence also. The accounts of Periplus of Erithrean Sea, Strabo and Megasthanes[1] prove the existence of seafaring and ship-building in ancient India. The ancient Indian political entities were land powers[2] and did not exercise power over the seas. Therefore, they supported the freedom of the seas.

A deviation from this aspect is seen in Kautilya's *Arthasastra* wherein he suggests control of State over the sea. In the statecraft suggested by Kautilya in *Arthasastra*, a Superintendent of Ships was appointed to take care of navigation in the external and internal waters.[3] In this context, C.J. Chacko[4] concludes that strict delimitation of seas is not seen in ancient India:

> It is difficult to assert, however, whether the term 'sea' as used in those distant times implied the clear divisions which modern international law makes between *the territorial*, or *marginal sea*, and *high or open sea*.

The Indian rulers broke the monopoly of sea trade, whenever the freedom of the seas was threatened. When Sumatra monopolised the sea route to China, Rajendra I of the Chola Empire broke the monopoly and established freedom of the seas.[5] Another evidence to existence of freedom of the seas is the prohibition of piracy. Kautilya directed to destroy the pirate ships.[6]

China concentrated on territory and its protection.[7] It did not aim at empowering the naval defence because sea was left as vast and needed no conquest. China had to pay the price as it underwent six times invasion.

Mare Liberum vs. Mare Clausum

In the modern law of the seas, the freedom of the seas was imbued after a much heated debate by the international lawyers of Europe. The debate is on *mare liberum* versus *mare clausum*. It means whether the seas should be open or closed. This debate opened after the discovery of the new world for the Europeans. It began due to the clash amongst the European powers to gain economic and political power especially in the East Indies. For the Portuguese, only Christians had the right to own property. Therefore, they introduced the cartazes system and imposed *mare clausum* in the Indian Ocean.[8] Due to the monopoly exercised by the Portuguese in the Indian Ocean, the Dutch could not trade freely in India. Therefore, Hugo Grotius, the advocate of the Dutch East India Company suggested *mare liberum*. He took the cue from freedom of the seas practised in Asia since ancient times:[9]

> ... whatever may be said about some other rules of international law, freedom of the seas, which has been the pith and substance of the modern law of the sea, is one principle which Europe acquired from Asia through Grotius, but only after a long struggle and for a different purpose.

Grotius borrowed supportive arguments from Francisco de Vitoria who propagated that non-Europeans cannot be converted to Christianity forcefully.[10] Grotius argued that the political entities of India should be recognised and therefore, India was not *terra nullius* as argued by the Portuguese.[11] Moreover, the Portuguese cannot claim title by conversion because St. Thomas converted many people into Christianity long before the Portuguese advent.[12]

Later, the Dutch established monopoly of sea trade in many parts of India. The gaining superiority of English naval power and its increasing interest in trade in East Indies was sensed as a threat by the Dutch. Therefore, the Dutch despatched a delegation to England. Grotius was a part of the delegation. He put forward an argument that there was no freedom of the seas and *mare clausum* was to be followed. The English quoted *Mare Liberum* and justified their freedom of the seas and freedom to trade. Later, the English gained untrammelled power over the seas and colonised vast territories. John Selden claimed *Mare Clausum* to claim right over English sea.

At the end of the eighteenth century, the industrial revolution gained impetus in Europe. Freedom of the seas was an imperative for importing raw materials to Europe and export manufactured goods to colonies. Therefore, freedom of the seas was accepted as a necessity and integral part of law of the seas in the colonial India. The significance of *mare liberum* was realised by Europe and Grotius was declared as the father of international law.[13]

Delimitation of the Seas

Under the United Nations Convention on Law of the Sea (hereafter UNCLOS), sea is divided into territorial sea, contiguous zone, exclusive economic zone and high seas. The delimitation of sea was finalised in UNCLOS, 1982, after debate over the limit of territorial sea (ranging from three nautical miles to twelve nautical miles). Finally, the territorial sea was marked as twelve mile limit.

China applied the delimitation of seas for the first time in a treaty concluded in 1864 with Prussia. The treaties formulated after this one, mentioned "inner ocean" or territorial waters.[14] Some of the third world States including China supported the inclusion of Exclusive Economic Zone in UNCLOS because they believed that coastal States should have sovereignty over the adjacent seas.[15] Moreover, the delimitation of EEZ would restrict the interference from developed countries which could easily explore and exploit the natural resources in the EEZ.[16] Because of the compromise in the UNCLOS negotiations, EEZ was included in the delimitation of the seas. In the *Libya/Malta Continental Shelf* Case[17] the International Court of Justice held that the practice of the States prove that EEZ has become a part of customary international law.

UNCLOS demarcates Exclusive Economic Zone as a separate part of the seas. EEZ is not a part of high seas.[18] The coastal State exercises some rights in the EEZ like the right to exploit natural and marine resources under Article 56 of the UNCLOS.[19] Some States like the US demarcate "security zones" which are not under the purview of UNCLOS.

UNCLOS and Freedom of the Seas

The first attempt of codification of law of the sea was at the Conference on the Progressive Codification of International Law at the Hague in 1930. China supported a three-mile limit. Due to disagreement by parties, a conclusion could not be reached as to the limitation of territorial sea. In 1958, the First United Nations Conference on the Law of the Sea was conducted in Geneva. Again a decision on delimitation could not be reached. Since the process of decolonisation was incomplete, many nations were under the colonial rule. Therefore, China felt that the 1958 Convention was a reflection of the interests of the colonial powers.[20] The freedom of the seas was viewed by China as a tactic of the developed States to wield power over the sea and exploit the natural resources. China opposed the freedom of innocent passage because it implied freedom to the military vessels.[21] China opined that it was denial of the right to exercise sovereignty over its territorial waters. In the UNCLOS III negotiations, China felt the need for more power over territorial waters due to the long coastline possessed by China.[22] In the *travaux preparatories* also, China made it clear that prior notice for innocent passage of military vessels is required.[23] Since China could not achieve its aim in the UNCLOS, it continued oceanographic surveillance and surveys in the Exclusive Economic Zone against the provisions in the UNCLOS. Some more instances of violations of UNCLOS exist. During the cold war era, USSR ships conducted surveillance in various EEZs.[24] China has been conducting surveillance in Japanese waters.[25]

Despite the opposition and hindrances, freedom of the seas is upheld in UNCLOS. It is enunciated in Articles 36, 38, 58, 78 and 87 of the UNCLOS.[26] The rationale behind the freedom of the seas provided under UNCLOS is to prevent "international shipping being forced to take long and potentially dangerous detours".[27] Restrictions on freedom of the seas by one State may give persuasive power to other States to follow course. At the end, there will be disputes with regard to enclosing many areas which may lead to innumerable disputes.[28]

Freedom of the Seas and the South China Sea Dispute

China and Vietnam claim historic titles over the Paracel Islands and Spratly Islands in the South China Sea. China's claim to the islands is due to discovery of the islands way back in the 3rd century B.C. during the Tang Dynasty. Vietnam's claim over the islands is also through a historic title. China's claim is territorial rather than over the sea.[29] In the arbitration proceedings before an arbitral tribunal constituted under the UNCLOS, the Philippines challenged the claim of China on historic title as against the provisions of UNCLOS.

The dispute between the Philippines and China raises the question of "maritime claims" which can give rise to third party entitlements.[30] In this case, the question of freedom of the seas of other States which want to exercise their right of "innocent passage" in the maritime region claimed by China arises. One such example is the United States Freedom of Navigation Operations carried now and then.

The US uses the term "international waters" instead of EEZ. It used the term for the first time in 1995 in the Commander's Handbook on the Law of Naval Operations. It considers all waters seawards as "international waters". The US carried its Freedom of Navigation Operations in the South China Sea. The US "guided missile destroyer", USS Lassen passed through the Subi Reef in the South China Sea which is less than 12 nautical miles from the Spratly Islands claimed by China.[31] Some US naval ships passed through the South China Sea claiming the right of innocent passage. China claims the area to be its territorial sea. China demanded that the warships should give notice before entering its territorial sea. China's stand is that innocent passage of vessels is allowed under UNCLOS but, it does not mean military vessels have the right.[32] The purpose of the US is to show that it opposes the Chinese claims on the South China Sea and further, to assert the freedom of navigation.[33] The US is not a party to UNCLOS. However, the US recognises Part XI of the UNCLOS dealing with common heritage of mankind. It claims the right to surveillance in the Exclusive Economic Zones of other States. Taking a realistic stance, the emerging power of China in the world is perceived as a threat by the US in economic and political front. To show its prowess, US carries the freedom of navigation operations in the South China Sea. China does not want to forego the presence in the South China Sea region due to its strategic location and richness of natural resources. China opposes the US freedom of Navigation Operations. It is to be noted that freedom of the seas is an integral part of UNCLOS but the freedom is not untrammelled to the extent that a permanent installation is erected in the maritime zones by third party.[34]

Article 58 of the UNCLOS does not prohibit military operations in the EEZ. If China has problems with the military exercises of the US then it should enter into bilateral treaty rather than oppose UNCLOS which is not consistent with China's arguments.[35] The interventionist policies of the US and its hegemony are condemned by most of the nations today. It has different set of standards in international relations. The US has rules which do not allow interference or military might to be shown in its adjacent airspace and international waters. The US claims "security interest beyond its territorial sea and its airspaces".[36]

The final award in the South China Sea dispute was issued by the Arbitral Tribunal on 12 July 2016. The Arbitral Tribunal was constituted under Annex VII of the UNCLOS. China refused to participate in the proceedings because it believed that the differences were political and the tribunal had no jurisdiction in the matter.[37] The issues in the arbitration dealt with "the status of certain maritime features in the South China Sea, the maritime entitlements such features are capable of generating, and the lawfulness of certain actions by the People's Republic of China in the South China Sea that were alleged by the Philippines to violate the Convention".[38] One of the primary questions dealt with was whether the maritime features are rocks or islands. The declaration of these features as islands would extend the territorial sea and EEZ limits of the sea under the jurisdiction of China (nevertheless, the Tribunal decided against China). The main contention raised by the Philippines was that China's claims in the South China Sea are volatile of UNCLOS, 1982. China and other States may try to limit the effect of the award but some parts of the award will be automatically applied.[39] Moreover, the award is non-appealable and binding on the parties to the disputes (whether they participate or not).[40] Since there is alleged interference in the EEZ by China, the Philippines has claims but the interference has impact on third party claims and the freedom of the seas itself.[41] The third party claims like the military exercise in the EEZ is provided under UNCLOS but China has violated the rights of the Philippines by using the living resources in EEZ of the Philippines. The third party claims to freedom of the seas is to the extent of freedom of navigation but not to erect permanent installations. To uphold the freedom, some obligations are to be followed, be it on the part of China or the US. The freedom of the seas is upheld after long struggle and heated debates. It is an international obligation of each State to uphold the freedom.

Conclusion

Freedom of the seas was followed in Asia since ancient times. The vastness of sea and concentration over acquiring power over land upheld the freedom for long. The freedom of the seas also led to freedom of trade. The advent of Europeans in Asia, was the beginning of a heated debate on *mare liberum* and *mare clausum*. Hugo Grotius was influenced by Asia and he wrote a treatise on *Mare Liberum*. The treatise earned him the position of father of international law. Earlier, freedom of the seas was a result of belief that sea was vast and a common heritage. Later, freedom of the seas became the necessity of the times for the Europeans to earn maximum profit in their international trade. The freedom of the seas became a basic doctrine of the negotiations of UNCLOS.

The developing countries stood for the freedom and finally, it was included in UNCLOS. Asia is emerging as a major centre of power in the post-Cold War period. The multipolarity of the world is demanding new power play in international law. Therefore, China and India are asserting power over the territorial sea and control over innocent passage. Such exercise of power by these States is a result of power politics and seems inevitable for them. In the times, when there is a turn to history, there is a need to remind the world, the history of international law and the emphasis of developing countries on certain freedoms which are put at stake by them today.

NOTES AND REFERENCES

1. Chakravarti, Ranabir (2001), "Introduction", Chakravarti, Ranabir (ed.), *Trade in Early India*, New Delhi: Oxford University Press, p. 65.
2. *Quarterly*, 440–454, p. 451.
3. *Kautilya's Arthasastra*, Translated by R. Shamasastry (1915), Mysore: Mysore Publishers in Chapter XXVIII: Book II.
4. Chacko, C. J. (1962), "International Law in India: Ancient India (Part III)", *Indian Journal of International Law*, Vol. 2, No.1, 48–63, p.50.
5. Rothermund, Dietmar (1988), *An Economic History of India: From Pre-Colonial times to 1986*, London: Croom Helm, p.10.
6. *Arthasastra* in Chapter XXVIII: Book II.
7. Gao, Zhiguo (2009), "China and the Law of the Sea" in Nordquist, Myron H. et al. (Eds.), *Freedom of Seas, Passage Rights and the 1982 Law of the Sea Convention*, Leiden: Martinus Nijhoff Publishers, 265–96, p. 267.
8. Mathew, K.S. (2014), "Portuguese Trade with India and the Theory of Royal Monopoly in the Sixteenth Century" in Chandra, Satish (ed.), *Essays in Medieval Indian Economic History*, Delhi: Primus Books, p. 272.
9. Anand 1981.
10. Alexandrowicz, C.H. (1954), "Is India a Federation?", *The International and Comparative Law Quarterly*, Vol. 3, No.3, 393–403, p. 359.
11. *Ibid*, p. 361.
12. *Ibid*
13. Anand, R.P. (1986), *Confrontation or Cooperation? International Law and the Developing Countries*, New Delhi: Banyan Publications, p. 63.
14. Gao, p. 268.
15. Paul (2016), p. 3.
16. Shaw, Malcolm N. (2003), *International* Law, Cambridge: Cambridge University Press, Fifth Edition, p. 492.
17. ICJ Reports (1985), p. 13.
18. Haiwen, Zhang (2010), "Is it Safeguarding the Freedom of Navigation or Maritime Hegemony of the United States?—Comments on Raul (Pete) Pedrozo's Article on Military Activities in the EEZ", *Chinese Journal of International Law*, Vol. 9, 31–47, p. 33.
19. Article 56 of the UNCLOS states that the coastal States have following rights:
    a) Sovereign rights for the purpose of exploring and exploiting, conserving and managing the natural resources, whether living or non-living, of the waters superjacent to the

seabed and of the seabed and its subsoil and with regard to other activities for the economic exploitation and exploration of the zone, such as the production of energy from the water, currents and winds;

b) Jurisdiction with regard to (i) the architecture and use of artificial islands, installations and structures; (ii) marine scientific research; (iii) the protection and preservation of the marine environment.

20. Gao, p. 270.
21. *Ibid.*, 271.
22. *Ibid.*, 272.
23. *Ibid.*, 11.
24. *Ibid.*, 15.
25. *Ibid.*, 16.
26. Article 36 states as follows:

This part does not apply to a strait used for international navigation if there exists through the strait a route through the high seas or through an exclusive economic zone of similar convenience with respect to navigational and hydrographical characteristics; in such routes, the other relevant Parts of this Convention, including the provisions regarding the freedoms of navigation and overflight, apply.

Article 38 provides that:

a) In straits referred to in article 37, all ships and aircraft enjoy the right of transit passage, which shall not be impeded; except that, if the strait is formed by an island of a State bordering the strait and its mainland, transit passage shall not apply if there exists seaward of the island a route through the high seas or through an exclusive economic zone of similar convenience with respect to navigational and hydrographical characteristics.

b) Transit passage means the exercise in accordance with this Part of the freedom of navigation and overflight solely for the purpose of continuous and expeditious transit of the strait between one part of the high seas or an exclusive economic zone. However, the requirement of continuous and expeditious transit does not preclude passage through the strait for the purpose of entering, leaving or returning from a State bordering the strait, subject to the conditions of entry of that State.

c) Any activity which is not an exercise of the right of transit passage through a strait remains subject to the other applicable provisions of this Convention.

Article 58 deal with "rights and duties of other States in the exclusive economic zone":

a) In the exclusive economic zone, all States, whether coastal or land-locked, enjoy, subject to the relevant provisions of this Convention, the freedoms referred to in article 87 of navigation and overflight and of the laying of submarine cables and pipelines, and other internationally lawful uses of the sea related to these freedoms, such as those associated with the operation of ships, aircraft and submarine cables and pipeline, and compatible with the other provisions of this Convention.

b) Articles 88 to 115 and other pertinent rules of international law apply to the exclusive economic zone in so far as they are not incompatible with this Part.

c) In exercising their rights and performing their duties under this Convention in the exclusive economic zone, States shall have due regard to the rights and duties of the coastal State and shall comply with the laws and regulations adopted by the coastal State in accordance with the provisions of this Convention and other rules of international law in so far as they are not incompatible with this Part.

Article 78 elucidates the "legal status of the superjacent waters and air space and the rights and freedoms of other States":

a) The rights of the coastal State over the continental shelf do not affect the legal status of the superjacent waters or of the air space above those waters.

b) The exercise of the rights of the coastal State over the continental shelf must not infringe or result in any unjustifiable interference with navigation and other rights and freedoms of other States as provided for in this Convention.

Article 87 provides that "The high seas shall be reserved for peaceful purposes."

27. Paul, Michael, 2016, "The United States, China and the Freedom of the Seas", *SWP Comments*, Vol. 15, 1–4, p. 3.
28. Paul at p. 3.
29. Fry, James D. and Loja, Melissa H., 2014, "The Roots of Historic Title: Non-Western Per-Colonial Normative Systems and Legal Resolution of Territorial Disputes", *Leiden Journal of International Law*, 727–54, p.750.
30. Pemmaraju, Sreenivasa Rao (2016), "The South China Sea Arbitration (The Philippines v. China): Assessment of the Award on Jurisdiction and Admissibility, *Chinese Journal of International Law*, 265–307, p. 270.
31. Paul at p. 1.
32. Ku, Julian, Fravel, Taylor M. and Cook, Malcolm (2016), "Freedom of Navigation Operations in the South China Sea Aren't Enough", URL: http://foreignpolicy.com/2016/05/16/freedom-of-navigation-operations-in-the-south-china-sea-arent-enough-unclos-fonop-philippines-tribunal/.
33. Ibid
34. Pemmaraju, p. 299.
35. Pedrozo, p. 27.
36. Haiwen, p. 33.
37. Ted L. McDorman (2016), "The South China Sea Arbitration", URL: https://www.asil.org/insights/volume/20/issue/17/south-china-sea-arbitration, 20(17)
38. Talmon, Stefan (2017), "The South China Sea Arbitration and the Finality of 'Final' Awards", *Journal of International Dispute Settlement*, 1–14, p. 1.
39. *Ibid.*, p.13.
40. Ted L McDorman with reference to Annex VII, Article 11 of UNCLOS.
41. *The South China Sea Arbitral Award of 12 July 2016*, pp. 285–286.

13

The Effectiveness of International Institutions in Restraining China's Behaviour in the South China Sea Conflict: A Critical Analysis

Pranav Kumar

ABSTRACT

As argued by liberal-institutionalists and social constructivists, treaties, International laws, regimes and International Organizations (IOs) have been instrumental in shaping and restraining the behaviour of states. Social constructivists consider the institutions as social power that influences formulation of state preferences and choices. China, most of the times, seems to defy the aforementioned theorization. Be a member of any institutional arrangement or not, China's behaviour has rarely been influenced by the so called social power that gets manifested through the institutions. The Chinese defiance to the international institutions becomes much more prominent when it comes to confrontation with the Chinese perceived 'national interest'. China's behaviour and assertiveness in the ongoing South China Sea (SCS) conflict is an interesting case to understand it. Be the seizure of a US navy unmanned underwater vehicle by China or rejecting the principle of arbitration-one of the major institutions accepted in peaceful resolution of interstate conflicts since The Hague conferences (1899, 1907) as a means of conflict resolutions in the said conflict, or flaunting the UNCLOS; the international institutions seem to have failed in restraining Chinese behaviour in the South China Sea. By taking the South China Sea conflict as a case, the paper, first identifies the institutions that can be/are considered as social power in shaping China's behaviour. Further, it analyses the effectiveness and capability of the international institutions in restraining China's behaviour. The paper will also endeavour to critically analyse the assumptions made by the social constructivists in this context. Finally, an attempt would be made to understand as to why the international institutions have been not very successful in restraining the Chinese behaviour.

Introduction

International Institutions (IIs) remain to be point of discussion in the most of the IR theory history. However, meaning and scope of IIs have changed over a period of time. Unlike as understood until 1960s, when International Intuitions' (IIs) were considered as formal international organizations, IIs are now being considered as the sources of rules that govern elements of world politics and the organisations which help implement those rules. During the post-Cold War period, emphasis has been given to recognize the importance of international institutions for maintaining world order (Keohane 1998: 82), peace-making and peace-building. Liberal Institutionalists are pioneers in showing great optimism towards the role of IIs in dampening the impact of power politics and 'relative gain'. The most significant work in this respect is Keohane's *After Hegemony*, in which while accepting the centrality of neorealism's individualism, he highlights pivotal role of International institutions in building cooperation among nation-states (Keohane 1998: 82). Most of the time the Global Organizations like the UN, which was considered as a custodian of global peace, could not be successful in achieving their designated goal. However, it was recognized by policymakers and academicians that for systemic coordination on any global issue, 'systematic policy coordination' is required, and institutions are essential for such coordination (Keohane 1998: 83).

Theories of international politics during the Cold War were

overwhelmingly materialistic, reflecting a view of the world in which states pursued "national interests" shaped by geopolitical and economic realities. In the 1980s, research on international regimes moved from attempts to describe the phenomena of interdependence and international regimes to closer analysis of the conditions under which countries cooperate. Their arguments revolve around the pertinent question as to how does cooperation occur among sovereign states and how do international institutions affect it (Keohane 2004: 29). The neoliberals believe that the ambit of international institutions has broadened because of complex interdependence and the intended efforts by 'rational' states to manage it. Often deriving from international conventions or treaties, regimes are agreements between states to promote common interests in a defined sphere of influence (Bateman 2009: 1). The regimes can be defined as structures of rules and norms that could be more or less informal (Keohane 1998: 83).

In a broader sense the institutions, as Keohane believe, can be described as the phenomena of interdependence and international regimes that create conditions under which countries cooperate (Keohane 1998: 83) by influencing the process and creating the capability for states to cooperate in mutually beneficial ways by dampening uncertainty, and reducing the costs of making and enforcing agreements, i.e. transaction cost. Keohane reiterates that IIs rarely engage in centralized enforcement of agreements, but they do reinforce practices of reciprocity, which provide incentives for governments to keep their own commitments to ensure that others do so as well. Even powerful states have an interest, most of the time, in following the rules of well-established international institutions, since general conformity to rules makes the behaviour of other states more predictable to engender collaborative actions (Keohane 1998: 83). However, he emphasizes that IIs/regimes should not impose themselves on states; rather they should respond to the demand by states for cooperation. And hence, according to him the International regimes are generally self-enforcing through mutual monitoring and predictable behavior. Bateman argues that international regimes do not erode states' sovereignty; rather they can be considered as a restriction to states' behaviour. Although there can be dispute procedures and sanctions to guarantee the implementation of the rules and in some cases the regimes can get more legitimacy by evolving as formal international organizations can also be established to ensure the respect of international regimes (Bateman 2009:1), the fundamental function of a regime remains to be of either facilitating cooperation among states or restrict states' behaviour in one way or other.

Like regime theorists from the neo-liberal school of thought, the English School also highlights the role of IIs. But unlike the regime theorists, their focus remains to be on historical perspective not on contemporary. The regime theory is concerned with 'particular human constructed arrangements, formally or informally organized' (Keohane 1988: 383). Whereas the English School is concerned primarily with 'historically constructed normative structures' (Alderson and Hurrel 2000: 2007 as cited in Buzan 2014: 31). Onuf (2002) argues that the IIs 'evolve' over the period of time, unlike as the liberal who term them 'designed' (Buzan 2014: 31). According to the English School, the IIs and nation-states of 'international society' are mutually constitutive. Unlike as argued by the regime theorists that the difference is complemented and reinforced by the method called rational choice based on 'self-interest' (Kratochwil and Ruggie 1986; Wæver 1998: 89–92 as cited in Buzan 2014: 31), for the English School the same is entrusted upon more on history, normative political theory and international legal theory (Hurrell 2001 as cited in Buzan 2014: 31) guided by common interest and shared value among the actors and the mechanism of international order (Evans and Wilson 1992: 337–9; Buzan 1993; Hurrell 1993; Dunne 1995: 140–3; as cited in Buzan 2014: 31). As far as the issues, around which the IIs are formed, are concerned, unlike as elaborated by the Regime theory that the institutionalization takes place around economic and technological issues, the English School concentrates mainly on the politico-military sectors and the issue of human rights (Buzan 2014: 31). This distinction is highly important to understand the effectiveness of IIs in the SCS.

Similarly, Social Constructivists consider the IIs as 'Social Power'. According to them, State's behaviour is defined by identity and interest, which in turn is defined by international forces. The international force refers to the norms that are embedded in international society. The international organizations transmit the norms to states, which shape national policies by 'teaching' states what their interests should be (Jackson 2006: 169). Hence, in a nutshell, it can be concluded that the role of IIs in shaping and restraining state's behaviour has been highly appreciated by various branches of international theory.

The South China Sea Conflict

The South China Sea has been considered as one of the major sources of conflict and discontent in East and South-East Asia. Conflict resolution and peace-building in the region has been a herculean task that the parties to the conflict and international community have been confronting with. The shadow of conflict has been looming large over the relationship between the parties (Bateman 2009: 1). If geo-economic centre of gravity is shifting from the West to the East, the South China Sea—situated between the East and South-East Asia—can be termed as the centre of gravity making the shift possible, as the region has vital sea lines of communication (SLOCs) between these two parts of Asia (Bateman 2009: 1). The SCS is a conduit for about $5 trillion annual international trade, including vital energy flows.

As far as the SCS conflict is concerned, six major claimants—the Philippines, Malaysia, Vietnam, Brunei, People's Republic of China (China), Republic of China (Taiwan)—stake overlapping and conflicting territorial and maritime claims (Schofield 2009: 11; Fels 2016: 25). The claims are centred on two island archipelagoes, namely, Paracel Islands in the northwest and the Spratly Islands in the south (Schofield 2009: 8) and are aimed at the scramble for region's natural resources such as fishery stocks, natural gas and oil reserves (Fels 2016: 25; Djalal 2009: 175). According to the United States Energy Information Administration (EIA) estimates, the proved and probable reserves in the SCS are about 11 billion barrels of oil resources and about 190 trillion cubic feet of natural gas reserves (Ohnesorge 2016: 25). All the claimants, barring Brunei, have military presence in the region. There are multiple claims, from bilateral, to trilateral, to multilateral (Djalal 2009: 175).

Table 1: Claimants and Central Area of Dispute in the South China Sea

Country	*Area*		
	South China Sea	*Spratly Islands*	*Parcel Islands*
Brunei	UNCLOS	No formal claim	None
People's Republic of China	All	All	All
Malaysia	UNCLOS	Three islands	None
The Philippines	Significant Proportions	Eight islands	None
Republic of China (Taiwan)	All	All	All
Vietnam	All	All	All

Source: Ohnesorge (2016: 29) on the basis of U.S. Energy Information Administration (2013).

Paracel islands, which were snatched away from Vietnam by China by using force in 1974, remain a bone of contention between Vietnam and China. Both of them stake their claims over the archipelago with the help of some historical facts in their favour. However, the main source of territorial dispute in the China Sea remains to be the Spratly Islands. Out of the islands, rocks, and reefs that form the archipelago; Vietnam controls 22, China controls 14, the Philippines controls 11, Malaysia controls 10, and Taiwan controls 1. Even though, Brunei does not occupy any feature, it claims certain portions of the nearby sea as its EEZ or continental shelf (Djalal 2009: 176).

How Effective IIs Are?

The long road towards peace and cooperation in the South China Sea started way back in the late 1980s. But, the major theme of the paper is to understand which international institution-international law, regime, international organization take effect in this context? And to understand that how much these IIs, if any, are effective in restraining China's aggression in the region.

Legal Regimes & UNCLOS

Maritime Sovereignty and Rights

The United Nations Convention on Law of Seas UNCLOS I (1958), UNCLOS II (1960), UNCLOS III (1982) are the most significant institutional arrangements that can be applied to the SCS conflict. The latest UNCLOS, which was signed in 1982 after a prolonged negotiation and entered into force in 1994, has been termed as 'Constitution for the Oceans', as it provides the most comprehensive agreement in the sphere of international law. (Ohnesorge 2016: 33). The UNCLOS aims at establishing a maritime regime that endeavours to facilitate maritime cooperation, setting procedures for the resolution of territorial disputes and introducing new concepts, rights and responsibilities (Bateman 2009: 1). With ratification by Azerbaijan on 16 June 2016, there are 168 states parties to the UNCLOS including all the claimant states of the SCS with an exception of Taiwan (UN 2017). Legal fixation of maritime zones to coastal states, states' right over the maritime zone, delimitation of the maritime zone, defining certain features and related provisions are the characteristic features of the UNCLOS (Ohnesorge 2016: 33). The delimitation of a maritime zone is done on the basis of a line called baseline, which is considered as starting point for determining the maritime zone. The UNCLOS identifies following maritime zones: (1) internal waters (Art 8), the (2) territorial sea (Arts 3-4), the (3) contiguous zone (Art 33), the (4) exclusive economic zone (Arts 55-58), the (5) continental shelf (Part VI; Art 76-79), the (6) high seas (Part VII), and the (7) Area (seabed and ocean floor and subsoil thereof; Part XI). Apart from the identified zones, the offshore features such as islands, rocks, and reefs are the important features in the SCS conflict (Beckman as cited in Ohnesorge 2016: 34; UN 2017).

As mentioned earlier, since all the state parties to the SCS conflicts barring Taiwan ratified the UNCLOS and in 2002 the parties reaffirmed their commitment to the Convention in their joint Declaration on the Code of the Conduct of Parties in the SCS (Ohnesorge 2016: 33), the UNCLOS constitutes a common institutional foundation which may construct cooperative arrangements in the region (Beckman 2009: 226). Beckman identifies following two Articles that can provide a legal basis for cooperation among the claimant states:

1. Firstly, Article 74 that delimits the EEZ.
2. Secondly, Article 123 that places a general obligation on states bordering a "semi-enclosed sea" (Beckman 2009: 226). On the basis of the parameters prescribed by the UNCLOS the SCS falls under the category of the 'semi-enclosed sea'.

Dispute Settlement

Under Part XV of the UNCLOS there are provisions on disputes over maritime boundaries. Under Article 74 (1) of UNCLOS, the states are obliged to 'achieve an equitable solution'. The UNCLOS further, under 74 (2), elaborates that if bilaterally or multilaterally no agreement is reached, the Part XV can be referred to (Ohnesorge 2016: 35). Party deals with measures and provisions of peaceful settlement under the Convention (Ohnesorge 2016: 47). Article 279 of Part XV set obligation for states that the 'States Parties shall settle any dispute between them concerning the interpretation or application of this Convention by peaceful means' (UN 2016: 129). The Article 282 deals with exploring the possibility of general, regional or bilateral agreement, and in case the peaceful efforts fail the case can be submitted to the procedures that entail binding decision (UN 2016: 130). The Philippines used this clause to approach Permanent Court of Arbitration in 2013, in which decision was delivered in 2016 (Firestein 2016).

However, the Article 298 of the UNCLOS provides an escape clause for any party of the Convention. The Article reads thus: 'When signing, ratifying or acceding to this Convention or at any time thereafter, a State may, without prejudice to the obligations arising under section 1, declare in writing that it does not accept any one or more of the procedures (UN 2016: 136).' On 25 August 2006, China declined to accept the compulsory dispute settlement procedure by evoking Article 298(1). This means that any compulsory dispute settlement procedures will not be applicable to any case involving China (Beckman 2009: 223).

According to Article 287(1):

> 'one or more of the following means for the settlement of disputes concerning the interpretation or application of this Convention: (a) the International Tribunal for the Law of the Sea established in accordance with Annex VI; (b) the International Court of Justice; (c) an arbitral tribunal constituted in accordance with Annex VII; (d) a special arbitral tribunal constituted in accordance with Annex VIII for one or more of the categories of disputes specified therein.' (UN 2016: 131).

In Southeast Asia, two disputes concerning sovereignty over offshore islands have been referred to the ICJ. The first dispute was between Indonesia and Malaysia in which the ICJ delivered its decision in 2001; and the second was between Malaysia and Singapore in which the ICJ delivered its decision in 2008 (Beckman 2009: 223). Beckman has shown pessimism about possibility of referring any dispute to either ICJ or to the International Tribunal on account of: firstly, the greater strategic importance of the region This is because, as he believes, the strategic importance of the region is so high that the claimants consider it a 'zero-sum game' scenario, and secondly, China's interest in negotiation than invoking the Article 287 (1) (Beckman 2009: 223).

Limitations of UNCLOS

The first limitation of the UNCLOS remains to be absence of any provisions when the parties to the conflict have conflicting claims owing to its silence on sovereignty over the defined features (Ohnesorge 2016: 33). As Beckman puts it, the UNCLOS has no provisions setting out how sovereignty disputes over offshore islands are to be resolved (Beckman 2009: 222).

Secondly, confusion related to the determining the baseline is yet another challenge that complicates the claims made by various claimants in the SCS.

According to Art. 5 of the UNCLOS the 'normal baseline' is defined as 'the low-water line along the coast' (UN 2016). However, the UNCLOS also delineates the exceptions of the normal baseline. One of them is the 'straight baseline' defined under the Article 7. Moreover, under Article 7 yet another criterion for defining baseline for reefs is laid down. Similar kind of exceptions for demarcating the baselines for bays, mouth of rivers, etc., are also there. Hence, the ambiguity regarding demarcating baselines and exceptions to the 'normal baselines' have been major cause of litigation (Ohnesorge 2016: 34) in the SCS. The 'strait baseline' can be drawn: (a) in localities where the coastline is deeply indented and cut into; or (b) if there is a fringe of islands along the coast. Some of the claimants to the geographic features in the South China Sea have employed the straight baseline method despite the fact that they do not meet the criteria laid down in Article 7. This casts some doubt on the validity of the outer limit of their EEZ claims in the South China Sea. Beckman argues that the ICJ has delivered a judgment in the *Qatar–Bahrain* case and under para 212 of the judgment the court observed that method of straight line *must be applied restrictively* (Beckman 2009: 225). Unfortunately, the strait line method is not used restrictively in the SCS, rather the claimants used it invariably.

Thirdly, the offshore features also become highly important in the SCS, as according to Article 121 (2) of the UNCLOS the islands will have their own maritime zones very similar to those of the mainland coasts. Hence, the islands would also have extensive contiguous and Exclusive Economic Zone (EEZ); although, the 'rock' would not have its contiguous zone and EEZ. Hence, the distinction between an 'island' and a 'rock' itself makes a big difference, which engender conflicting claims (Schofield 2009: 12). As far the SCS is concerned, on the basis of the principles laid down under UNCLOS, majority of the Spratly Islands will not qualify to be called as islands (Schofield 2009: 13).

Fourthly, the dispute settlement regime set down in UNCLOS has been described as "the most complex system ever included in any global convention" (Ohnesorge 2016: 47).

In a nutshell, as summarized by Beckman, the potential disputes in the South China Sea relate primarily to (1) sovereignty disputes over geographic features in the Spratly Islands archipelago; and (2) overlapping maritime boundaries. UNCLOS has clear limitations with respect to both categories of disputes (Beckman 2009: 222). Robert Beckman further elaborates that the four questions, which are addressed in UNCLOS, are among the central topics of relevance for the dispute:

1. Which maritime zones may be claimed deriving from the territory of adjacent states and which rights do states enjoy in them?
2. Which offshore features may be subject to sovereignty claims?
3. Which maritime zones may be claimed deriving from offshore features and which rights go along with them?
4. How can claims be harmonized in instances where they overlap or conflict with claims from other states? (Beckman 2013 as cited in Ohnesorge 2016: 33)

Association of Southeast Asian Nations (ASEAN)

ASEAN along with its extended arm is the most important Regional Organization that has been indirectly and directly playing active and conscious role in engendering cooperation and building peace in the region. The efforts have been made through diplomatic consultations and track II diplomacy between the members of the ASEAN and China. Particularly, since late 1980s regular and periodic efforts have been made to build a cooperative management regime for the South China Sea. Several rounds of workshops were organized annually to defuse the potential for conflict in the region. This resulted in the agreement between ASEAN and China in 2002, 'the Declaration on the Conduct of Parties in the South China Sea', as well as a range of recent measures for functional cooperation. But, the initiatives have been successful in very limited manner (Bateman 2009: 1).

China: An Elephant in the Room

China, riding on its unprecedented economic performance, has been showcasing its prowess in Asia and beyond to such an extent that scholars have started to argue that Chinese challenge to American power in Asia is no longer a future possibility but a current reality (White 2016: 7). The problem that remains important to understand is the 'Thucydides trap' according to which rising and declining great powers are set to clash militarily with each other. China claims the South China Sea islands on historical reasons. It has based its claim on a map produced in 1947 by the Republic of China, indicating nine undefined, discontinued, and dashed lines (Djalal 2009: 176). This claim was renewed in 1958 at which time China claimed a 12-nautical-miles territorial sea and declared that "no foreign vessels for military use and no foreign aircraft may enter China's territorial sea and the airspace above it without the permission of the government of the PRC." China claims all the features encompassed by those nine undefined and dashed lines, although it began to occupy some of them only recently. Taiwan's claim in the South China Sea was basically similar to that of China. The Chinese claim was originally described in the Taiwanese/KMT map of 1947 (Djalal 2009: 176). One former Chinese People's Liberation Army Navy (PLAN) admiral argued, "[W]hoever controls the Spratlys will reap huge economic and military benefits (Ohnesorge 2016: 29).

Why China's Behaviour Is Not Restrained by IIs?

The lack of agreed maritime jurisdiction and the limitations of the institutions are major reasons behind inability of IIs in controlling or restraining Chinese muscle-flexing in the region. The SCS has an obvious strategic importance for the claimant nation-states, China and other extra regional players. The aggressive Chinese naval plan has not only created anxious moments for the littoral countries, but also for other major maritime powers (Bateman 2009: 2). The strategic significance of the South China Sea to non-littoral countries could not be ignored. (Djalal 2009: 175). There are the political factors that inhibited the process of cooperation as well. The South China Sea is surrounded by countries that are vastly different from one another. The issue has been further compounded by the claims of Taiwan (Djalal 2009: 175).

Conclusion

To conclude, empirically it is established that even though IIs have tried to address the SCS conflict but have been successful in limited way. The legal regime UNCLOS and the 2002 Declaration of the Parties can be considered as the bright spots. However, these institutional arrangements are successful in only maintaining status-quo to some extent and in not letting to escalate the conflict into a war. These IIs have been unsuccessful in evolving any effective institution that can restrain China's aggressive posturing in the region. Apparently, the IIs also provide scope for confusion and misinterpretation that China has been using to cater its narrow interest. Hence, the IIs have been more successful in controlling behaviour of weaker countries than that of the stronger nation-states having substantial power capability and intention to (mis)use the provisions and arrangements to satisfy self constructed national interest.

NOTES AND REFERENCES

Allison, G. (2012, August, 21), Thucydides trap has been sprung in the Pacific, *Financial Times.* As cited in Fels, Enrico & Vu. Truong-Minh eds (2016), *Power politics in Asia's contested waters: Territorial disputes in the South China Sea*, Heidelberg: Springer

Bateman, Sam & Emmers, Ralf (2009), *Security and International Politics in the South China Sea*, London, New York: Routledge.

Bateman, Sam (2009), The prospects for a cooperative management regime, in Bateman, Sam & Emmers, Ralf (2009), *Security and International Politics in the South China Sea*, London, New York: Routledge.

Beckman, Robert C. (2009), Legal regimes for cooperation in the South China Sea, in Bateman, Sam & Emmers, Ralf. Eds. (2009), *Security and International Politics in the South China Sea*, London, New York: Routledge.

Beckman, R. (2013a), The South China Sea: The evolving dispute between China and her maritime neighbours, *Geomatics World,* 3(21), 18–21.

Beckman, R. (2013b), The UN convention on the law of the sea and the maritime disputes in the South China Sea, *American Journal of International Law*, 107(1), 142–163.

Buzan, Barry (2014), *An introduction to the English School of International Relations*, Cambridge: Polity Press.

Djalal, Hasjim (2009), The south China Sea: The long road towards peace and cooperation, in Bateman, Sam & Emmers, Ralf (2009), *Security and International Politics in the South China Sea*, London, New York: Routledge.

Erskine, Toni, ed. (2003), *Can Institutions have Responsibilities?*, Houndsmills: Palgrave Macmillan.

Fels, Enrico & Truong-Minh, Vu., eds (2016), *Power politics in Asia's contested waters: Territorial disputes in the South China Sea*, Heidelberg: Springer.

Firestein, David J. (2016, August 16), The US-China perception gap in the South China Sea, *The Diplomat*, http://thediplomat.com/2016/08/the-us-china-perception-gap-in-the-south-china-sea.

Katzenstein, P.J, Keohane, R.O., & Krasner, S.D. (1998), International Organization and the Study of World Politics, *International Organization*, 52(4), 645-685.

Keohane (1998), "International institutions: Can interdependence work?," *Foreign Policy*, Washington: Spring.

Keohane (1984), *After Hegemony: Cooperation and discord in the world political economy*, New Jersey: Princeton University Press.

Keohane. Robert O. (2004), *Power and governance in a partially globalized world*, London: Routledge.

Krasner, Stephen D. (1982), Structural causes and regime consequences: Regimes as intervening variables, *International Organization*, 36, 2.

Newman, Edward (2007), *A Crisis in Global Institutions?*, London, New York: Routledge.

Ohnesorge, Hendrik W. (2016), A sea of troubles: international law and the Spitsbergen plus approach to conflict management in the south china sea. In Fels, Enrico & Truong-Minh, Vu., eds (2016), *Power politics in Asia's contested waters: territorial disputes in the South China Sea*, Heidelberg: Springer.

Risse-Kappen (1995), *Bringing transnational relations back*, Cambridge: CUP.

Schofield, Clive (2009), Dangerous ground: A geopolitical overview of the South China Sea, in Bateman, Sam & Emmers, Ralf (2009), *Security and international politics in the South China Sea*, London, New York: Routledge

UN (2017), http://www.un.org/depts/los/reference_files/chronological_lists_ of_ratifications.htm. Retrieved on 13 May 2017.

White, H. (2010, September), Power Shift. Australia's future between Washington and Beijing. *Quarterly Essay*, 39, 2. In Fels, Enrico & Truong-Minh, Vu. Eds. (2016), *Power politics in Asia's contested waters: Territorial disputes in the South China Sea*. Heidelberg: Springer.

14

Global Governance and Rule-Based Order: Issue of South China Sea

Yeshi Choedon

ABSTRACT

The United Nations has been established primarily to find collective solutions to the common problems. Making rules is one of the principal activities of the United Nations with the intention to bring about the rule-based international order. In that spirit, through the Convention on Law of the Sea (UNCLOS), the United Nations attempted to set rules and responsibilities among the member countries for the use of seas and oceans of the world. China was actively involved in the negotiation, and later it accepted the convention in 1982. In the context of the rise of China in the 1990s and with increasing need for resources for its rapid economic growth, China has been engaged in expanding its activities in the South China Sea (SCS). It led to disputes with countries around the SCS over the use of islands and maritime issues, damaging Beijing's claim for peaceful rise of China. On 22 January 2013, the Philippines initiated arbitration proceedings with the Permanent Court of Arbitration (PCA) in The Hague, the Netherlands, to clarify its conflicting claims with China in the SCS.

This paper intends to delve on the source of Conflict, why only seven out of 15 submissions made by the Philippines had been taken by the Court. It discusses the significance of the award on the jurisdiction of the Tribunal as well as merits of the case. It highlights the reaction of China in the aftermath of the verdict and the likely consequences. It also discusses the implications of the case for rule-based international order. It ends with a discussion on institutional lessons learned from this experience and what needs to be done to improve global governance relating to oceans and seas as they will continue to play a significant role in the globalized era.

Introduction

The increasing interconnectedness and interdependence of the world due to the advancement of science and technology made it imperative to devise new ways of managing relations among the states. Neither the state system has withered away as predicted by the scholars in the 1990s, nor led to pulling of sovereignty to form a global government. Instead, a concept of global governance has become relevant to manage the complex relationship among the states in the globalized world. The global governance involves pulling of sovereignty, but it led to strengthening the state system as an important actor in it. There are other pieces of global governance and various actors, apart from the states, to deal with various common concerns, which the states themselves alone are not in a position to tackle (Karns and Mingst, 2005:3-33). The inter-governmental organizations (IGOs) are important pieces of global governance, and its main role is to provide a forum to devise norms and standards on common issues and establish mechanisms to sort out the differences in interpretation of those agreed upon norms and sometimes set up monitoring, dispute settlement, and enforcement mechanisms as well.

One such global common issue has been the contestation among the states over use and control of oceans and seas. The states geared their expansionistic agenda towards seas and oceans as the land territories acquired settled legal borders with no scope of further expansion. Seas and oceans have become significant in the globalized world for a navigational route for global trade, overseas flights, maritime resources and military strategic perspective. The disputes over the use and control of the seas and oceans along with the outer space replaced the land bounded territorial disputes since the mid-1980s. Under such contextual situation, the states agreed upon the global norms and mechanism to settle the disputes relating to seas and oceans under the aegis of the United Nations in the form of UN Convention on Law of the Sea (UNCLOS) in 1982.

This paper first highlights some of the main provisions of the UNCLOS and its recommended mechanisms for settlement of disputes. It then traces the origin of the SCS disputes and developments manifesting in the Philippines filing the case against China over the dispute. The central focus of the paper is on the discussion on the award of Arbitral Tribunal on the points raised by the Philippines and reaction of the parties to the disputes as well as other stakeholders. It is followed by the discussion on the trajectory adopted by China and Southeast Asian countries in the wake of the ruling on the dispute and how their policies and activities are likely to impact the regional security. It ends with a discussion on what needs to be done to improve the management of governance and good order at sea.

Main Provisions of the UNCLOS and Mechanisms

UNCLOS is the most celebrated multilateral treaty on seas and oceans framed under the aegis of the United Nations to facilitate interaction of commerce, people, cultures, and ideas to generate international pluralism and global prosperity. It has become the constitution of seas and oceans of the world. It came into existence on 10 December 1982 and entered into force 12 years later, i.e. on 16 November 1994. The Convention establishes a comprehensive legal framework to regulate all ocean space, its uses, and resources. It contains, among other things, provisions relating to the territorial sea, the contiguous zone, the continental shelf, the exclusive economic zone and the high seas. It also provides for the protection and preservation of the marine environment, for marine scientific research and the development and transfer of marine technology. One of the most important parts of the Convention concerns the exploration for and exploitation of the resources of the seabed and ocean floor and subsoil thereof, beyond the limits of national jurisdiction. The Convention declares the seas and oceans and their resources to be "the common heritage of mankind" (United Nations, 1982).

Part XV of the Convention lays down a comprehensive system for the settlement of disputes that might arise on the interpretation and application of the Convention. It requires States Parties to settle their disputes concerning the interpretation or application of the Convention by peaceful means as indicated in the Charter of the United Nations. However, if parties to a dispute fail to settle by peaceful means of their own choice, they are obliged to resort to the compulsory dispute settlement procedures entailing binding decisions, subject to limitations and exceptions contained in the Convention. The Convention provides for four alternative means for the settlement of disputes: the International Tribunal for the Law of the Sea, the International Court of Justice, an arbitral tribunal constituted by Annex VII to the Convention, and a special arbitral tribunal constituted by Annex VIII to the Convention.

Origin and Development of the SCS Dispute

The dispute over the SCS is important to showcase the role of international norms in global governance in general and how the international norms specifically protect the rights of the smaller states against the claims of powerful states, thus managing relationship among the asymmetric power states.

In 1947, the Nationalist government of the Republic of China published a map with a U-shaped series of lines in the form of a nine-dash line delineating its maritime claim of sovereignty in the SCS. This cartographic feature persisted in maps published after the Communist Party came to power in the mainland in 1949. China remained relatively inactive between 1949 and the mid-1970s in the SCS. It was only from the mid-1990s, China began its strategy of "creeping assertiveness' based on its claim of historic rights to sovereignty over the islands within the U-shaped line and the waters within the region. These assertions of historic rights and its enhanced activities caused considerable friction with the Southeast Asian neighbours (Thayer, 2014:51). Despite the requirement under Part IX of the UNCLOS for cooperation among all the countries bordering a water body, the countries around SCS could not develop an effective regional regime for cooperative marine management and good order at sea. This is because of the several sovereignty disputes over islands and reefs in the sea and the consequent lack of agreed maritime jurisdiction (Bateman, 2014: 119–36).

China's aggressive assertion of sovereignty over the SCS in the first half of 2001 has raised the security stakes for the Southeast states as well as all maritime powers that sail through the waters of SCS. In an attempt to deal with increasing function, ASEAN and China, issued a Declaration on the Conduct of Parties in the SCS (DOC) in 2002. It was "soft law" that required the littoral countries to cooperate on certain marine activities. However, because of its non-binding nature, it falls short of constituting a successful regime for providing security and cooperative management in the SCS. A very little progress has been made in implementing and adhering to the DOC.

Due to increase in disputes over the SCS, the international diplomatic pressures exerted were to find peaceful settlement of the disputes. Under these pressures, ASEAN and China adopted the Guidelines for the Implementation of the DOC in 2011. Immediately after the Guidelines were adopted, the Philippines Foreign Secretary Albert del Rosario noted that they would need more 'teeth' to make them effective. To quote Rosario: "The necessary elements to make the guidelines succeed are still incomplete. We're looking for the participants to be honorable. Beyond that, there's not much room for us to exact consequences for misbehavior" (Thayer, 2014:46).

The Philippines Filing the Case

China's historical claim of sovereignty over most of the SCS conflicted with the claims by Vietnam, the Philippines, Malaysia, Indonesia, Brunei, and Taiwan. The SCS became contentious as one-third of global maritime traffic, carrying oil and raw materials to Asia and Asian consumer goods to the world. It is also endowed with rich fishing grounds and potential energy and mineral reserves beneath the seabed (Fenby, 2001: 32). The confrontations with Japan, Vietnam, and the Philippines over the use of waters and islands increased as the Xi Jinping administration, unlike the previous administrations, a high profile policy at global level without hesitation of projecting its power. China adopted a more militarized posture in the disputed areas of the SCS with the intention to establish "facts on the ground" situation. It carried out the construction of islands reclaimed from the sea, and built airstrips and naval patrol vessels. China's decision to deploy its coast guard as a coercive arm of its state policy to consolidate and protect its maritime interests has an unsettling effect on the countries in the region. China's policy of "might makes rights, "and numerical superiority of coast guard vessels ensures continued dominance and bullying tactics towards smaller claimants of the SCS (Morris, 2016).

China's aggressive policies and postures not only raised regional tensions but also provoked the smaller countries of the Southeast Asian region resorted to countering China's military threat by seeking security under US strategic umbrella (Fenby, 2001: 32). Among the Southeast Asian states, the Philippines took an unusual soft approach to Chinese claims in the SCS. The relations between the Philippines and China turned from bad to worse and became virtually frozen since China seized the Scarborough Shoal in mid-2012. Manila increased its defence budget and took various measures to modernize its military capability for territorial defence. It also aligned more closely with the US and increased defence cooperation (Thayer, 2014:25).

As the Philippines found itself involved in a tussle with much stronger state with much more influence, economic and military capabilities, it sought a level playing field by filing a suit against China in accordance with the mechanism provided in the UNCLOS. By resorting to an international mechanism, the Philippines wanted to internationalize its dispute with China, increase the credibility of its claims against Beijing and sought the assistance to deal with the bullying neighbour. China's claim to historic rights within the nine-dash line, including the Exclusive Economic Zone (EEZ) of the Philippines, was the major reason for the Philippines to opt for arbitration proceedings through the Arbitral Tribunal provided by Annex VII to the UNCLOS. On 22 January 2013, the Philippines initiated the proceedings by 15 points submission to seek clarification on the conflicting claims of China in the SCS (Permanent Court of Arbitration, 2015:3-4). China consistently and firmly contended that the submissions before the Tribunal involved the issues of sovereignty and maritime boundary delimitation and both of these issues were beyond the scope of UNCLOS dispute settlement. As China believed that the Tribunal did not possess jurisdiction, it had decided not to appear or participate in the proceedings. The arbitration proceeded in its absence in accordance with the provisions of UNCLOS.

China also criticized the composition of the Arbitral Tribunal to examine the submission. According to UNCLOS Annex VII, both parties of a dispute are entitled to appoint one judge each and rest of the members the Tribunal are to be appointed by the president of the Hamburg-based International Tribunal for the Law of Sea (ITLOS). The Philippines appointed a German arbitrator Rudiger Wolfrum as its choice. China had ceded its rights to appoint a judge by declining to participate in the arbitration. As a result, UNCLOS rules that Japan's Shunji Yanai, then president of International Tribunal for the Law of Sea (ITLOS), to appoint four other arbitrators. The Chinese state-run media accused Yanai of bias in selecting the arbitrators and stated that a Japanese national unfit to play such a key role in the case as Japan itself has maritime disputes with China. China's ambassador to Indonesia, Xie Feng, claimed that Yanai "went to great pains to form a temporary tribunal" that can "hardly be considered as universally representative" (Johnson, 2016).

Despite China's non-participation and criticism of the composition of the Tribunal, over the next three years, the five judges assigned to this case deliberated on the Philippines' 15 submissions. First, it examined its jurisdiction over the case as China raised an objection on that account. The Tribunal rejected China's contention that the dispute is regarding Maritime Boundary Delimitation and therefore excluded from Dispute Settlement by Article 298 of the UNCLOS. It observed that a dispute concerning whether a State has an entitlement to a maritime zone is a distinct matter and there is no confusion. The Tribunal came to the conclusion that all fifteen submissions fall within the interpretive and applicative scope of UNCLOS and not relate to sovereignty and maritime boundary delimitation. It also arrived at the conclusion that a formal 'dispute' existed between the parties on interpretation and application of the provisions of the UNCLOS (Permanent Court of Arbitration, 2015: 1-2).

Ruling by the Arbitral Tribunal

The five judges on the Arbitral Tribunal finally rendered their judgment in a "unanimous Award" on 12 July 2016. In essence, the Philippines' claims on the SCS have been vindicated at the expense of China's claims of historic rights behind the infamous nine-dash line. The three most important points of judgment were attributing Chinese moves in the SCS to the aggravation of tensions in the region; condemning China as a leading source of ecosystem degradation, and infringing on the rights of the Philippines from lawfully exercising its maritime rights.

Regarding 'nine-dash line' and China's claim to historic rights, the Tribunal said that it did not find any grounds for China's territorial claims in the SCS within the so-called 'nine-dash line.' It concluded that China's historic rights to resources in the waters of the SCS were nullified by the entry into force of the Convention (Arbitral Tribunal, 2016:111). The Tribunal considered that prior to the Convention, the waters of the SCS beyond the territorial sea were legally part of the high seas, in which vessels from any State could freely navigate and fish. Accordingly, the Tribunal concluded that historical navigation and fishing by China in the waters of the SCS represented the exercise of high seas freedoms, rather than a historic right, and that there was no evidence that China had historically exercised exclusive control over the waters of the SCS or prevented other States from exploiting their resources. The Tribunal found that China's claim to historic rights to resources was incompatible with the detailed allocation of rights and maritime zones in the UNCLOS. Thus, the ruling rejected the historic rights claim of China on the basis of the provisions of UNCLOS. However, the tribunal did not rule that the nine-dash line per se is illegal or invalid. China is under no obligation to formally denounce the nine-dash line (Arbitral Tribunal, 2016: 112-115).

Furthermore, it stressed that China had no right to claim an exclusive economic zone around the Spratly Islands. Under Articles 13 and 121 of the Convention, features that are above water at high tide generate an entitlement to at least a 12 nautical mile territorial sea, whereas features that are submerged at high tide generate no entitlement to maritime zones. The Tribunal concluded that all of the features in the Spratly Islands are "rocks" that do not generate an exclusive economic zone or continental shelf (Arbitral Tribunal, 2016:254). The Tribunal also held that the Convention does not provide for a group of islands such as the Spratly Islands to generate maritime zones collectively as a unit.

The Court also determined that the construction of artificial structures on the Spratly Archipelago reefs and shoals and attempts to pass them off as fully natural islands is illegal. Having found that Mischief Reef, Second Thomas Shoal, and Reed Bank are submerged at high tide, form part of the exclusive economic zone and continental shelf of the Philippines, the Tribunal concluded that the Convention is clear in allocating rights to the Philippines with respect to sea areas in its exclusive economic zone. The Tribunal found as a matter of fact that China had (a) interfered with Philippine petroleum exploration at Reed Bank, (b) purported to prohibit fishing by Philippine vessels within the Philippines' exclusive economic zone, (c) protected and failed to prevent Chinese fishermen from fishing within the Philippines' exclusive economic zone at Mischief Reef and Second Thomas Shoal, and (d) constructed installations and artificial islands at Mischief Reef without the authorization of the Philippines. The Tribunal, therefore, concluded that China had violated the Philippines' sovereign rights with respect to its exclusive economic zone and continental shelf (Arbitral Tribunal, 2016: 279-286).

The Tribunal next examined traditional fishing at Scarborough Shoal and concluded that fishermen from the Philippines, as well as fishermen from China and other countries, had long fished at the Shoal and had traditional fishing rights in the Area. Although the Tribunal emphasized that it was not deciding sovereignty over Scarborough Shoal, it found that China had violated its duty to respect the traditional fishing rights of the Philippine fishermen by halting access to the Shoal after May 2012 (Arbitral Tribunal, 2016:315-316). The tribunal also found that China's vessels had breached several UNCLOS articles governing safety and navigation at sea (Arbitral Tribunal, 2016:431-435).

The Tribunal found that Beijing's activities on the Spratly Islands were also deemed as detrimental to the region's natural ecosystem. China's large-scale land reclamation and construction of artificial islands at seven features in the Spratly Islands has caused severe harm to the coral reef environment and that China has violated its obligation under Articles 192 and 194 of the Convention to preserve and protect the marine environment with respect to fragile ecosystems and the habitat of depleted, threatened, or endangered species. The Tribunal also found that the Chinese fishermen have engaged in the harvesting of endangered sea turtles, coral, and giant clams on a substantial scale in the SCS, using methods that inflict severe damage on the coral reef environment. The Tribunal found that Chinese authorities were aware of these activities and failed to fulfil their due diligence obligations under the Convention to stop them. The tribunal held that these construction activities were unlawful because they aggravated and extended the ongoing dispute that was before the international tribunal. In addition, China's construction activities destroyed evidence of the natural condition of the features in question, even though the status of such features was a matter pending before the tribunal (Arbitral Tribunal, 2016: 378).

The Reactions to the Ruling

The award of the Tribunal has not only clarified in several ways how UNCLOS applies to the complex disputes in the SCS, but it has also brought home to all concerned the importance of UNCLOS in establishing a rules-based order for the oceans and seas. All the parties to the convention have an obligation to adhere to the rulings of the dispute settlement mechanism, and there is no appellate court to appeal against the ruling. In case the parties to the dispute refuse to comply with the verdict, there is no enforcement mechanism.

China reacted furiously to the judgment of the Tribunal, refused to accept and execute it on the ground of lack of jurisdiction as well as the illegal constitution of the Tribunal. The Chinese President Xi Jinping said that China's "territorial sovereignty and maritime rights" in the seas would not be affected by the ruling, which declared large areas of the sea to be neutral international waters or EEZ of other countries. He insisted China was still "committed to resolving disputes" with neighbours (*The Guardian*, 2016). China released a white paper against the verdict on 13 July and insisted that it has claimed over the strategic region for 2000 years. It stated that awards rendered by the Tribunal were null and void and had no binding force. It stated "China does not accept or recognize those awards. China opposes and will never accept any claim or action based on those awards" (Xinhua, 2016). Through the denunciation of the verdict and raising the issue of legality and fairness, China seems to be attempting to avoid being branded a violator of international law. The more stringent reaction of China and refusal to comply with the judgment, the more it appears that China has a moral responsibility to implement it.

The Philippines, despite the favourable nature of the award, has reacted carefully. There was a change in political leadership in the Philippines due to the election just 13 days before the verdict. The new President of the Philippines Rodrigo Duterte preferred to adopt reconciliatory rather than confrontationist approach to China. The Philippines foreign ministry called for "restraint and sobriety" after the tribunal issued a decision favourable to Manila (The Straits Times, 2016 A). The Southeast Asian countries also welcomed the judgment but exhibited restrained reaction. The Judgement had an impact on the other Southeastern Asian countries, such as Vietnam, Malaysia, Brunei, and Indonesia, who have a dispute with China over the SCS. The ruling has clarified numerous issues. Specifically, the tribunal ruling states that China has no historic rights to resources in the EEZs of other states within the nine-dashline and that none of the disputed islands is entitled to an EEZ of its own has an impact on their dispute with China. It means that China has no legal basis under UNCLOS to claim that it has a right to share the fishing or hydrocarbon resources in the EEZs of the ASEAN claimants bordering the SCS. Thus, the positions of other smaller neighbours of China in Southeast Asia were strengthened by this ruling.

The USA welcomed the judgement, and the State Department called on both parties to comply with their obligations. The similar position has been taken by the majority of the other states, highlighting the need for adherence to international norms and respecting the institution.

The Arbitral Tribunal provided level playing field for the Philippines and in the process built up international support for its position. The conciliatory position of the new leadership of the Philippines, as well as cautious approach of the other Southeast Asian countries, indicate that they prefer to give China cooling off period and find a face-saving device to recalibrate its policy towards the SCS after the highly embarrassing ruling of the Tribunal.

The disputes with its smaller neighbours, refusal to participate in the tribunal's proceedings as well as rejecting the judgment displayed China as an outlier that flouts international law. Thus, the judgment hurt China's international standing. China seems to have realized this, and therefore it has not pursued an open, aggressive path in response to the ruling despite dumping up publicity of its firm stance against it. The ruling gave Manila as well as other smaller neighbors a bargaining chip to use in their negotiations with Beijing. Efforts should have been focused on building a high level of trust and confidence to resolve the issues through constructive dialogue and consultation and aim towards the mutual exploration of the seabed and joint management rather than seeking sovereignty over the SCS.

However, the development since the verdict indicates that this was much not been a change in China's policy and behaviour in the SCS. After the tribunal verdict, China agreed to expedite the talks to bring about the legally binding code of conduct (COC) preferred by the members of the ASEAN and to stop its "unilateral action" (Straits Times, 2016 B). China must have taken this position to deflect criticism away from its rejection of the Tribunal's award and instead project the image of a cooperative partner. In the first half of 2017, ASEAN and Chinese officials met three times to discuss the COC. However, China has been resisting any hint of enforcement mechanisms or consequences of violations. On 6 August 2017, Foreign ministers from Southeast Asia and China adopted the framework of COC on maritime disputes. They hailed the progress, but the critics see it as a tactic of China to buy time to consolidate its maritime power (Channel News Asia, 2017). The framework emphasizes that the COC "is not an instrument to settle territorial disputes or maritime delimitation issues." It is expected to promote "mutual trust, cooperation, and confidence, prevent incidents, manage incidents should they occur and create a favourable environment for the peaceful resolution of disputes" (The Straits Times, 2017). The negotiations are likely to be lengthy and frustrating as there is a difference of view between ASEAN countries and China, specifically on the issue of 'legally binding' code. China prefers a non-binding instrument that can be leveraged to improve regional trust, rather than resolve overlapping claims, whereas the many of the ASEAN members held the position that the COC must be legally-binding.

ASEAN Secretary-General Le Luong Minh is reported to have said, "A framework is a framework. But the framework will hopefully pave the way towards meaningful and substantive negotiations towards the conclusion of a COC. It must be able not only to prevent but also to manage incidents of the kind that have taken place so far. For that COC to be effective, it will have to be legally binding" (The Straits Times, 2017). The adoption of the framework makes it appear that China is cooperating and that they are making progress towards establishing a COC.

In terms of behaviour on the ground, China's reclamation project has moved at a brisk pace with reports of new military installations appearing frequently. There is no one at the present moment to challenge China's activities in the SCS. Under Rodrigo Duterte, the Philippines has turned from China's chief regional rival into an ally. Although a U.S. warship has sailed near a Chinese-controlled island in the disputed SCS on May 24, 2017, to exercise freedom of navigation, Donald Trump seems less willing than his predecessor to enforce a rules-based order. Because of the uncertainty of the US policy under the new administration and its preoccupation with the North Korean crisis, other Southeast Asian countries seem resigned to China's island-building. Further, there is a lack of unity among the countries of ASEAN to take a common position against China expansionism in the SCS and in negotiating a legally binding commitment. Extended talks on a COC give an appearance of engagement to find a regional solution, while probably mean that China gets the freedom to consolidate its gains with minimal interference from rivals near or far. In the process, China gets an opportunity to establish 'fact on the ground' without much of international attention.

Conclusion

The global governance is expected to bring about rule-based order to manage relations and disputes among the states in the globalized world. It is expected that power-based order is replaced by norm-based one where even the small states are assumed to get level playing field in relation to powerful states. This kind of global governance prevents the power asymmetry among the states from indulging in bullying and coercive tactics of the big over the small powers.

Through such mechanism of global governance at the seas and oceans, the above discussion shows that the Philippines, a small state, could bring its grievance against the big power, China, to seek clarification on a number of issues and ruling over the differences of their interpretation and application of the provisions of the UNCLOS. Till the announcement of the ruling of the Arbitral Tribunal ruling, the process went on as designed in the piece of governance relating to seas and oceans, despite China's refusal to participate.

The disputes with its smaller neighbours, its refusal to participate in the tribunal's proceedings as well as rejecting the judgment, displayed China as an outlier that flouts international law. As China has been projecting itself as the emerging superpower of the World, this image of outlier hurt its international standing. China seems to have realized this, and, therefore, it has not pursued an aggressive path in response to the ruling.

After the verdict, it was expected that China and Southeast Asian countries would focus on constructive dialogue and consultation and aim towards the mutual exploration of the SCS seabed and joint management of the sea. However, the development since the verdict indicates that nothing much has been changed in China's policy and behaviour in the SCS. After the tribunal verdict, China agreed to expedite the talks to bring about the legally binding COC. However, there is not much tangible progress on that front as China has been resisting any hint of enforcement mechanisms or consequences of violations. On the other hand, China's reclamation project has moved at a brisk pace with reports of new military installations appearing frequently. There is no one at the present moment willing with the capability to challenge China's activities in the SCS. The US administration under the leadership of Donald Trump seems less willing than his predecessor to enforce a rules-based order. Because of the uncertainty of the US policy, the Southeast Asian countries seem resigned to their fate. Further, through the divide and rule policy, China could prevent emerging of common position among the countries of the ASEAN against China's expansionism in the SCS. These circumstantial factors enable China to consolidate its gains.

Thus, despite prevalence of the global governance and rule-based order through UNCLOS, China as a hegemonic power continue to bully and coerce small powers in the Southeast Asian region, avoiding any overt confrontation and yet carry on covert activities to establish 'fact on the ground' to promote its own interests and facilitate the projection its power in the sea. These developments not only increase security risk of the Southeast Asian region but also pose a challenge to the existing global order. This situation obviously points to the need for strengthened global governance mechanism in the SCS with enforcement and monitoring mechanisms to ensure compliance with global norms and rulings by the global institution. It should not be left alone to the Southeast Asian countries to deal with China. There is a need for more active participation not only of the other states concerned with China's activities in the SCS but also non-state actors like media, epistemic community, and concerned international organizations focusing on seas, trade, and security.

NOTES AND REFERENCES

Arbitral Tribunal (2016), "The South China Sea Arbitration Award of 12 July 2016", https://pca-cpa.org/wp-content/uploads/sites/175/2016/07/PH-CN-20160712-Award.pdf

Bateman, Sam (2014), "Maritime boundary Delimitation, Excessive claims and effective Regime Building in the South China Sea", in Song, Yann-huei; Zhou, Keyuan and Bateman, W.S.G. (eds.) *Major Law and Policy Issues in the South China Sea: European and American Perspectives*, Surrey: Routledge.

Channel News Asia (2017), "ASEAN, China adopt framework for crafting code on South China Sea", 7 August, http://www.channelnewsasia.com/news/asiapacific/asean—china-adopt-framework-for-crafting-code-on-south-china-sea-9100694

Fenby, Jonathan (2001), "The Great Wall of Sand China's aggressive claims to sovereignty in the South China Sea have angered its Asian neighbours and raised fears of a showdown with the US", *New Statesman*, 13-19 May.

Johnson, Jesse (2016), "Beijing turns on Japanese judge as Hague tribunal ruling over SCS near", *The Japan Times*, July 8.

Karns, Margaret and Mingst, Karen A. (2005), *International Organizations: The Politics and Processes of Global Governance*, Colorado: Lynne Rienner

Morris, Lyle J. (2016), "The Crucial SCS Ruling NO One is Talking About", *The Diplomat*, Sept 09.

Permanent Court of Arbitration (2015), "Arbitration between the Republic of the Philippines and the People's Republic of China", *Press Release*, 29 October https://www.pcacases.com/web/sendAttach/1503

Thayer, Carlyle, A. (2014), "China-ASEAN and the South China Sea: Chinese Assertiveness and Southeast Asian Responses", in Song, Yann-huei; Zhou, Keyuan and Bateman, W.S.G. (eds.) *Major Law and Policy Issues in the South China Sea: European and American Perspectives*, Surrey: Routledge.

The Guardian (2016), "Beijing rejects tribunal's ruling in South China Sea case", 12 July, https://www.theguardian.com/world/2016/jul/12/philippines-wins-south-china-sea-case-against-china

The Straits Times (2016 A), "The Philippines welcomes South China Sea ruling, urges restraint and sobriety," 12 July, http://www.straitstimes.com/asia/se-asia/philippines-urges-restraint-and-sobriety-after-south-china-sea-ruling

The Straits Times (2016 B), "ASEAN urges self-restraint in South China Sea activities, no mention of tribunal ruling", 25 July, http://www.straitstimes.com/asia/se-asia/asean-foreign-ministers-address-south-china-sea-issue-in-communique-but-not-tribunal

The Straits Times (2017), "ASEAN, China adopt framework of code of conduct for South China Sea", 6 August, http://www.straitstimes.com/asia/se-asia/chinas-foreign-minister-says-maritime-code-negotiations-with-asean-to-start-this-year

United Nations (1982), *Convention on Law of the Sea,* 10 December, *http://www.un.org/depts/los/convention_agreements/texts/unclos/unclos_e.pdf*

Xinhua (2016), "China Focus: China issues white paper on settling disputes with the Philippines," on 13 July, http://news.xinhuanet.com/english/2016-07/13/c_135510278.htm

15

Chinese Expansionism and its Implications for Regional Security

M. Venkataraman

ABSTRACT

Recent international political discourse has largely been dominated by China's role in the world at large and specifically with regard to the conflicting claims over South China Sea islands by China and few other East Asian countries. The issue has been dragging for decades without settlement but has only generated increasing worries not only among those involved but otherwise too. Behind this entire episode is the expansionist design of China unrelenting as always and adamant in its claims. In fact, it is not just the South China Sea islands that is under dispute but several other territorial claims that China is yet to settle including those with India. The basic argument of this paper is that expansionism cannot happen without political consolidation and attempts to legitimize political control and rule over the country. The Chinese political consolidation attempts can be traced to history and the consequent internal political make up contributing to adopting strategies aimed at dominating and dealing with the outside world in its own terms. In fact, what is interesting to note in the Chinese case is the unique political and economic systems that it has been able to adopt in order to consolidate political power. Hence, the question raised here is to what extent the consolidation of political power contributes to expansionist designs of China? And if so, what are the implications for regional security? This paper aims at answering these questions and provides alternatives by describing and analyzing the domestic compulsions that China has been grappling with and the implications thereof.

Introduction

The rise of China has not been without controversies when looked at from the perspective of the role it has played on certain international political issues. In particular, the focus is on the Asia–Pacific region where China's activities have drawn increasing criticisms and challenges from among the regional and distant countries alike. The North Korean military standoff is one issue drawing world attention and that apart it is China's recent military activities in South China Sea that have even more added fuel to fire. The case in point is its activity in South China Sea which is claimed by few other countries—the Philippines, Malaysia, Vietnam and Taiwan—as well. The issue has been lingering for several decades without any resolution in sight so far owing largely to the Chinese unrelenting position of sovereignty over all islands, rather China has only been placing military installations with anti-aircraft missile batteries, air craft hangers, re-fuelling facilities and radar systems on the islands. Besides, in at least three of the Spratly island chain China has constructed air strips and placed surface to surface artillery and surface-to-air missiles. Such militarization of the islands and assertion of claims over territory by military means is yet another example of China's fewer adherences to international norms and standards. This has caused grave concern among many including that of India and other distant countries like the U.S. which has been clamouring for freedom of navigation and free trade in that part of the world. If one looks at the volume of trade in the Asia-Pacific region, then any potential military confrontation would have devastating effect on the political, economic and strategic interests of the U.S. and other countries like South Korea and Japan, all of whom have intense trade ties with each other and allies of the U.S.

Thus, the objective of this article is to analyze the rationale behind China's expansionist policies and the implications it has on regional security and stability. The discussion follows a qualitative approach and used descriptive and analytical methods. It has relied extensively on secondary data with the use of relevant literatures including prominent books and journal articles besides e-resources. These are used in understanding the reality of Chinese expansionism. Chinese nationalism or its self-image is also within focus as an explanatory factor in the intricacy of these prime issues of international relations. The article proceeds to clarify the concepts used and then to outline the historical connections of Chinese expansionism. Thereafter, it proceeds to analyze the behavioural patterns as exhibited by its new foreign policy postures and military modernization programmes, and finally to draw conclusions in the form of implications to regional security.

Clarifying the Concepts

What possibly defines Chinese expansionism? What are its measurable indicators? In fact, expansionism as a concept has no universally acceptable definition. It can happen in various ways through various methods and exhibited in various manifestations. To some it can mean economic and to some others military expansionism both of which have been the hall marks of international politics at various times and by various actors. Expansionism, for the purpose of this article, is seen essentially as a foreign policy act in which behaviours of countries provide clues to whether they accede to international norms and rules or not.[1] Such behaviours are observable ones and could be identified to argue if they fit into acceptable standards. For example, foreign policy pronouncements of countries are indicators of the degree to which they assert themselves to a particular issue. Many of most such pronouncements could be mere rhetoric but when combined with military actions they indicate the assertiveness.[2] The argument of this article is that foreign policy assertiveness when combined with military actions tantamount to a potential threat indicating expansionist tendencies. In the case of China too one can notice such assertiveness, which is expansionist in nature. As far as China is concerned it is its nationalistic ideology that is reflected in an increasingly assertive and militaristic manner in contravention to established international norms and principles.

What then is nationalistic ideology? Definitions of nation and state abound but what is important to point out is how the concepts of nation and state combine to form nationalism, which is nothing but an ideology that emphasizes collective interests of the community to advance their well-being.[3] John Hall (1993, p.1)[4] clarifies that "it is the belief in the primacy of a particular nation, real or constructed; the logic of this position tends to move nationalism from cultural to political forms, and to entail popular mobilization". Here one can observe that there is a political interest attached to nationalism in order to mobilize the feelings and sentiments of the diverse people into a collective fold as per its national interests. Such mobilization is achieved through many ways such as by way of establishing certain political institutions, political education, threat from abroad and such others. In the case of China too, these methods have been the hallmarks much before it proclaimed itself People's Republic and from then on the national interest is defined by the Chinese Communist Party (CCP).[5] And, therefore, the assertive behaviour is a product of its attempt to bring out supreme loyalty to the nation as exhibited by its militaristic behaviour.

The militaristic nature is an essential ingredient of expansionism and has formed part and parcel of Chinese strategic culture. What then is strategic culture? Undoubtedly, national cultural attributes provide clues as to how a country behaves with one another and its tendency to use force.[6] The term has been of recent origin and one of the earliest scholars to define this was Jack Snyder. He defined it as "the body of attitudes and beliefs that guides and circumscribes thought on strategic questions, influences the way strategic issues are formulated, and sets the vocabulary and perceptual parameters of strategic debate".[7] However, Johnston defines it as "ranked grand strategic preferences derived from central paradigmatic assumptions about the nature of conflict and the enemy, and collectively shared by decision makers."[8] For the purpose of this article the strategic culture focuses on the uses of military for strategic purposes.

The discussion on Chinese strategic culture posits two set of views. One that is based on the principles of Confucianism and peaceful co-existence and avoiding war while the other opposed to that and based on real politik behaviour emphasizing the use of force to threats to security. This dualism in Chinese culture has continued and is also reflected in Mao's theory on contradictions, which stressed that conflict is not only inevitable but also desirable. Hence, nations should be prepared militarily and the one that is weak will always be invaded.[9] The study on Seven Military Classics one of which includes the Sun Tzu's Art of War accepts the situation of constant state of war in international politics and justifies the use of coercive force as the most efficacious means to deter and defeat enemies to achieve security.[10] As will be seen below, the strategic culture of China extended to protecting the strategic periphery from where China historically received threats to its political control.[11] And the realpolitik cultural behaviour is more evident in China today as Chinese leaders are more than willing to the use of force in international politics.[12]

Historical Connections

It is an undeniable fact that nation-building process, like that in many other countries, has its roots in history. In the case of China too one can observe that historical developments during the times of Imperial China have impacted subsequent generations tremendously and have continued to be so reflecting on their expansionist tendencies. Among many others, two inter-related features of history stand out as applicable in today's context. One is the need for domestic consolidation of rule and the second is lack of tolerance to criticisms against the government.

There have been many imperial dynasties and emperors who have passed through the long Chinese civilization. A cursory glance at Chinese history reveals that their history is replete with examples of the struggle for control over power because the vast and diverse country was facing periodic invasions from within and outside, particularly the Mongols, and hence the need to consolidate power. Of particular to note is that of the rule under Emperor Chin Shi Huang, the founder of Chin dynasty and the first emperor who unified China and brought it under his central control. This was sometime in 221 B.C. when emperor Chin succeeded in unifying China by warfare with many rival feudal kingdoms and ruled ruthlessly as a tyrant. Of course there were several other dynasties ruling China before this period such as the Shang dynasty in 1766 B.C. However, the dynasty of Chin Shi Huang is notable not only for unifying China but also for creating what later came to be known as the Chinese heartland.[13] The Great Wall of China was built during his rule as he desired to prevent invasions from the north of the country particularly from Hun invasions. The Great Wall is historic and a semblance of not only Chinese architecture and fortification but also the importance attached to security.[14]

It should be noted here that the consolidation of political control in effect meant protecting its borders which included the periphery from where China historically received threats to its rule and control through invasions. Michael Swaine notes that China's periphery region was vast and it included not only continental areas like Xinjian, Outer and Inner Mongolia, Tibet, and Korea but maritime regions as well.[15] And like that of the Chin dynasty, control over the periphery or dominance by any means was equally considered important. To quote Michael Swaine:

> Even when periphery areas did not pose a significant security threat to the Chinese heartland, or during times of relative Chinese weakness, the symbolic maintenance of a sinocentric order nonetheless remained an important objective of the Chinese state, to sustain the political legitimacy and authority of the Chinese order and, it was hoped, to deter potential adversaries.[16]

With regard to the second feature, the intolerance towards criticisms was followed right from the Chin dynasty as it was conceived as a threat to the sovereign rule and would not help consolidate political power. In other words, for power to be consolidated criticisms cannot be tolerated. As noted above, the rule of Chin Shi Huang was ruthless and he ruled like a tyrant—a policy followed by subsequent rulers as well.

If one compares the above two features of historical China with that of contemporary China, then it is easy to observe that both have been the features applicable today as well. As will be seen in subsequent sections, China both during the Mao era and the present President Xi Jinping times have made strident efforts to stay put in power. Also, criticisms and opposition to rule were not accepted in Mao era and so was during Deng Xiaoping and also the current rule of Xi Jinping. We have the examples in the form of the Hundred Flowers Movement, the Great Proletarian Cultural Revolution (GPCR), Tianenmen Massacre, etc., that depicts the historical connections of such behaviour and the reactions on the part of the government's intolerance towards such oppositions and criticisms. That apart, even today China is being criticised for human rights violations. For example, the Human Rights Watch in its 2014 report points out the continued hard line approach of the Chinese government on human rights by way of curbing media, Internet and cultural expressions.[17]

Expansion and consolidation of rule and territory was followed by subsequent Chinese dynasties as well. Of noteworthy is that of the Han dynasty which expanded and controlled the neighbouring states of China—the Vietnam and Korea. In fact, maritime expansionism is also said to have taken place. This happened during the Sung dynasty between 960 A.D. and 1279 A.D. when China secured maritime trade routes that ran from Southeast Asia into Indian Ocean region as far as Java in Indonesia.

Hence, what could be discerned from the above is that the Chinese nation building process was tough and much of what we see as the larger territorial size of today's China was a product of expansion and consolidation of territory within China reaching the maximum extent during the later years of the Manchu Dynasty. However, the expansion of territory into modern times has not been shelved totally. One can note that with the proclamation of the People's Republic in October 1949 and the coming to power by the Chinese Communist Party (CCP) under Chairman Mao tse-Tung, these historic features touch upon the behaviour of China vis-a-vis the outside world. The Chinese economic growth and the consequent military modernization programme is one such development that has provided all the more assertiveness to its behaviour. The section below will delve into the details.

China's Military Modernization Programme

The threat of invasions from within and from abroad during the imperial era gave a fillip to securing borders and need for maintaining large army. Challenges to territorial security and defending it were a necessity for the kings who were able to accomplish it through force and constant warfare. In fact, the military history of China tells us that defending the territory was a prerequisite for making advancements in science and technology in the society. In the modern context of China the Japanese invasion of Manchuria in 1931 provided both a nationalistic glue as well as military solidarity to what was a peasant guerrilla force to win over and proclaim People's Republic in 1949 and change into what is called the People's Army or People's Liberation Army (PLA) as the largest standing army in the world.

In fact, modernization of military came along with other programmes launched in 1978-79 by Chairman Deng Xiaoping. Speaking on the occasion of inauguration of the national conference on science in March 1978 Chairman Deng emphasized:

> Unless we modernize our country, raise our scientific and technological level, develop our productive forces and thus strengthen our country and improve the material and cultural life of our people — unless we do all this, our socialist political and economic system cannot be fully consolidated, and there can be no sure guarantee for the country's security...the more our agriculture, industry, national defence and science and technology are modernized, the stronger we will be in the struggle against forces which sabotage socialism, and the more our people will support the socialist system.[18]

From then on, China's economic rise was unstoppable. As was noted by Deng himself, it was one of building "Socialism with Chinese Characteristics". Commensurate with its economic growth and achieving the status of the second largest economic power in the world, the Chinese military spending has also been rising steadily over the years leading to impressive modernization of its military arm particularly since the launch of modernization.

It should be noted that Chinese military modernization programme should be understood as one of fulfilling the goals of Chinese Communist Party, which is to sustain its monopoly on political power. As has been the case historically, there has been excessive reliance on the military to maintain order domestically. And control over the military was also felt essential. It was along this line that military reforms were launched by Deng Xiaoping and continued by the present President Xi Jinping. As will be seen below, President Xi Jinping established full control not only over the party but also on the military.

The success in economic growth has lent the capacity to spend for its military. However, there are inconsistencies in the exact reporting of China's military spending. For example, the official figures released by the Chinese government put the country's 2015 defence budget at $146 billion (currently a little over USD 150 billion), an increase of about 11 percent from the budget of $131 billion in 2014 where as the U.S. Department of Defense (DOD) estimates it to exceed $180 billion while the Stockholm International Peace Research Institute (SIPRI) estimates the overall figure to be at $214 billion. The same is true of the previous year as $165 billion by the US Department of Defence, $180 billion by the International Institute for Strategic Studies (IISS) and SIPRI at $199 billion.[19] Be that as it may, there is certainly an increase in the defence budget as for example from $5.86 billion in 1989 to $143 billion in 2011.[20] The publishing of defence white papers notwithstanding such inconsistencies only reveal the lack of transparency in defence spending.[21] Whatever it is, as compared to its neighbours—Japan, South Korea, Vietnam and other Southeast Asian countries—China's defence budget is by far greater and in fact second only to the U.S. In the case of India, it is four times higher.

New Foreign Policy Postures and the Rationale for Modernisation

The Chinese military modernization programme was part of the larger foreign policy strategy to reorient the military to tackle new types of threats arising in the changed world, and to become an avenue to maintain political power and finally ward off threats particularly arising in the periphery through identifying areas of modernization. Along this line, new foreign policy postures have been visible under the leadership of President Xi Jinping who in 2013 made it clear to guide Chinese foreign policy along more activist lines.[22] In fact, much of what we see in today's China as assertive postures such as the announcement of new East Asia Air Defense Identification Zone (ADIZ), the string of pearls strategy, One Belt One Road (OBOR) strategy and such others were taken during the leadership of President Xi Jinping. Although this sounds benevolent, it also indicates the larger economic and foreign policy strategy of China. All such new activist policies require revamping the Chinese military and expansion in naval power. As will be seen below, in the process of such modernization and new direction in foreign policy China also sought to consolidate its political power.

With regard to modernization three principal areas were focussed: increased military spending, reforming the organizational structure to provide the ability to fight and maintain control over the military and the areas of modernization in the respective services.

As regards the purpose, the Chinese Defense White Paper 2015 mentions that the armed forces strategic tasks among other things are: dealing with military threats and safeguarding the sovereignty and security of China's territorial land, air and sea; to safeguard China's interests in new domains; and to maintain strategic deterrence and carry out nuclear counter attack.[23] The White Paper further elaborates on the strategic doctrine with regard to all three services. Notable among them is the need to reorient the PLA Army (PLAA) from theatre defence to trans-theatre mobility adapting to different regions with the ability for joint operations and for the PLA Navy (PLAN) to shift its focus to protecting open seas by building a combined multi-functional and efficient marine combat force structure with a capability for strategic deterrence and counter attack, maritime manoeuvres, joint operations at sea, comprehensive defence and comprehensive support.[24]

With regard to the structure, the Chinese Communist Party (CPC) continues to maintain the overall leadership of the armed forces through the Chairman of the Central Military Commission (CMC) who is elected by the Chinese National People's Congress (NPC) and with a mandate to supervise the overall work of the armed forces. Decisions on war and peace are made by the NPC when the Standing Committee, which decides not only on war and peace but also general or partial mobilization of the country, was in recess. The Chinese President, as Chairman of the CMC, directs and exercises unified command of the armed forces.[25] Accordingly, President Xi Jinping, as commander of all armed forces, possesses operational command over all of China's armed forces and its branches, military doctrine development, logistics, and civil military relations.

The recent announcement of reforms in the military structure reducing the region-wide command to form five-theatre commands—the Eastern, Western, Northern, Southern and Central—with focus on joint combat[26] is a move undertaken with a twin purpose of continued control of the armed forces by the CPC and adapting the Chinese military to the changes in the external environment. In the words of Jiang Jie, the reforms became imperative in view of the expansion in the missions that China has embarked from one of "safeguarding national security to more global tasks such as overseas peacekeeping and escort missions".[27] Besides, downsizing the army strength to 2 million by 2017 has also been planned.

In the area of modernization of weapons, both qualitative and quantitative improvements have been made. Traditional weaknesses in conventional armaments have been overcome with appropriate training, inclusion of technology and newer weapons capable of handling new areas like counter space, cyber operations and electronic warfare.[28] A good part of the defence budget has been allocated towards procurement of weapons and equipments besides producing a wide variety of weapons including light arms and ammunition, armour, artillery, combat aircraft, conventional and nuclear submarines, tactical missiles and ballistic missiles and such others as part of its huge military-industrial complex.[29] The PLA Air Force (PLAAF) has also been equally modernized on a scale unprecedented in China's history acquiring stealth fighter programs. Besides, China's nuclear arsenal consists of several ICBMs, sea-based deterrents, MRBMs, and deploying several anti-ship ballistic missiles as part of its PLA Navy (PLAN) modernization.[30] In fact, during the military parade celebrating the 70th anniversary of victory in the World War II, China displayed several of its upgraded ballistic missile systems (IRBMs and ICBMs) for the first time demonstrating the strides that Beijing has been making in the area of ballistic missile research and development.[31]

And similarly, sustaining economic growth is vital as part of its core vital interests which to a very large extent has turned towards the sea and dependent on sea. The Chinese sea borne commerce has increased tremendously. It is not the intention of this article to delve on this aspect in detail but suffice here to say that Chinese focus on maritime region has become all the more evident. Much of China's trade and energy today passes through the seas. With threats arising from over the land largely decreased, the attention has now shifted to the seas. Hence, the growing Chinese economic activity stretching far and beyond its national borders into the maritime realm requires protection of sea lanes of communication and secured energy supplies.[32] This has led to the ambitious modernization programme of the PLAN. Accordingly, the PLAN has revitalized its force combatants and naval procurement has shifted from large numbers of low quality to less numbers of highly capable forces with focus on modernizing its submarine forces. Currently, PLAN possesses roughly 60 submarines of all categories and this is expected to grow further. Of particular to note is the possession of Jin Class and Shang Class submarines with an aircraft carrier. Owing to such efforts the gap that existed between PLAN and other modern navies has been narrowed with improved competency as compared to a decade ago.[33]

What can be ascertained from the above is that the modernization programme has indeed yielded results with the help of sound economic basics achieved during the past four decades. When seen from the prism of Chinese expansionism, the military modernization becomes all the more important.

Implications for Regional Security

The Chinese economic growth combined with modernized military and maritime power is reflected in the expansionist behaviour of China with regard to claiming all of SCS islands and questioning the maritime rights of other claimants and the right to free passage of high seas. In fact, the starting point of Chinese expansionism in the SCS is dated to the 1974 sea battle with Vietnamese Navy over Paracel islands from which China dislodged Vietnam.[34] And since then there have been periodic efforts by China to claim one after the other. The 1988 forcible eviction of Vietnam troops from Johnson south reef and seizure of Subi reef from the Philippines and thereafter the seizure of Mischief reef again from the Philippines in 1992 besides seizing the Scarborough shoal in 2012 are evidences depicting continued Chinese expansionist behaviour.[35]

However, efforts to put pressure on China by legal means did not yield results. Rather it only contributed to further militarization. It was the Philippines that took up the case with the Permanent Court of Arbitration on Chinese claims of islands falling within the nine-dash islands.[36] Understandably, the verdict from the Tribunal was not supportive of China and said in clear terms that the Chinese claims were illegal.[37] Such international legal pressures only added fuel to fire as China increased its military activities in the islands.

This shows that China only upped its stance on the conflicting claims by utilizing its modernized military and not relenting to international pressure. This depicts that China is bent on securing economic resources and strategic access without hindrances to protect its vital national interests. It is clear hence that sustaining economic growth has been felt imperative by the Chinese leaders to consolidate political power.

The response from among the Southeast Asian neighbours and other claimants of South China Sea islands is mixed. Interesting to note is the changed position of the Philippines government soon after Tribunal rejected the Chinese claims. In the joint statement released during the 50th Anniversary Summit of the formation of ASEAN in April 2017, the Philippine President Rodrigo Duterte toned down the stand of the organization without any mention of the militarization of South China Sea islands and reference to the verdict of the arbitration tribunal against China was removed.[38]

It is not only the Philippines that has softened its tone but some other ASEAN partners as well dividing the organization's position on the issue. China's close ally Cambodia was the other ASEAN member to oppose inclusion of South China Sea dispute in the communiqué. Be that as it may the point to note is that China succeeded in ensuring that disputes of such kind would be dealt only at the bilateral level than at the multilateral level.

In essence this implies that China has extended its geo-political influence much beyond its immediate shores to include Southeast Asia and considers that part of the world to be within its domination and control. The presence of huge numbers of overseas Chinese in the region provides China with an opportunity to extend its influence. In fact, even during the times of Mao-tse Tung, Southeast Asia was considered to be China's sphere of influence. Chairman Mao hence stated: "We must without fail get hold of Southeast Asia, including South Vietnam, Thailand, Burma, Malaysia, Singapore ... After we get hold of Southeast Asia, the wind from the East will prevail over the wind from the West".[39] Even if this did not become a reality what could be discerned from this is the desire to become a regional hegemon minus the U.S.

However, apprehensive of this development, the U.S. has only increased its military presence both to safeguard its historic allies—Japan and South Korea—and to ensure freedom of navigation and thereby prevent any such Chinese ambitions to fructify. Notable fall out is the strengthening of bilateral military ties between India and the U.S. in the form of joint naval exercises called the Malabar exercise. The exercise cannot be ruled out as routine because this time what was supposed to be bilateral took the form of multilateral exercise with Japan joining as the third member. The July 2017 exercise focused on Anti-submarine warfare and used aircraft carriers for the first time. The exercise was a sign of the military preparedness and coming together of like-minded partners supporting each other at the military to military level.

Conclusions

To conclude, Chinese political history is replete with attempts at consolidation of power and military invasions. With the proclamation of the People's Republic the Chinese political concourse had semblances of historical connections and committed to sustain what was perceived to be Chinese tradition and culture. And it was this via-medium that helped provide the rationality and justification to hold on to political power by post-1949 rulers of China, of course with the help of the military. This strategy worked well for China to help steer the country towards the path of economic development embracing in the process the best practices of the world through participating in the globalized world. The opening up of the economy along with identifying the four major areas of modernization which included the military sphere was well conceived by post-Mao rulers upon the justification of "Socialism with Chinese Characteristics". The benefits of such policies was astounding as Chinese economic growth drove the country to the place of second largest economic power in the world and providing the necessary money power to help modernize its military to a very great extent. The enlarged economy requires both sustenance and unimpeded resources. What has come to stay, in this changed situation, is the continued activist role of China and much talked about hegemonic ambitions and expansionist tendencies will continue to be a time tested phenomenon.

NOTES AND REFERENCES

1. See for an excellent argument along this line, Alastair Iain Johnston, "Is China a Status-Quo Power"? *International Security*, Vol. 27, no. 4, 2003, pp. 5–56.
2. Alastair Iain Johnston, "How New and Assertive is China's New Assertiveness"?, *International Security*, Vol. 37, no. 4, 2013, pp. 7–48.
3. Xiaoyu Chen, "The Nationalist Ideology of the Chinese Military", Occasional Papers reprints series in contemporary Asian Studies, no.3, U.S, 1998, p. 5.
4. John A. Hall, "Nationalisms Classified and Explained", *Daedalus*, Vol. 122 no. 3, USA, p. 1.
5. Xiaoyu Chen, "The Nationalist Ideology of the Chinese Military", Occasional Papers reprints series in contemporary Asian Studies, no.3, U.S, 1998, pp. 5-12. For an interesting elaboration of the different phases of Chinese nationalism, see Jean-Pierre Cabastan, "The Many Facets of Chinese Nationalism", China Perspectives, https://chinaperspectives.revues.org/2793, accessed 7th September 2017 and Maria Hsia Chang & Xiaoyu Chen, "The Nationalist Ideology of Chinese Military", *Journal of Strategic Studies*, vol. 21, no.1. 1998, pp. 44–64.
6. Andrew Scobell, "China and Strategic Culture", Strategic Studies Institute, U.S Army War College, 2002.
7. "Strategic Culture and Grand Strategy in Chinese History", http://www.southasiaanalysis.org/paper32, p.32 accessed 4th September 2017.
8. Johnston, Alastair Iain, "Cultural realism and strategy in Maoist China", The culture of national security: Norms and identity" *World Politics* (1996): pp. 216–68.
9. Ibid, pp. 229-230.
10. Warren I. Cohen, "China's Strategic Culture", *The Atlantic*, https://www.theatlantic.com/magazine/archive/1997/03/chinas-strategic-culture/376815/ March 1997, accessed 4th September 2017.
11. Michael D. Swaine, Ashley J. Tellis, *Interpreting China's Grand Strategy: Past, Present and Future*, RAND Corporation, California, 2000, pp. 24–25.
12. Andrew Scobell, "China and Strategic Culture", Strategic Studies Institute, U.S. Army War College, 2002. p. 3.
13. Michael D. Swaine, Ashley J. Tellis, no.11, pp. 23–24.
14. Andrew Scobell argues deftly in his article opposing the view that depicts Great Wall as China's symbol of defensive strategic culture which cannot be accepted. See for more details on this, Andrew Scobell, "China's Real Strategic Culture: A Great Wall of Imagination", *Contemporary Security Policy*, vol. 35, no. 2, 2014, pp. 211–26.
15. Michael D. Swaine, Ashley J. Tellis, no.11, pp. 24–25.
16. Ibid, p. 26.
17. "China: Political Repression at High Mark", https://www.hrw.org/news/2015/01/29/china-political-repression-high-mark accessed 6th September 2017.
18. Deng Xiaoping, "Speech at the Opening Ceremony of the National Conference on Science, March 18, 1978", *Selected Works of Deng Xiaoping*, vol.11, Beijing: Foreign Languages Press, 1984
19. Centre for Strategic and International Studies, http://chinapower.csis.org/military-spending/ accessed 7th September 2017
20. Binh Nguyen, "The People's Liberation Army Navy: The Motivations Behind Beijing's Naval Modernization".
21. China's defense budget, http://www.globalsecurity.org/military/world/china/budget.htm accessed 8th October 2016.

22. Nien-chung Chang-Liao, "China's New Foreign Policy under Xi Jinping", *Asian Security,* Vol. 12, No. 2, 2016, p. 83.
23. Anthony H. Cordesman and Steve, Colley et. al, "Chinese Strategy and Military Modernization in 2015: A Comparative Analysis" 2015, Centre for Strategic and International Studies, Washington, D.C., p. 3.
24. Ibid.
25. Anthony H. Cordesman and Steve, Colley et. al, "Chinese Strategy and Military Modernization in 2015: A Comparative Analysis" 2015, Centre for Strategic and International Studies, Washington, D.C., p. 3.
26. China revamps military command structure, The Hindu, Feb 3, 2016) http://www.thehindu.com/news/international/china-revamps-military-command-structure/article8185344.ece accessed 26th October 2016.
27. Jiang Jie, "China unveils military revamp", *Global Times,* 2015, http://www.globaltimes.cn/content/955220.shtml accessed 26th October 2016.
28. Annual Report to Congress, Military and Security Developments involving the People's Republic of China, 2015, Office of the Secretary of Defense, Washington D.C.
29. Anthony H. Cordesman and Steve, Colley et. al, no.23, p. 152.
30. Ibid, p. 180.
31. "Chapter I, Part II: China's ballistic missiles", International Institute of Strategic Studies (IISS), The Military Balance 2016, p. 8.
32. James R. Holmes and Toshi Yoshihara, "*Chinese Naval Strategy in the 21st Century: The Turn to Mahan*", Routledge, London, 2008, pp. 2–3 .
33. People's Liberation Army Navy: A Modern Navy with Chinese Characteristics, https://fas.org/irp/agency/oni/pla-navy.pdf, accessed 28th October 2016. Huge differences in number (except for air craft carrier where China has only one) could be seen with India in all aspects of Navy—destroyers, frigates, surface warships, submarines and others. See for details in all services, Comparison of World Military Power Strengths, Global Firepower, http://www.globalfirepower.com/countries-comparisondetail.asp?form= form&country1= India&country2=China, accessed 29th October 2016.
34. Toshi Yoshihara, "The 1974 Paracel Sea Battle", Naval War College, vol. 69, no. 2, Spring 2016, pp. 41–42.
35. "Implications of Chinese Activities in South China Sea and Benham Rise", Institute of Maritime and Ocean Affairs, http://www.imoa.ph/implications-chinese-activities-south-china-sea-benham-rise/ accessed 10th September 2017.
36. Zhiguo Gao and Bing Bing Jia, "The Nine-Dash Line in the South China Sea: History, Status, and Implications", *The American Journal of International Law,* vol. 107, no. 1, 2013, pp. 98–124
37. See for details on the verdict, Press release, Permanent Court of Arbitration, Netherlands, 12 July 2016
38. Raul Dancel, "Asean calls for peaceful end to territorial conflicts", *Straits Times,* Singapore, May 2017, http://www.straitstimes.com/asia/se-asia/asean-calls-for-peaceful-end-to-territorial-conflicts accessed 10th September 2017.
39. V. Suryanarayan, "People's Republic of China's Policy towards Overseas Chinese", South Asia Analysis Group, 2012, http://www.southasiaanalysis.org/node/1044 accessed 10th September 2017.

16

Gunboat Diplomacy in the South China Sea and its Implications for Regional Security

Vignesh R

ABSTRACT

Currently the South China Sea (SCS) has become one of the most militarised maritime regions in the World. China's extensive territorial claims over the SCS contradict the provisions of international maritime laws and its continuous defiance to adhere to the rules of the international legal bodies like the Permanent Court of Arbitration (PCA) has bought the focus of the international community to the SCS. This has resulted in both China and the other claimants of the Southeast Nations most notably Vietnam and the Philippines engaging coercive naval diplomacy against each other to consolidate their territorial claims over the SCS. The military build-up in the SCS is further intensified as extra-regional powers like the USA and Japan who have also involved themselves in the dispute to support Vietnam and the Philippines against China. As the SCS is an adjoining maritime region to the Indian Ocean, India also is closely monitoring the developments in the SCS disputes. The present scenario in the SCS is reminiscent of the nineteenth century when the colonial powers like the US and the European nations intimidated each other in the coasts of Latin America and Africa to consolidate their colonial claims through the aggressive deployment of their naval forces or gunboat diplomacy as it is termed in the field of security studies. This paper will analyse the on-going Gunboat Diplomacy in the SCS between China, Vietnam and Extra-regional powers. This paper will also focus on the implications for the regional stability of Southeast Asia and its impact on India's maritime security.

Definition and History of Gunboat Diplomacy

In the subject of security studies and international relations the term 'gunboat diplomacy' refers to the coercive display of a nation's naval force against a target nation for the purpose of enforcing the former's political will over the target nation. The most prolific writer on the subject of gunboat diplomacy was British naval strategic thinker Sir James Cable who defines the concept as:[1]

> *Gunboat Diplomacy is the use or threat of limited naval force, otherwise than as act of war, in order to secure advantage or to avert loss, either in the furtherance of an international dispute or else against foreign nationals within the territory of the jurisdiction of their own state.*

The essential objective of a successful Gunboat Diplomacy is not to initiate war but to intimidate and force the target nation to concede political will of the nation conducting gunboat diplomacy. It needs to be noted that in Gunboat Diplomacy the navy is used only as an instrument of diplomacy to achieve a political objective. Therefore, gunboat diplomacy is carried out by a nation to achieve political objectives and not military objectives. Hence, without a political objective there can be no gunboat diplomacy.[2] This form of diplomacy belongs to the Realist School of Thought in the international relations that propagates peace through strength. Renowned maritime strategists like Alfred Thayer Mahan and Julian Corbett were proponents of gunboat diplomacy. Historically during the mid-nineteenth century the World witnessed the consolidation of European and American Imperialism throughout the continents of Asia, Africa and Latin America. The sea-routes were the primary mode of connectivity for these imperial powers with their respective colonies. Hence, the naval forces of the imperial powers played a very crucial role in the control of their colonies. As the territorial influence of these imperial powers overlapped each other, confrontation between them started. The navies of the colonial powers soon became instruments of coercive military diplomacy for consolidating their territorial influence and to deter the rival power.

The advent of modern warships only emerged during the beginning of the twentieth century with the construction of HMS Dreadnought by the British Navy in 1906. The HMS Dreadnought can be stated as the forefather of the modern warships as the entire hull of the ships was designed specifically around its armaments. However, the naval ships of the mid-nineteenth century (pre-dreadnought era) were simply characterised by guns or cannons mounted on ordinary ships and boats, which led them to be referred as gunboats. Hence, when these gunboats were used to showcase colonial powers military might for the purpose of intimidating the rival powers and consolidating their territorial claims, it was termed as gunboat diplomacy. Throughout the era when the colonial powers like the European Nations and America dominated the World, gunboat diplomacy was common between them for asserting their sphere of influence in the coasts of Africa, Asia and Latin America. After the First and the Second World Wars, the relevance of Gunboat Diplomacy significantly got reduced due to the advent of nuclear weapons and the nuclear deterrence became the instrument of coercive diplomacy between the United States of America and the Soviet Union during the Cold War.

Relevance of Gunboat Diplomacy in the 21st Century

Following the end of the Cold War and advent of globalisation there has been a paradigm shift in the international geopolitics and global security. Despite the fact that the number of nations that possess nuclear weapons has increased after the end of the Cold War, the relevance of nuclear deterrence as a tool of coercive diplomacy has significantly decreased in comparison to the times of Cold War. As majority of the nations have become democratic and economically interdependent, the threat of using nuclear weapons has become implausible. Also the nations are affected by violence perpetuated by global terrorism against which nuclear deterrence is ineffectual. The global interdependence as a result of globalisation and the rise of Non-State Actors (NSA) are some of the reasons as to why the relevance of nuclear deterrence was reduced significantly except for a few instances like the sabre-rattling of North Korea in the recent times. It is due to these transformations in the geo-politics that nations are again resorting to coercive military diplomacy using conventional weapon platforms including naval vessels.

The rapid increase in population coupled with declining resources is driving developing nations resource hungry. Hence, in the twenty-first century resource conflict would be a principal factor in instigating military confrontation between nations. Water bodies like seas and oceans will be the principal arena where the resource conflict between nations will manifest. The reason for this is the fact that a nation's economy and population is heavily dependent on the seas for a multitude of reasons like fisheries, offshore oil fields and economic shipping.[3] As a result oceanic regions like the Indian Ocean Region (IOR) and the South China Sea (SCS) have become potential regions where armed conflicts between nations are highly probable. The littoral states of both the IOR and the SCS are highly populated developing states which are hugely dependent on oceanic resources for their economic development. Maritime territorial disputes are also more complicated to resolve than the land disputes due to the fact that access to high seas are considered to be free to all nations according to the provisions laid out by the United Nations Convention on the Law of the Sea (UNCLOS) namely:[4]

1. Freedom of Transit
2. Freedom of the High Seas
3. International Servitudes
4. Geographic Equality

These provisions enable all nations the free access to high seas for commercial shipping, however, dispute arises when a particular nation restricts the other nation's access to high seas in a particular maritime region by claiming certain islands and atolls in the region as its own. When a nation makes such territorial claims citing some historic assumptions, it leads to a complicated maritime dispute. This is the fundamental cause of the on-going SCS dispute where China is claiming the entire SCS as its own maritime territory on the basis of its self-proclaimed "nine-dash line" concept and ignoring the provisions of UNCLOS on maritime territorial claim. To assert its claim over the SCS, China has deployed its naval forces to intimidate the Southeast Asian nations like Vietnam and the Philippines to whom areas of the SCS legitimately belong in accordance with the provisions of the UNCLOS. This has resulted in intense militarisation of the SCS and escalating tensions in Southeast Asia and its neighbouring regions.

The SCS Dispute: A Case Study of Modern Gunboat Diplomacy

The on-going maritime dispute in the SCS is the most appropriate case study for understanding relevance of gunboat diplomacy in the twenty-first century.

The geo-strategic location of the SCS is one of the main reasons for why China seeks to bring the entire maritime area under their influence as it is a semi-enclosed sea of three and half a million square kilometres which extends from the eastern end of the Singapore Strait to the Taiwan Strait. The littoral states of the SCS are Indonesia, Malaysia, Brunei, the Philippines, Vietnam, China and Taiwan. The SCS is extremely vital to international shipping because one-third of the world's shipping transits the sea on the route between Europe and the Middle East to East Asia. The SCS also has rich fisheries resources and there are potentially huge oil and gas reserves beneath its seabed.[5] The SCS dispute is a very complicated maritime dispute as multiple nations are involved in it. The developments in the SCS dispute will have a far reaching impact on South and South East Asia's geo-political stability and security to which India's national security and interest are invariably linked. The SCS dispute has developed from a minor regional dispute in the second half of the twentieth century to a major international maritime dispute that involves various extra-regional actors. This has eventually resulted in the intensive militarisation of the region by the different belligerents of the dispute.

Since China is a large and economically powerful nation, it is able to project an aggressive naval posture and resort to gunboat diplomacy in the region in support of its territorial claims against the ASEAN nations which are geographically small and militarily weaker compared to China. The extra-regional parties to the dispute like the US and Japan are invariably concerned with the safety of the freedom of navigation in the SCS as it is very vital for their shipping and economic interest in the region. The US and Japan are aware of the fact that the ASEAN nations alone cannot counter the aggressive Chinese claims in the region and hence they have decided to support the ASEAN nations directly. The ASEAN nations also realised that China's influence in the region can only be counter-balanced by the involvement of India and hence nations like Vietnam have increased their military cooperation with India exponentially. This has made India indirectly involved in the SCS dispute. But, just like in the Cold War fearing mass destruction that would be caused by direct confrontation between them, the nations would rather engage in coercive military diplomacy or gunboat diplomacy against each other in the SCS dispute. Apart from the political disputes in the SCS, this paper will specifically focus on the patterns of naval confrontation among the disputed parties of the SCS in order to study and understand the modern gunboat diplomacy. Sir James Cable in his book, *Gunboat Diplomacy 1919-1979:*

Political Applications of Limited Naval, has laid out four principal features of gunboat diplomacy which are as follows:

1. Definitive Force
2. Purposeful Force
3. Catalytic Force
4. Expressive Force

For understanding gunboat diplomacy in the SCS, the patterns of naval contestations between the disputed parties should not be viewed as mere random confrontations. Rather the aggressive conduct must be carefully analysed in accordance with the four principal features of gunboat diplomacy laid out by James Cable. The various moves made by the Chinese navy and the counter moves made by the combined navies of the US and Vietnam must be classified into the four features of gunboat diplomacy.

Definitive Force

According to James Cable definitive force refers to the use of a limited naval force for projecting a credible threat to the target nation so that it concedes the demands of the nation resorting to gunboat diplomacy.[6] A nation deploys its warships in a disputed maritime region where it has staked its claims by conducting aggressive naval patrolling or drills for the purpose of sending a strong message to the other claimant state of the disputed maritime region. An example of definitive force used in the SCS dispute is when China conducts drills in the disputed South China Sea by deploying its first aircraft carrier along with number of destroyers in January 2017.[7] China's decision to deploy its first aircraft carrier in the SCS came just months after the verdict given by the Permanent Court of Arbitration (PCA) on the SCS dispute where it invalidated China's claim over SCS in favour of the Philippines. However, China rejected the PCA verdict and continued to stake its claim over the SCS. Hence, China's showcase of definitive force in the SCS through the deployment of aircraft carrier is a symbolic defiance of the PCA verdict and reassertion of its expansive territorial claims in the region by ignoring the international law.

Purposeful Force

In this feature of gunboat diplomacy a limited and selective naval force is employed purposefully in order to change the policy or the character of the target nation whose relationship to the assailant nation is hostile.[8] In the case of purposeful force a nation employs its naval assets in response to the gunboat diplomacy carried out by the other nation. In purposeful force, naval assets that are employed are specifically chosen to counter the opponent's naval assets. For example, if the opponent employs it's naval carriers for conducting gunboat diplomacy, then as a response naval carriers would be deployed to confront them. In February 2017, after Donald Trump assumed office he deployed American aircraft-carrier strike group led by USS Carl Vinson to conduct naval and air operations in the South China Sea for challenging Beijing's expansive maritime claims in the region.[9] It should be noted that this is an example of purposeful force as the American Carrier battle group (CBR) was deployed in response to China's deployment of its aircraft carrier in the region in the month of January. The USA had employed purposeful force in this case in an attempt to force China to cease its aggressive deployment of its naval forces in the SCS for staking territorial claims in the maritime region. The US's deployment of CBR in the SCS sent a strong message to China that the smaller Southeast Asian states have America's backing.

Catalytic Force

James Cable explains Catalytic force as the readiness and positioning of the naval forces for a crisis that has not yet started or is expected to start. If a crisis arises that may cause a potential threat to any particular nation then in that case the nation that feels threatened from the impending crisis can preemptively deploy limited naval force to deter the potential opponent.[10] The catalytic force is rather a precautionary or cautious approach of deploying the naval force when a crisis is suspected to arise. On March 2017 Japan dispatched its largest warship on a three-month tour through the South China Sea in its biggest show of naval force in the region since World War II. Japan's Izumo helicopter carrier initiated naval exercise with the American Navy in the disputed region of SCS.[11] Here Japan's action of deploying its helicopter carrier in the SCS is due to the fact that Japan is insecure with the Chinese actions in the region. Japan has a vast amount of its economic shipping that transit through the SCS. Japan's feels threatened that the aggressive Chinese claims in the SCS would hinder the secure transit of its shipping. Moreover, Japan already has a longstanding dispute with China in the East China Sea with regards to the Senkaku Islands. Hence, Japan had decided to employ catalytic force in the SCS against China to assert its position in the disputed maritime region.

Expressive Force

Under expressive force naval vessels are employed to emphasise attitudes, to lend credibility to otherwise unconvincing statements. Unlike the previous features of gunboat diplomacy which are symbolic, vague and uncertain, the expressive force is more focused, decisive and not a mere flag showing by a nation's naval forces.[12] In expressive force, a nation's military forces conduct activities like conducting live fire drills or seizing and sabotaging the assets of the opponent. In July 2017, the Chinese naval ships belonging to the SCS fleet which are responsible for the China's Navy operations in the disputed region engaged in live fire drills in a naval exercise.[13] This exercise is viewed by many observers as directed towards China's opponents in the SCS dispute. In another important incident that happened in December 2016 the Chinese Navy seized an American underwater drone in front of the American ship that launched it. This incident caused a diplomatic furore between the USA and China with the American Government condemning the Chinese actions and demanded the immediate return of the American drone.[14] Expressive force is the most overt display of coercion with the use of limited naval power against another nation without actually engaging in a direct conflict.

Overall, these four types of gunboat diplomacy and its examples in the ongoing SCS dispute represent the action-reaction model of naval confrontation between the navies of China, the US, Japan and the Southeast Asian states. What is certain that is this pattern of naval confrontation will continue in the SCS without any actual escalation to overt conflict due to the mutual fear among the disputed parties of enormous costs that would be involved in waging modern warfare.

Implications of Gunboat Diplomacy in the SCS

This raging gunboat diplomacy in the SCS will certainly have a long-standing impact on the regional stability of Southeast Asia. This paper has identified four major implications as the result of the gunboat diplomacy in the SCS which are enumerated follows:

1. **Naval Arms Race:** The gunboat diplomacy in the SCS will lead to the increasing military spending among the littoral nations of the South China Sea especially the smaller nations like Vietnam and the Philippines which are essentially developing nations. The maritime dispute in the SCS has resulted in expensive naval arms race that is

driving the Southeast nations to divert their national income more towards military funding rather towards social and infrastructural development.

2. **Threat to Freedom of Navigation:** As far as commercial shipping is concerned, in the South and South East Asian Region the SCS acts as the transits route for massive amounts of economic cargo transported through this region. The multilateral gunboat diplomacy in the SCS will certainly cause threat to the freedom of navigation in the region which will hamper the secure transit of economic shipping of various nations. As the region consists of developing nations, they heavily rely on the economic and oil shipping to fuel their growing economy and if shipping gets affected then the entire economy of Southeast Asia would suffer.
3. **Threat to Regional Stability and Cooperation:** The Association of Southeast Asian Nations (ASEAN) is an effective regional grouping and has achieved significant success in the regional economic and political development. However, the intensification of the SCS dispute and the ensuing gunboat diplomacy will certainly affect the regional stability and cooperation. The involvement of extra-regional actors in SCS's gunboat diplomacy has further aggravated the instability in the region and undermines an amicable regional solution for the SCS problem which is essentially a regional territorial dispute.
4. **Threat to the Fragile Eco-System of the SCS:** The marine ecosystem of SCS is very fragile due to the coral reefs. However, China's construction activities that include the construction of artificial islands and dredging activities to set up refuelling stations for its warships is creating enormous environmental damage to the marine ecosystem of the SCS which will seriously affect the fisheries resources in the region.

Importance of Indian Gunboat Diplomacy in the SCS

In the recent times China has been conducting gunboat diplomacy in the IOR against India. In 2013, two Chinese Naval submarines had docked in the China built Hambantota port in Sri Lanka that caused concern among the Indian Strategic community. Most recently, the Chinese Navy had increased its naval presence in the IOR as a response to the recent impasse between

India and China over the Dolkam tri-junction in Bhutan. India had been subjected to gunboat diplomacy in the past such as during the 1971 India-Pakistan War when the US dispatched its Seventh Carrier fleet in the Bay of Bengal in support of its ally, Pakistan, and to intimidate India. But, India was able to thwart the American gunboat diplomacy with the support the erstwhile Soviet Union. Today India has become the regional power and is at a transition stage of becoming a global power. Therefore India is in the process of rapid naval modernisation that includes the induction of two additional aircraft carriers within the next ten years along with one carrier already in service. This would make the Indian Navy a blue water navy and it will be capable of deterring any gunboat diplomacy on its own. Apart from this, India would able to project its own gunboat diplomacy to secure its national interests. There are several reasons for the SCS is vital for India's maritime security. This paper has identified some major factors on how the on-going gunboat diplomacy in the SCS is important for India's maritime security and they are enumerated as follows:

- An opportunity to containing China within the SCS to restrict its Navy's ingress into the IOR.
- To adhere to commitments of India's 'Act East Policy' and to assist the ASEAN in defending their maritime sovereignty.
- The protection of the free shipping in the SCS is also essential for India's economy as large volumes of Indian goods are exported to the region and simultaneously large amount of goods are imported into India from Southeast Asia.

Conclusion

Overall, the SCS dispute can only be expected to further intensify due to China's blunt rejection of the PCA verdict. This would lead to increasing military buildup in the region that would lead to constant gunboat diplomacy carried out by China, the US, Japan, Vietnam, Philippines and other Southeast Asian Nations. China's rejection of the PCA verdict signifies the triumph of realpolitik over institutionalism where nations resort to military forces and hard diplomacy to resolve their disputes. This has eventually led the disputed parties of the SCS to extensively use their navy for coercive naval diplomacy or gunboat diplomacy. There is also high probability that the gunboat diplomacy in the SCS can even extend to the IOR which is strategically very important. Hence, any gunboat diplomacy in the IOR would directly threaten India's maritime security as a result of which India is closely monitoring the developments in the SCS. As both India and China are expected to operate multiple aircraft carriers by 2025, gunboat diplomacy between the Indian and the Chinese Navies will be a regular affair in the near future. Many strategic thinkers have stated that gunboat diplomacy is an outdated concept and has no relevance in the twenty-first century. However, the SCS dispute validates the relevance of gunboat diplomacy in a contemporary maritime dispute and its impact in the modern geo-politics.

NOTES AND REFERENCES

1. Cable, James (1981), "Gunboat Diplomacy 1919-1979: Political Applications of Limited Naval Force", Basingstoke: Palgrave Macmillan, p. 39.
2. Gosh, P.K. (2008), *Revisiting gunboat diplomacy: An instrument of threat or use of limited naval force*, Abington: Taylor & Francis, p. 2.
3. United States Institute of Peace (2007), *Natural Resources, Conflict and Conflict Resolution*, Washington DC: United States Institute of Peace, p. 8.
4. United Nations (1994), *United Nations Convention on Law of the Sea*, New York: United Nations, p. 64.
5. Beckman, Robert (2012), *Geopolitics, International Law and the South China Sea*, Tokyo: University of Tokyo, p. 2.
6. Cable, James (1981), "Gunboat Diplomacy 1919-1979: Political Applications of Limited Naval Force", Basingstoke: Palgrave Macmillan, p. 41.
7. Reuters (2016), "China's aircraft carrier to drill in Western Pacific", *The Reuters*, Retrieved from http://www.reuters.com/article/us-china-defence/chinas-aircraft-carrier-to-drill-in-western-pacific-idUSKBN14E025?il=0.
8. Cable, James (1981), "Gunboat Diplomacy 1919-1979: Political Applications of Limited Naval Force", Basingstoke: Palgrave Macmillan, p. 58.
9. Panda, Ankit (2017). "US Carrier Strike Group Arrives in the South China Sea", *The Diplomat*, Retrieved from http://thediplomat.com/2017/02/us-carrier-strike-group-arrives-in-the-south-china-sea/.
10. Cable, James (1981), "Gunboat Diplomacy 1919-1979: Political Applications of Limited Naval Force", Basingstoke: Palgrave Macmillan, p. 46.
11. Aljazeera (2017), "South China Sea: Japan to Deploy its Largest Warship", *Al Jazeera*, Retrieved from http://www.aljazeera.com/news/2017/03/south-china-sea-japan-deploy-largest-warship-170313130210567.html
12. Cable, James (1981), "Gunboat Diplomacy 1919-1979: Political Applications of Limited Naval Force", Basingstoke: Palgrave Macmillan, p. 62.
13. Gady, Franz Stefan (2017), "Chinese Navy Conducts Live-Fire Drill in Mediterranean Sea", *The Diplomat*, Retrieved from http://thediplomat.com/2017/07/chinese-navy-conducts-live-fire-drill-in-mediterranean-sea/.
14. Hunt, Katie & Jiang, Steven (2016), "China: Seized underwater drone 'tip of the iceberg' when it comes to US Surveillance", *The CNN*, Retrieved from http://edition.cnn.com/2016/12/18/politics/china-us-underwater-vehicle-south-china-sea/index.html

REFERENCES

Aljazeera (2017), "South China Sea: Japan to Deploy its Largest Warship", *Al Jazeera*. Retrieved from http://www.aljazeera.com/news/2017/03/south-china-sea-japan-deploy-largest-warship-170313130210567.html.

Beckman, Robert (2012), *Geopolitics, International Law and the South China Sea*, Tokyo: University of Tokyo.

Cable, James (1981), "Gunboat Diplomacy 1919-1979: Political Applications of Limited Naval Force", Basingstoke: Palgrave Macmillan.

Gady, Franz Stefan (2017), "Chinese Navy Conducts Live-Fire Drill in Mediterranean Sea", *The Diplomat*, Retrieved from http://thediplomat.com/2017/07/chinese-navy-conducts-live-fire-drill-in-mediterranean-sea/.

Gosh, P.K. (2008), *Revisiting gunboat diplomacy: An instrument of threat or use of limited naval force*, Abington: Taylor & Francis.

Hunt, Katie & Jiang, Steven (2016), "China: Seized underwater drone 'tip of the iceberg' when it comes to US Surveillance:, *The CNN*, Retrieved from http://edition.cnn.com/2016/12/18/politics/china-us-underwater-vehicle-south-china-sea/index.html.

Panda, Ankit (2017), "US Carrier Strike Group Arrives in the South China Sea", *The Diplomat*, Retrieved from http://thediplomat.com/2017/02/us-carrier-strike-group-arrives-in-the-south-china-sea/.

Reuters (2016), "China's aircraft carrier to drill in Western Pacific", *The Reuters*, Retrieved from http://www.reuters.com/article/us-china-defence/chinas-aircraft-carrier-to-drill-in-western-pacific-idUSKBN14E025?il=0.

United Nations (1994), *United Nations Convention on Law of the Sea*, New York: United Nations.

United States Institute of Peace (2007), *Natural Resources, Conflict and Conflict Resolution*. Washington DC: United States Institute of Peace.

17

Changing Contours of the US Foreign Policy and the South China Sea

Ramesh Babu V

ABSTRACT

As the world's largest trading nation, China has a deep vested interest in ensuring the trade routes in the South China Sea remain open, and Beijing has no interest in military conflict with regional powers. Although China's South China Sea policy is inconsistent with some of the norms and institutions of the rules-based liberal world order, Beijing does not seek to undermine this order as a whole and remains supportive of key elements of the international system. To avoid needlessly entangling itself in the South China Sea dispute, the United States should not support the territorial claims of any state and should make clear that the U.S.-Philippine Mutual Defense Treaty does not apply to disputed territory and waters claimed by the Philippines. In fact, the United States should encourage claimant states to agree on de facto jurisdiction over disputed areas and to jointly exploit resources while more permanent resolutions are negotiated. Washington should also understand that ratifying the United Nations Convention on the Law of the Sea will have little effect on the South China Sea dispute.

Introduction

No relationship will be as important to the twenty-first century as the one between the United States, the world's great power, and China, the world's rising power. China's development is directly transforming the lives of one-fifth of the world's population, and is otherwise influencing billions more.

The overall message is that while the United States should not turn a blind eye to the economic, political, and security challenges posed by China's rise and should be clear that any aggressive behaviour on China's part would be met with strong opposition, U.S. strategy toward China must focus on creating and taking advantage of opportunities to build on common interests in the region and as regards a number of global concerns.

Every Chinese move in disputed maritime territories is analysed as though it's an existential threat to America's lifelines. There's no doubt that China's growing assertiveness in waters far from its own coasts has sparked great angst in the region. The "nine-dash line" that Beijing pushes as the basis of its claims includes virtually the whole of the South China Sea, including areas claimed by its neighbours, like Vietnam and the Philippines.[1]

The importance of the sea lanes in the South China Sea through which merchandise goods worth trillions of dollars pass each year cannot be overstated. But those sea lanes have never been under serious threat (in peacetime), as the United States and China share an economic interest in the uninterrupted flow of commerce. Historically, U.S. national security interests in the South China Sea (SCS) have been limited and consistent since the first clipper ship, the *Empress of China*, sailed to Canton (now Guangzhou) in 1784. The United States has always sought freedom of navigation which today includes air, space and commercial access in Asia. Freedom of navigation does reflect a vital interest that the United States can and should defend, unilaterally, if necessary. To that end, U.S. Navy exercises in the SCS should be stepped up and coordinated with allies and strategic partners to underscore continuing U.S. presence and commitment. The Trump administration's assertive naval operation on August 10, 2017, near the Chinese-controlled islet Mischief Reef was a good example of such U.S. resolve and continuing presence. But, China's protest notwithstanding, ultimately, such tactics can have only a marginal effect on China's own actions. China is willing and able to go much further than the United States.

Importance of South China Sea

An estimated $5.3 trillion worth of trade passes through the SCS each year. That number accounts for a significant portion of the manufactured products and raw materials entering and leaving East Asia's powerhouse economies of China, Japan, South Korea, and Taiwan. The downstream connections of those flows of goods and raw materials to the economies of Oceania, Southeast and South Asia, Africa, the Middle East, and Europe make the SCS an important transit point for global trade. The SCS dispute is one of the globe's most complex and volatile geopolitical flashpoints. Involving a patchwork of overlapping territorial and maritime claims by China, Taiwan, Vietnam, the Philippines, Malaysia, Brunei, and Indonesia, the dispute centres on numerous atolls and islands and vast tracts of sea, encompassed within China's so-called Nine-Dash Line. In addition to issues of territorial sovereignty, maritime jurisdiction, resource access, and shipping routes, the SCS dispute is driven by nationalist sentiment. This conflict rouses widespread and sometimes violent public feelings in China, Vietnam, and the Philippines, in particular, and is regularly used by leaders in claimant states to mobilize political support. Given the value of this trade corridor for U.S. allies and partners like Japan, South Korea, Taiwan, Thailand, the Philippines, Singapore, and Australia, analysts also claim that China's SCS policy poses a severe potential threat to the economic health of the United States' Asian allies and partners. Such fears about the threat of China's SCS policy to global trade do not bear scrutiny.[2] The SCS dispute looms large as a diplomatic and security challenge for the United States. Claimant states include U.S. allies and partners like the Philippines and Malaysia, as well as increasingly close friends like Vietnam. It also involves China—the United States' largest trading partner and the only likely military peer competitor of the United States in the coming decades. The SCS conflict has already strained ties between Southeast Asian claimant states and China and has become a key point of diplomatic and strategic tension between China and the United States.[3] Although the SCS dispute involves five Southeast Asian states, senior U.S. officials like former and current secretaries of state John Kerry and Rex Tillerson focus on China's SCS policy as the primary source of instability and tension. Unlike the smaller claims made by the five Southeast Asian states to portions of the SCS contiguous to their coasts, China seeks to assert territorial sovereignty and maritime jurisdiction over the bulk of the SCS between roughly 62 per cent and 90 per cent of this sea. The territorial and maritime demands of the combined five Southeast Asian contestants and China stretch more than 800 nautical miles from the Chinese island province of Hainan and encompass islands, rocks, reefs, and waters claimed by Vietnam, the Philippines, Malaysia, Brunei, and Indonesia.

China's forceful declarations to so-called inviolable historic rights over the SCS are matched by regular forced evictions of fishing vessels from neighbouring states and numerous cases of naval brinkmanship with Southeast Asian states and non claimant states like the United States and Australia. By dredging up sand onto seven shallow underwater features in the Spratly Islands, China created more than 3,200 acres of territory between 2013 and 2015. That amounts to nearly 17 times more land creation in 2 years than all of the other claimant states combined in the past 40 years. With China able to station an expanding arsenal of missiles, fighter jets, and even strategic bombers on its newly created artificial islands, those constructions could eventually serve a fleet of "unsinkable aircraft carriers." At the same time, China has failed to justify its territorial and maritime claims in a manner consistent with the United Nations Convention on the Law of the Sea (UNCLOS), and refuses to recognize the adverse award against it rendered on July 12, 2016, by the Arbitral Tribunal assembled at the Permanent Court of Arbitration under the auspices of UNCLOS, Regional and Global Security.[4]

China's Ambitions and US Role in South China Sea

People in the region watching Beijing stake claims to disputed South China Sea rocks and shoals have no illusions that China is being deterred by the United States. They have come to understand the reality of an asymmetry of respective Chinese and U.S. geopolitical interests. Beijing's interest in the South China Sea is political and strategic in nature. Island building is aimed at asserting sovereignty to reverse the "century of humiliation," which has become a key to legitimacy for the Chinese Communist Party. Strategically, China is pushing out its defence perimeter and enhancing China's maritime sway in the region. But for the United States, the South China Sea is just one part of the larger, complex U.S.-China relationship. Former President Barack Obama's policy priorities for China were the Paris climate change accords and the Iran nuclear deal; Donald Trump's policy priorities for China are North Korea and trade. Look no further than Secretary of State Rex Tillerson's appearance at meeting of the ASEAN Regional Forum: Though the meeting was held one year after an international tribunal at The Hague rejected all of China's territorial claims, the issue that dominated the discussions was North Korea. The lingering disputes in the South China Sea were a second-order matter, and in the chairman's statement only "some member states" expressed "concerns" regarding the South China Sea.[5]

China knows that the Trump administration lacks a comprehensive strategy toward the Asia-Pacific region. Whatever its shortcomings in terms of implementation, the Obama administration's "pivot to Asia" did conceptually integrate the diplomatic, military, and economic elements of a comprehensive regional strategy. In contrast, the present administration's rejection of the hard-fought Trans-Pacific Partnership was a strategic shock and a blow to U.S. credibility. That has left Chinese projects like the Belt and Road Initiative and the Asian Infrastructure Investment Bank unchallenged. Like the global financial crisis of 2008, perceived U.S. weakness has emboldened China. But even in the face of the Obama administration's cautions against unilateral change and support for a rules-based international order, Beijing disregarded U.S. diplomacy, trashed The Hague tribunal's ruling against its sovereignty claims in the South China Sea, and effectively changed the status quo. The Chinese bet, correctly, that, as long as shipping lanes are not threatened, the United States will not risk war with a nuclear weapons state over rocks and reefs to which it has no claims, just to defend the U.N. Convention on the Law of the Sea (UNCLOS), which it won't ever ratify. Washington's absence from the governance councils at UNCLOS makes it easier for Beijing to push its largely bogus interpretations of the treaty.[6]

The president-elect tweeted, in reference to China's construction of artificial islands for military purposes in the South China Sea: "Did China ask for our permission?" Still, it is premature to conclude that Trump will really take a harder line on China than the Obama administration has over the South China Sea issue. The tweet may simply have been Trump firing back at China for criticizing his telephone conversation with Taiwanese President Tsai Ing-wen two days earlier. Also, China's seizure of a U.S. Navy's underwater drone in the South China Sea later that month was not a sufficient test of Trump's South China Policy, although he criticized the incident on Twitter. From the very beginning of his presidential campaign, Trump has viewed China not through a national security lens, but primarily as an economic competitor and as a challenge. He sees China as a currency manipulator that is taking jobs and wealth away from Americans through an increasing trade deficit. He also accuses China of stealing industrial secrets through cyber attacks and thinks that if the U.S. eliminates the trade deficit with China and applies economic pressure, China will stop reclaiming reefs in the South China Sea.

Yet, Trump simultaneously does not appear to be a believer in the Thucydides trap (which posits that confrontation between an emerging power and an existing power is inevitable). He has said that he would aim for peaceful coexistence with China and seek to build relations based on common interests. This is not incompatible with the "new type of major country relations" which China has been calling for under President Xi Jinping. The top foreign policy priority for the Trump administration will be containing Islamic extremists such as the Islamic State. Trump has said he will significantly expand U.S. military power, increasing the Army's numbers from 490,000 to 540,000, fighter jets from 1,113 to at least 1,200, Marines from 23 battalions to 36 battalions, and surface vessels and submarines in the U.S. Navy from 276 to 350.[7]

It is not yet clear what policy the Trump administration will pursue with respect to the South China Sea and what role this expanded military force will play in the region. The Chinese leadership is perhaps very keen to know. China has a history of testing the crisis response capabilities of incoming U.S. administrations. In April 2001, soon after the inauguration of the administration of George W. Bush, a Chinese fighter jet collided with a U.S. EP-3 reconnaissance airplane over international waters off Hainan Island, which severely strained relations. At that time, China demanded an apology from the United States and succeeded in drawing an expression of regret from the Bush administration. In March 2009, soon after Barack Obama had taken over the presidency, Chinese warships, government-owned vessels and fishing vessels obstructed the navigation of USNS *Impeccable*, an ocean surveillance ship, in the South China Sea. The Obama administration responded by dispatching the guided missile destroyer USS *Chung-Hoon* to protect the *Impeccable*.

Since China saw its claims to the South China Sea voted down by the International Court of Arbitration based on the U.N. Convention of the Law of the Sea, Beijing has ostensibly been refraining from provocative acts. But it has continued to build facilities on the artificial islands it has created. China chose the East China Sea, rather than the South China Sea, to test the Trump administration and the strength of the U.S.-Japan alliance. This would no doubt please the Philippines President Rodrigo Duterte, who has been keen to make overtures to China. Alternatively, Beijing may target Taiwan, to punish Tsai for her phone call with Trump in addition to the recent demonstration deployment of its aircraft carrier in the South China Sea.[8]

Chinese Threat

China has a history of using force to advance its territorial and maritime claims in the SCS, including two brief naval clashes with Vietnam in 1974 and 1988 that saw China gain control of disputed maritime features in the Paracel and Spratly Islands, respectively. More recently, China seized Mischief Reef in 1994 and Scarborough Shoal in 2012, each located within 135 nautical miles of the Philippine territory, while coercive tactics against competing claimant states have increased in frequency since 2008. Recent years have also witnessed a series of confrontations between Chinese vessels and the U.S. Navy. Tensions remain high in the wake of the long-standing attempted Chinese naval blockade of the Philippine marines stationed on Second Thomas Shoal, the 2014 deployment of a Chinese oil platform approximately 120 nautical miles off the Vietnamese coast, and China's interdiction of Philippine fishermen entering Scarborough Shoal which satellite imagery suggests may be on-going despite a tentative rapprochement between Manila and Beijing. Although the likelihood of large-scale military conflict between China and one or more Southeast Asian claimant states is low, the risk of accidents and small-scale skirmishes escalating to military confrontation remains.[9]

A Sino-Philippine naval skirmish in turn poses the real though small, risk of igniting a military conflict involving major Asia Pacific powers. With the U.S.-Philippine Mutual Defense Treaty calling on the United States to "act to meet the common dangers" of any "armed attack" on the Philippine "armed forces, public vessels or aircraft in the Pacific," the United States is likely to support the Philippines in the event of a Sino-Philippine naval clash. Such a Sino-Philippine military conflict could also draw in U.S.-allied regional actors, such as Japan, South Korea, Australia, and Thailand. The risk of the SCS dispute morphing into a major military conflict increased with the Obama administration's "pivot" to Asia. U.S. officials displayed greater willingness to criticize and challenge China's territorial and maritime claims and actions in the SCS. Among other initiatives, the United States stepped up its diplomatic opposition to China's SCS policy, reaffirmed its commitment to resolving the SCS dispute in accordance with international law, and sought to bolster the maritime surveillance and defence capabilities of Southeast Asian claimant states. The Trump administration has given mixed signals on the SCS, ranging from the critical but measured statements from Secretary of State Tillerson to the former White House chief strategist Steve Bannon's provocative comment before the 2016 presidential election that the United States will go to "war in the South China Sea in five to 10 years".[10]

The economic dimension of the U.S. "pivot" to Asia might have ended with the Trump administration's withdrawal from the Trans-Pacific Partnership trade pact, and yet the harder-edged security aspects of the "pivot" look likely to live on in the SCS. Notwithstanding China's record of aggression in the SCS, Beijing has thus far been careful to use force only in circumstances where the risk to regional and global security is low. Even China's most aggressive actions in the SCS its brief naval clashes with Vietnam in January 1974 in the Paracel Islands and in March 1988 in the Spratly Islands were extremely unlikely to spark a larger military conflict. China may be willing to resort to military aggression in the SCS, but it has been willing to do so only against weak or isolated adversaries and when the risk of sparking a large-scale conflict is low. China's SCS policy continues to exhibit pragmatism and strategic opportunism. Since the reinvigorated U.S. effort to manage the SCS dispute in the wake of the Obama administration's "pivot" to Asia, China's SCS policy has included a suite of what might be described as "soft" forms of coercion. Featuring prominently are such tactics as:

- the creation or expansion of disputed maritime features,
- the recalibration of China's military command structure to place greater strategic emphasis on China's territorial and maritime claims in the SCS, and
- an increased tempo of naval patrols and surveillance by the maritime militias (i.e., irregular Chinese navy).[11]

Through its maritime militias, fishermen, and coast guard, China admittedly continues to deploy force, including evicting fishermen from competing claimant states and blockading the Philippine marines stationed on Second Thomas Shoal. However, in addition to keeping such uses of force at relatively low levels, China's overall SCS policy is weighted toward softer forms of coercion. Rather than, for example, launching naval assaults on Philippine, Vietnamese, or Malaysian outposts in disputed waters, China will probably continue its pragmatic and strategically opportunistic SCS policy. That policy might include tactics such as expanding the size and sophistication of its artificial islands and taking control of and developing the more than 200 maritime features which the Chinese military officials have said are still unoccupied in the SCS. Such tactics are likely to aggravate regional tensions.

Yet, although they can be expected to elicit objections internationally, these forms of soft coercion are unlikely to provoke military conflict. Soft coercion will, therefore, probably allow China to slowly but surely consolidate and expand its area of 'de facto' control over the SCS without endangering regional and global security. Of course, the risk of escalation cannot be ruled out. The uptick in China's island-building activities in the SCS has coincided with its efforts to integrate Chinese-controlled maritime features into China's defence architecture and power projection capabilities.

The United States and its Asian allies and partners should, therefore, remain alert to changes in behaviour and possible threats to regional and global security. Nevertheless, notwithstanding a dramatic and unexpected change in prevailing conditions, such threats seem unlikely to emerge in the short to medium term. For now, China can be expected to carefully calibrate its tactics in the SCS to avoid the kind of escalation that risks culminating in a military conflict with a neighbour or great power.[12]

China and International Court of Law

China has sought to exploit hydrocarbon and fishery resources over which Vietnam, the Philippines, Malaysia, Brunei, and Indonesia are likely to have sole jurisdiction because of the location of these resources within their exclusive economic zones (EEZs) that extend up to 200 nautical miles from their coasts. In 2016, China also rejected arbitration of the SCS dispute, immediately dismissing the adverse award against it by the UNCLOS Arbitral Tribunal. The Arbitral Tribunal which was approached by the Philippines considered the legality of China's Nine-Dash Line, the status of numerous SCS maritime features, Chinese island construction within the Philippine EEZ, and resource exploitation in disputed waters, among other issues. In addition to numerous other adverse findings against China, the Arbitral Tribunal concluded that "there was no legal basis for China to claim historic rights to resources within the sea areas falling within the 'Nine-Dash Line,'" and that "China had violated the Philippines' sovereign rights in its EEZ." Meanwhile, senior Chinese officials such as former foreign minister Yang Jiechi have implicitly endorsed the illiberal doctrine that "might makes right" in the SCS and indicated that Southeast Asian states should adopt a deferential position vis-à-vis China[13]. In fact, although China judges that it's national interest is best served by circumventing international institutions and norms in a particular geographic region (the SCS) and with respect to a particular conflict (the SCS dispute), China generally supports the existing order elsewhere. Rightly or wrongly, Beijing simply considers disputed islands in the SCS to be an "integral part of Chinese territory". Unsurprisingly, China will not allow its general support for the rules-based liberal world order to impede its efforts to ensure that the SCS becomes Chinese "blue national territory". True, Beijing has also long violated the political and individual rights of its citizens and sought to aid Chinese companies with industrial espionage and protectionist measures.[14]

Freedom of Navigation and the U.S. Military and Allied Forces

The U.S. freedom of navigation and over flight program aims to assert the freedom of all vessels and aircraft to conduct innocent passage in and over the territorial seas of all countries (up to 12 nautical miles from the baseline, which is usually the low-water line of a coastal state). This program also asserts the freedom of all vessels and aircraft to conduct military exercises, gather intelligence, and perform other activities inconsistent with innocent passage in and over the EEZs of all states (between 12 and 200 nautical miles from baselines). Crucially, the U.S. freedom of navigation and over flight program is conducted in territorial seas and EEZs without prior consent. China, Argentina, India, Indonesia, Malaysia, Vietnam, and a number of other states reject the U.S. interpretation of freedom of navigation rights under UNCLOS a treaty the United States seeks to comply with despite not having ratified. China insists that innocent passage within its territorial seas requires prior permission and strongly opposes foreign military vessels and aircraft even approaching Chinese-controlled maritime features in the SCS. China has sought to demonstrate its opposition to the U.S. freedom of navigation and over flight program by publicly objecting to those operations and periodically tailing and harassing U.S. vessels and aircraft. China has similarly criticized and sought to disrupt U.S. allies from conducting freedom of navigation and over flight operations in the SCS. China's tailing, surveillance, and verbal warnings directed at U.S. and allied vessels and aircraft raise the risks associated with freedom of navigation and over flight operations in the SCS. Such tactics could easily lead to a repeat of the tense diplomatic standoff that followed the deadly 2001 collision between a U.S. EP-3E Aries II surveillance aircraft and a Chinese fighter jet. Notwithstanding the risk of incidents of this nature, even China's deployment of additional military capabilities to disputed maritime features does not seriously threaten freedom of navigation. China would need to risk precisely the kind of confrontation that it has for the sake of its own strategic interests heretofore sought to avoid. China would likely need to directly attack and inflict serious material damage on the U.S. and allied sea and air assets to have a realistic chance of ending these operations. The deep economic and security costs of such a military confrontation with the world's greatest military power and China's largest trading partner mean that Beijing has strong prudential grounds to avoid disrupting U.S. and allied freedom of navigation and over flight operations. However, China is developing military capabilities that will dramatically increase its ability to block the vessels and aircraft of the U.S. military and allied forces. China's evolving anti-access/area denial (A2/AD) capabilities typically counter-maritime and counter-air systems designed to destroy surface ships and aircraft are aimed at making power projection into the seas adjoining China may be costly if not impossible in the event of military conflict. Such capabilities could be deployed to seriously threaten the freedom of navigation and over flight program throughout the first island chain, which runs from the southern end of the Japanese island of Kyushu to roughly the southern tip of China's Nine-Dash Line, thereby including the bulk of the SCS. Despite the growing power and sophistication of China's A2/AD capabilities, they would pose a genuine threat to freedom of navigation and over flight only in the extreme scenario of a military confrontation on the Chinese littoral with the United States and its allies.[15]

Conclusion

China saw its claims to the South China Sea voted down by the International Court of Arbitration based on the U.N. Convention of the Law of the Sea, Beijing has ostensibly been refraining from provocative acts. But, it has continued to build facilities on the artificial islands it has created. Rather than in the South China Sea, China could test the Trump administration and the strength of the US-Japan alliance in the East China Sea. This would no doubt please Philippines President Rodrigo Duterte, who has been keen to make overtures to China. Alternatively, Beijing may target Taiwan, to punish Tsai for her phone call with Trump in addition to the recent demonstration of deployment of its aircraft carrier in the South China Sea.

The Trump administration could avoid a major rupture in US-China relations by responding rationally to any provocation, while emphasizing freedom of navigation and the peaceful resolution of conflicts. It could also go too far in its response, and put itself on the path to confrontation. Or perhaps it will tacitly condone China's domination of the South China Sea in exchange for the elimination of the trade deficit, placing the emphasis on the peaceful coexistence of the two countries. Whichever path Washington takes, Trump's response to the likely Chinese provocations will become a major factor in determining the future of the South China Sea.

NOTES AND REFERENCES

1. "Top Trading Partners—November 2016," *U.S. Census Bureau*, https://www.census. gov/foreign-trade/statistics/high lights/toppartners.html.
2. Greg Austin, "Why Beijing Poses No Threat to South China Sea Commerce," *Straits Times*, May 28, 2015, http://www.straitstimes.com/opinion/why-beijing-poses-no-threat-to-south-china-seacommerce.
3. Department of State, "China: Maritime Claims in the South China Sea," *Limits in the Seas*, no. 143, December 2014, p. 4; Council on Foreign Relations, "China's Maritime Disputes," CFR InfoGuide Presentation, 2017, https://www.cfr.org/asia-and-pacific/chinas-maritime-disputes/ p31345#!/p31345
4. Ronald O'Rourke, *Maritime Territorial and Exclusive Economic Zone (EEZ) Disputes Involving China: Issues for Congress* (Washington: Congressional Research Service, 2016), pp. 27–28.
5. M. Taylor Fravel, *Strong Borders Secure Nation: Cooperation and Conflict in China's Territorial Disputes* (Princeton and Oxford: Princeton University Press, 2008), p. 376.
6. Council on Foreign Relations, n. 3, pp. 267–99.
7. M. Taylor Fravel, *The United States in the South China Sea Disputes* (Berlin: Stiftung Wissenschaft und Politik, 2012).
8. Peter Baker, "Trump Abandons Trans-Pacific Partnership, Osama's Signature Trade Deal," *New York Times*, January 23, 2017, https://www.nytimes. com/2017/01/23/ us/politics/tpp-trump-trade-nafta.html?_r=0.
9. Timothy A. Walton, "*China's Three Warfares*," (Herndon, VA: Delex Systems, 2012).
10. David C. Gompert, *War with China: Thinking Through the Unthinkable* (Santa Monica, CA: RAND Corporation, 2016), p. 27.
11. Jeff Stein, "Why Beijing Isn't Backing Down on South China Sea," *Newsweek*, October 10, 2015, http://www.newsweek.com/why-beijing-notbacking-down-south-china-sea-381973.
12. Gompert, n.10, p. 27.
13. Daniel Blumenthal, "What Happened to China's 'Peaceful Rise'?," *Foreign Policy*, October 21, 2010, http://foreignpolicy. com/2010/10/21/what-happened-to-chinas-peace ful-rise/
14. Patrick M. Cronin and Alexander Sullivan, *Preserving the Rules: Countering Coercion in Maritime Asia*,(Washington: Center for a New American Security, 2015).
15. Eric Heginbotham, *The U.S.-China Military Scorecard: Forces, Geography, and the Evolving Balance of Power 1996–2017* (Santa Monica, CA: RAND Corporation, 2015), pp. 117–18.

Index